Abitur 2019
mit Original-Prüfungsaufgaben und Lösungen

Mein Abi-Coach
Englisch
Grundkurs

So einfach lernt man mit dem Abi-Coach

1. Einfach planen

Auf diesen Seiten steht alles Wichtige rund um die Abiturprüfung und Hilfreiches für die Vorbereitung.

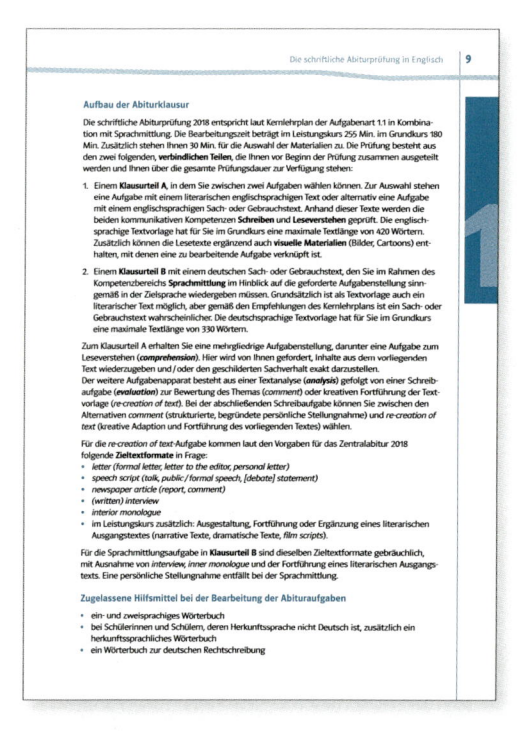

2. Einfach ausprobieren

Mit Übungs- und Probe-Abis feststellen, wie fit man ist. Mein Abi-Coach hilft mit Tipps und differenzierten Lösungen weiter.

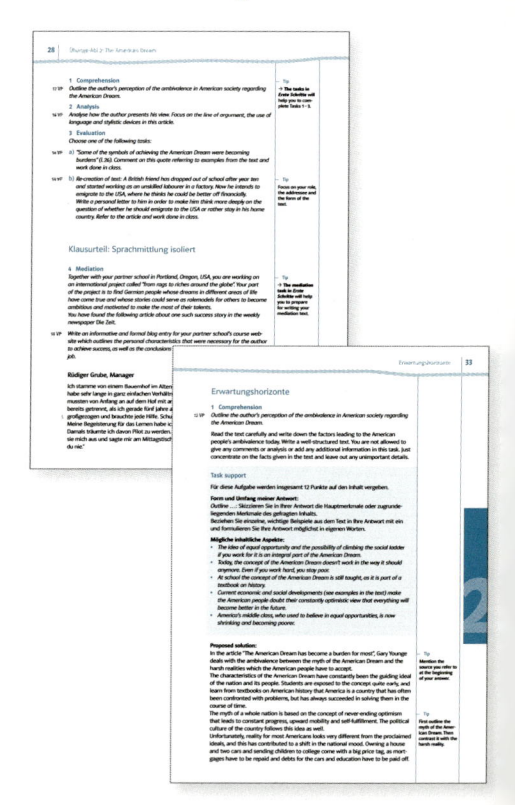

🌐 **Zum Tool für den individuellen Trainingsplan einfach bei www.klett.de ins Suchfeld eingeben: qn647v**

3. Einfach trainieren

Begleitende Übungen mit Lösungsvorschlägen unterstützen bei der Vorbereitung auf das schriftliche Abitur.

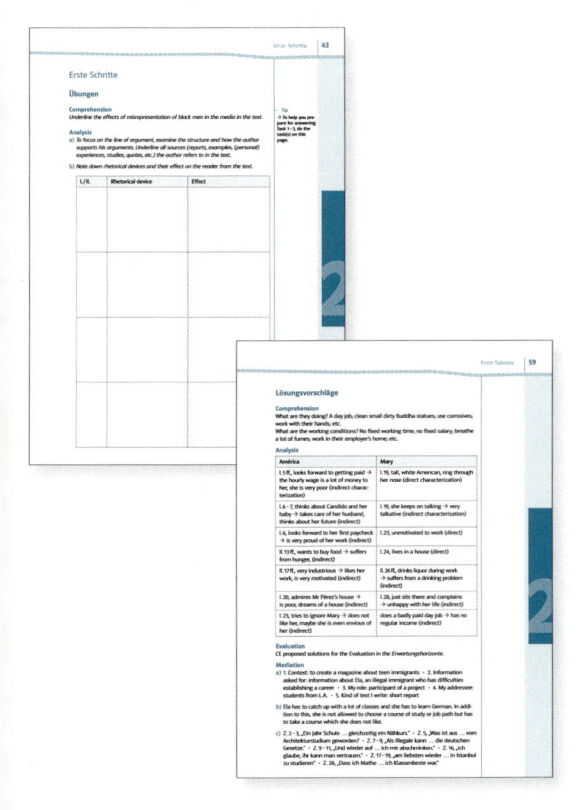

Hier hilft der Abi-Coach beim Training: Tipps zur Anwendung der abiturrelevanten Fertigkeiten und kompakte Zusammenfassungen des thematischen Grundwissens.

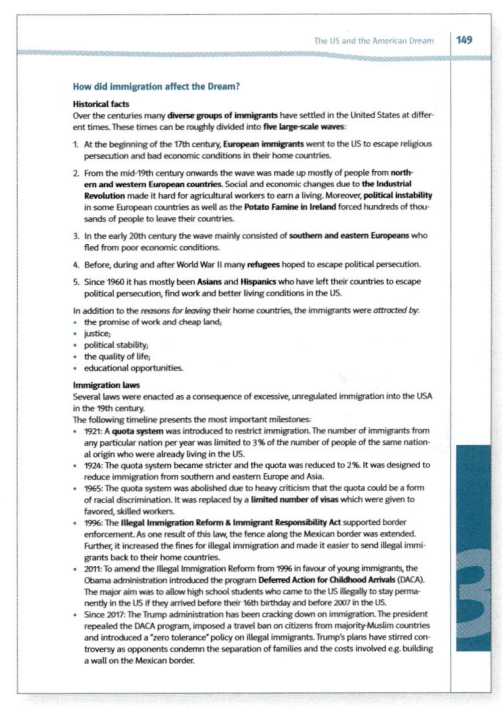

Abi – mach's einfach!
Mein Abi-Coach führt in drei Schritten zum erfolgreichen Abitur.

Abitur 2019 mit Original-Prüfungsaufgaben und Lösungen

Textquellen:
16 Copyright © 1989 by Amy Tan. First appeared in THE JOY LUCK CLUB. Reprinted by permission of the author and the Sandra Dijkstra Literary Agency.; **17** Der McDonald's Ausbildungsflash 2014, www.mcdonalds-ausbildung.de, (c) McDonald's Deutschland Inc. München; **27** Copyright Guardian News & Media Ltd 2018; **28–29** By Rüdiger Grube from „Mein Aufstieg war möglich, aber zu schwer", quotes collected by Marco Maurer, Zeit Online, 1. April 2015; **40** Copyright Guardian News & Media Ltd 2018; **41–42** Bundesamt für Migration und Flüchtlinge, Nürnberg, 29.09.2014; **54** Excerpt(s) from TORTILLA CURTAIN by T. C. Boyle, copyright © 1995 by T. Coraghessan Boyle. Used by permission of Viking Books, an imprint of Penguin Publishing Group, a division of Penguin Random House LLC. All rights reserved. Any third party use of this material, outside of this publication, is prohibited. Interested parties must apply directly to Penguin Random House LLC for permission.; **55–56** From „Plötzlich war ich Schatten" by Ela Aslan, Arena Verlag GmbH, Würzburg, 2012; **66** Copyright Guardian News & Media Ltd 2018. Zur besseren altersgemäßen Verständlichkeit wurde der Originaltext leicht verändert, ohne den Inhalt und/oder Sinn zu verändern.; **67–68** By Jannis Brühl, Süddeutsche Zeitung, 24.06.2015; **78** White House Website, September 10, 2014; **79–80** Süddeutsche Zeitung, München, 11. September 2015, Direkt aus dem dpa-Newskanal Berlin/Istanbul (dpa); **91** From THE HUNGER GAMES by Suzanne Collins, Scholastic Inc./Scholastic Press. Copyright © 2008 by Suzanne Collins. Reprinted by permission.; **92** Abiturprüfung 2014, Ministerium für Schule und Weiterbildung des Landes Nordrhein-Westfalen; **92–93** By Maikka Kost mit Prof. Angela Keppler, Badische Zeitung, 10. März 2012; **100** By Ed Miliband, labourlist.org, September 24, 2013 Zur besseren altersgemäßen Verständlichkeit wurde der Originaltext leicht verändert, ohne den Inhalt und/oder Sinn zu verändern.; **101** Abiturprüfung 2015, Ministerium für Schule und Weiterbildung des Landes Nordrhein-Westfalen; **102** Kölner Stadt-Anzeiger, 07.04.2015 © 2015 dpa; **111** www.whitehouse.gov; **112** Abiturprüfung 2016, Ministerium für Schule und Weiterbildung des Landes Nordrhein-Westfalen; **112–113** By Sven Becker et al., Der Spiegel, No. 9/2013; **121** Copyright Guardian News & Media Ltd 2018; **122** Abiturprüfung 2017, Originalprüfungsaufgaben des Ministeriums für Schule und Weiterbildung des Landes Nordrhein-Westfalen; **122–123** © 2014, Irena Güttel, dpa; **131** The Crossing, text copyright © 1987 Gary Paulsen; **132** Abiturprüfung 2018, Originalprüfungsaufgaben des Ministeriums für Schule und Weiterbildung des Landes Nordrhein-Westfalen; **132–133** Welt.de 20.04.2015, Dennis Betzholz, Per Hinrichs, Christine Kensche „Die Trgödie der Kinder-Flüchtlinge" (https://www.welt.de/vermischtes/article139802318/Die-Tragoedie-der-Kinder-Fluechtlinge.html); **147** James Truslow Adams, quotation from "The Epic of America", Little, Brown and Co., Boston, 1931

Bildquellen:
Cover shutterstock.com (Rawpixel), New York, NY; **101.1** Steve Bell, East Sussex; **142.1** Quelle: www.parliament.uk; **142.2** Getty Images (Bettmann), München; **150.1** Source: Bureau of the Census, U.S. Census of population, 1960; **151.1** Source: United States Census Bureau, 2014

Sollte es in einem Einzelfall nicht gelungen sein, den korrekten Rechteinhaber ausfindig zu machen, so werden berechtigte Ansprüche selbstverständlich im Rahmen der üblichen Regelungen abgegolten.

1. Auflage   1 5 4 3 2 1 | 22 21 20 19 18

Alle Drucke dieser Auflage sind unverändert und können im Unterricht nebeneinander verwendet werden. Die letzte Zahl bezeichnet das Jahr des Druckes.
Das Werk und seine Teile sind urheberrechtlich geschützt. Jede Nutzung in anderen als den gesetzlich zugelassenen Fällen bedarf der vorherigen schriftlichen Einwilligung des Verlages. Hinweis § 52 a UrhG: Weder das Werk noch seine Teile dürfen ohne eine solche Einwilligung eingescannt und in ein Netzwerk eingestellt werden. Dies gilt auch für Intranets von Schulen und sonstigen Bildungseinrichtungen. Fotomechanische oder andere Wiedergabeverfahren nur mit Genehmigung des Verlages.

© Ernst Klett Verlag GmbH, Stuttgart 2018. Alle Rechte vorbehalten. www.klett.de

Autor: Arnd Nadolny, Meine
Beratung: Nilgül Karabulut, Aachen
Redaktion: Steffen Auer; Hana Kim-Türk
Herstellung: Anette Wenzel
Layout: Petra Michel, Essen
Umschlaggestaltung: Petra Michel, Essen
Satz: Satzkiste GmbH, Stuttgart; Jürgen Kaufmann, Stuttgart
Druck: Medienhaus Plump GmbH, Rheinbreitbach

Printed in Germany
ISBN 978-3-12-601086-3

Inhalt

EINFACH PLANEN

Einführung 7

Die schriftliche Abiturprüfung in Englisch 8
Verbindliche Prüfungsthemen für das Abitur 2019 8
Aufbau der Abiturklausur 9
Zugelassene Hilfsmittel bei der Bearbeitung der Abituraufgaben 9

Bewertung 10
Anforderungsbereiche in der Abiturklausur 10

Meine Abiturvorbereitung 12
Allgemeine Tipps 12
Selbstevaluation 12
Tipps für die Prüfung 14

EINFACH AUSPROBIEREN

Abiture 15

Übungs-Abi 1: Prospects of young adults today 16
Klausurteil: Leseverstehen und Schreiben integriert 16
Klausurteil: Sprachmittlung isoliert 17
Erste Schritte 18
Erwartungshorizonte 21

Übungs-Abi 2: The US and the American Dream 27
Klausurteil: Leseverstehen und Schreiben integriert 27
Klausurteil: Sprachmittlung isoliert 28
Erste Schritte 30
Erwartungshorizonte 33

Übungs-Abi 3: The media 40
Klausurteil: Leseverstehen und Schreiben integriert 40
Klausurteil: Sprachmittlung isoliert 41
Erste Schritte 43
Erwartungshorizonte 46

Übungs-Abi 4: Global disparities 54
Klausurteil: Leseverstehen und Schreiben integriert 54
Klausurteil: Sprachmittlung isoliert 55
Erste Schritte 57
Erwartungshorizonte 60

Übungs-Abi 5: Rising nation India 66
Klausurteil: Leseverstehen und Schreiben integriert 66
Klausurteil: Sprachmittlung isoliert 67
Erste Schritte 69
Erwartungshorizonte 72

Übungs-Abi 6: The US and global security — 78
Klausurteil: Leseverstehen und Schreiben integriert — 78
Klausurteil: Sprachmittlung isoliert — 79
Erste Schritte — 81
Erwartungshorizonte — 84

Abitur 2014: Visions of the future — 91
Klausurteil: Leseverstehen und Schreiben integriert — 91
Klausurteil: Sprachmittlung isoliert — 92
Erwartungshorizonte — 94

Abitur 2015: Tradition and change in the UK — 100
Klausurteil: Leseverstehen und Schreiben integriert — 100
Klausurteil: Sprachmittlung isoliert — 102
Erwartungshorizonte — 103

Abitur 2016: The US and the American Dream — 111
Klausurteil: Leseverstehen und Schreiben integriert — 111
Klausurteil: Sprachmittlung isoliert — 112
Erwartungshorizonte — 114

Abitur 2017: Global challenges – communication — 121
Klausurteil: Leseverstehen und Schreiben integriert — 121
Klausurteil: Sprachmittlung isoliert — 122
Erwartungshorizonte — 124

Abitur 2018: The US and the American Dream — 131
Klausurteil: Leseverstehen und Schreiben integriert — 131
Klausurteil: Sprachmittlung isoliert — 132
Erwartungshorizonte — 134

EINFACH TRAINIEREN

Grundwissen und Skills — 140

Grundwissen — 141
The UK – tradition and change — 141
The US and the American Dream — 147
India — 157
Shakespeare's life and time — 160
Visions of the future — 162
Global challenges — 165
English as a lingua franca — 167

Skills — 168
Comprehension — 168
Analysis — 170
Evaluation — 174
Mediation — 175

Erfahren Sie in Kürze das Wichtigste für das Abitur.
Welche Themengebiete sind relevant, wie sind die Aufgabenteile gewichtet und wie
bereiten Sie sich am besten vor?

Einfach planen

Einführung

Die schriftliche Abiturprüfung in Englisch

Verbindliche Prüfungsthemen für das Abitur 2019

Ihre Prüfung im Abitur 2019 kann sich im Grundkurs auf folgende, zentrale Themen und Schwerpunkte beziehen. Einige Oberthemen können ähnliche oder identische Schwerpunkte beinhalten.

Lebensentwürfe, Studium, Ausbildung, Beruf international – Englisch als *lingua franca*
(*cf.* Übungs-Abi 1)
- *Studying and working in a globalised world*

Das Vereinigte Königreich im 21. Jahrhundert (*cf.* Abitur 2015)
- *Tradition and change in politics: multicultural society*

Amerikanischer Traum – Visionen und Lebenswirklichkeiten in den USA
(*cf.* Übungs-Abi 2, 3, 6; Abitur 2016; Abitur 2018)
- *American myths and realities: freedom and success*

Postkolonialismus – Lebenswirklichkeiten in einem weiteren anglophonen Kulturraum
(*cf.* Übungs-Abi 5)
- *India: faces of a rising nation*

Medien in ihrer Bedeutung für den Einzelnen und die Gesellschaft (*cf.* Abitur 2014)
- *The impact of Shakespearean drama on young audiences today: study of film scenes*
- *Visions of the future: utopia and dystopia*

Chancen und Risiken der Globalisierung (*cf.* Übungs-Abi 4; Abitur 2017)
- *Studying and working in a globalised world*
- *India: faces of a rising nation*
- *The impact of globalisation on culture and communication*

Für das Abitur wird von Ihnen erwartet, dass Sie Ihr erworbenes Grundwissen zu den hier genannten Themen selbständig anhand authentischer Quellen wie zum Beispiel englischer Tageszeitungen erweitern und die unterschiedlichen Informationen miteinander vernetzen.

Zudem reflektieren Sie Ihr erlerntes Grundwissen. Dies umfasst beispielsweise, dass Sie Aspekte der unterschiedlichen Themen vergleichen, mögliche Vor- und Nachteile erkennen und persönlich Stellung zu konkreten Fragestellungen beziehen.
Wie beurteilen Sie zum Beispiel bestimmte Entwicklungen der Globalisierung in den einzelnen Erdteilen? Wie steht es um den American Dream? Welche Auswirkungen hat das koloniale Erbe auf das heutige Großbritannien? etc.

Teil des Grundwissens ist auch, dass Sie sich der unterschiedlichen historischen und kulturellen Perspektiven auf spezifische Fragestellungen bewusst sind. Bedingt durch die historische Entwicklung weisen zum Beispiel ein Großteil der Bürger Englands eine relativ hohe Wertschätzung gegenüber der Monarchie auf. Berücksichtigen Sie solche und ähnliche kulturell bedingte Werthaltungen stets in Ihrem Urteil und zeigen Sie sich für interkulturelle Unterschiede sensibel.

Aufbau der Abiturklausur

Die schriftliche Abiturprüfung 2019 entspricht laut Kernlehrplan der Aufgabenart 1.1 in Kombination mit Sprachmittlung. Die Bearbeitungszeit beträgt im Leistungskurs 255 Min. im Grundkurs 180 Min. Zusätzlich stehen Ihnen 30 Min. für die Auswahl der Materialien zu. Die Prüfung besteht aus den zwei folgenden, **verbindlichen Teilen**, die Ihnen vor Beginn der Prüfung zusammen ausgeteilt werden und Ihnen über die gesamte Prüfungsdauer zur Verfügung stehen:

1. Einem **Klausurteil A**, in dem Sie zwischen zwei Aufgaben wählen können. Zur Auswahl stehen eine Aufgabe mit einem literarischen englischsprachigen Text oder alternativ eine Aufgabe mit einem englischsprachigen Sach- oder Gebrauchstext. Anhand dieser Texte werden die beiden kommunikativen Kompetenzen **Schreiben** und **Leseverstehen** geprüft. Die englischsprachige Textvorlage hat für Sie im Grundkurs eine maximale Textlänge von 420 Wörtern. Zusätzlich können die Lesetexte ergänzend auch **visuelle Materialien** (Bilder, Cartoons) enthalten, mit denen eine zu bearbeitende Aufgabe verknüpft ist.

2. Einem **Klausurteil B** mit einem deutschen Sach- oder Gebrauchstext, den Sie im Rahmen des Kompetenzbereichs **Sprachmittlung** im Hinblick auf die geforderte Aufgabenstellung sinngemäß in der Zielsprache wiedergeben müssen. Grundsätzlich ist als Textvorlage auch ein literarischer Text möglich, aber gemäß den Empfehlungen des Kernlehrplans ist ein Sach- oder Gebrauchstext wahrscheinlicher. Die deutschsprachige Textvorlage hat für Sie im Grundkurs eine maximale Textlänge von 330 Wörtern.

Zum Klausurteil A erhalten Sie eine mehrgliedrige Aufgabenstellung, darunter eine Aufgabe zum Leseverstehen (*comprehension*). Hier wird von Ihnen gefordert, Inhalte aus dem vorliegenden Text wiederzugeben und / oder den geschilderten Sachverhalt exakt darzustellen.
Der weitere Aufgabenapparat besteht aus einer Textanalyse (*analysis*) gefolgt von einer Schreibaufgabe (*evaluation*) zur Bewertung des Themas (*comment*) oder kreativen Fortführung der Textvorlage (*re-creation of text*). Bei der abschließenden Schreibaufgabe können Sie zwischen den Alternativen *comment* (strukturierte, begründete persönliche Stellungnahme) und *re-creation of text* (kreative Adaption und Fortführung des vorliegenden Textes) wählen.

Für die *re-creation of text*-Aufgabe kommen laut den Vorgaben für das Zentralabitur 2019 folgende **Zieltextformate** in Frage:
- *letter (formal letter, letter to the editor, personal letter)*
- *speech script (talk, public / formal speech, [debate] statement)*
- *newspaper article (report, comment)*
- *(written) interview*
- im Leistungskurs zusätzlich: Ausgestaltung, Fortführung oder Ergänzung eines literarischen Ausgangstextes (narrative Texte, dramatische Texte, *film scripts*).

Für die Sprachmittlungsaufgabe in **Klausurteil B** sind dieselben Zieltextformate gebräuchlich, mit Ausnahme von *interview* und der Fortführung eines literarischen Ausgangstexts. Eine persönliche Stellungnahme entfällt bei der Sprachmittlung.

Zugelassene Hilfsmittel bei der Bearbeitung der Abituraufgaben

- ein- und zweisprachiges Wörterbuch
- bei Schülerinnen und Schülern, deren Herkunftssprache nicht Deutsch ist, zusätzlich ein herkunftssprachliches Wörterbuch
- ein Wörterbuch zur deutschen Rechtschreibung

Bewertung

Klausurteil A mit Schreiben und Leseverstehen geht zu 70 Prozent, **Klausurteil B** mit Sprachmittlung zu 30 Prozent in die Gesamtbewertung ein. In der Tabelle ist eine Verteilung der Punkte auf Inhalt und Sprache abgebildet. Beachten Sie: Die Punkte für Sprache für Klausurteil A werden für den gesamten Teil A vergeben. Ebenso kann die Punkteverteilung geringfügig von dem Beispiel abweichen.

Klausurteil A	Inhalt	Sprache
Comprehension	12 Punkte	
Analysis	16 Punkte	63 Punkte
Evaluation	14 Punkte	
		Summe Klausurteil A: 105 Punkte

Klausurteil B	Inhalt	Sprache
Mediation	18 Punkte	27 Punkte
		Summe Klausurteil B: 45 Punkte

		Summe Klausurteil A und B gesamt: 150 Punkte

Anforderungsbereiche in der Abiturklausur

Der **Klausurteil A** deckt mit den Teilaufgaben drei Anforderungsbereiche ab.
In der ersten Teilaufgabe geht es um Verständnissicherung des zielsprachigen Textes (*comprehension*). Dabei geht es um die Wiedergabe von Textinhalten. Dies entspricht dem Anforderungsbereich I.

Mögliche Operatoren für den **Anforderungsbereich I** (*comprehension*):

describe	eine im Text geschilderte Person / Sache im Detail beschreiben
illustrate	anhand von im Text genannten Beispielen etwas erklären
outline	eine Person / Sache anhand ihrer wesentlichen Eigenschaften beschreiben
point out, find and explain certain aspects	eine Person / Sache / Aussage anhand ausgewählter und relevanter Textinhalte beschreiben / erklären
state	die wichtigsten Aspekte kurz und klar nennen
summarise, sum up	die wichtigsten Aspekte in einem zusammenhängenden Text zusammenfassen

Im Anforderungsbereich II (*analysis*) müssen Sie z. B. Textinhalte auswählen und verarbeiten oder verschiedene Aspekte des Textes vergleichen (*compare*) bzw. den Text unter inhaltlichen und sprachlichen Aspekten analysieren (*analyse, give a charactarisation, examine* etc.). Dieser Anforderungsbereich stellt gleichzeitig den Schwerpunkt Ihrer zu erbringenden Leistung dar. Dies ist in den meisten Fällen die 2. Teilaufgabe, die Sie zu bearbeiten haben.

Mögliche Operatoren für den **Anforderungsbereich II** (*analysis*):

analyse, examine	etwas im Detail beschreiben und anhand von Beispielen und Belegen erklären
give / write a characterisation of	einen Charakter ausführlich analysieren und beschreiben
compare	Ähnlichkeiten und Unterschiede herausarbeiten und darstellen
explain	einen Sachverhalt anhand von Argumenten und Beispielen ausführlich erklären
interpret	eine Motivation / Botschaft / Wirkung etc. anhand von Beispielen und Textbelegen darlegen

Die letzte Teilaufgabe entspricht Anforderungsbereich III. Hier werden Sie aufgefordert alternativ:
a) Textinhalte zu bewerten (*assess*), zu kommentieren (*comment*) oder eine Frage vor dem Hintergrund des Textes zu diskutieren (*evaluate / discuss*)

oder

b) eine *re-creation of text*-Aufgabe zu bearbeiten, indem Sie ausgehend von einer vorgegebenen Situation einen Text schreiben.

Mögliche Operatoren für den **Anforderungsbereich III** (*evaluation*):

assess / evaluate	Vor- und Nachteile zu einem Thema abwägen und in einem durchdacht strukturierten Text dazu Stellung nehmen
comment (on)	die eigene Meinung darlegen und durch Beispiele und geschickte Argumentation stützen
discuss	Pro und Contra zu einem Thema diskutieren und in ein persönliches Resümee fließen lassen
write (+ text type)	einen Text, passend zum vorgegebenen Kontext und der verlangten Textsorte, erstellen

Die Sprachmittlungsaufgabe des **Klausurteils B** deckt die Anforderungsbereiche I und II ab. Das heißt, die Aufgabe erfordert die Wiedergabe inhaltlicher Aspekte der deutschsprachigen Textvorlage und die richtige Auswahl und Verarbeitung von Textinhalten unter Berücksichtigung der gegebenen Situation, des Adressaten und gegebenenfalls kultureller Unterschiede der Ausgangs- und Zielkultur.

Mögliche Operatoren für den **Anforderungsbereich I** und **II** (*mediation*):

explain	einen Sachverhalt anhand von Argumenten und Beispielen ausführlich erklären unter Beachtung möglicher kultureller Missverständnisse
outline / present / summarise, sum up	eine Person / Sache anhand ihrer wesentlichen Eigenschaften beschreiben unter Beachtung möglicher kultureller Missverständnisse
write (+ text type)	entsprechend der Kriterien der Aufgabenstellung einen Text erstellen unter Beachtung möglicher kultureller Missverständnisse

Meine Abiturvorbereitung

Allgemeine Tipps

Fangen Sie frühzeitig mit der Abiturvorbereitung an. Je früher Sie anfangen, desto geringer fällt der Stressfaktor für Ihre Vorbereitung aus. Um Ihre Vorbereitung individuell zu planen, können Sie unter dem zu Beginn dieses Buches abgedruckten Online-Codes Ihren persönlichen Zeitplan erstellen. Mit diesem Trainingsplan haben Sie stets die Übersicht über bereits geschaffte und noch zu bearbeitende landeskundliche Inhalte und Prüfungsaufgaben.

Selbstevaluation

Anhand der Fragen zur Selbstevaluation können Sie Ihren aktuellen Lernstand einschätzen und Schwerpunkte für Ihre Vorbereitung setzen. Es ist empfehlenswert, die Selbstevaluation nach dem Durcharbeiten von ein bis drei Abitur-Aufgaben in *Mein Abi-Coach* anzuwenden.

Grundwissen

Folgende Themengebiete kann ich in Grundzügen beschreiben, erklären und ggf. aus verschiedenen Perspektiven beurteilen:

- ☐ The American Dream
- ☐ The United Kingdom
- ☐ Shakespeare and his time
- ☐ Globalisation
- ☐ The US in international politics
- ☐ Postcolonialism (India)
- ☐ Ethical issues of technological progress
- ☐ English as a lingua franca

Sprache

Die Selbstevaluation zur Sprache greift vor allem wichtige Aspekte für die Analyse- und Evaluationsaufgabe auf. Markieren Sie, wie sicher Sie die Anforderungen erfüllen.

Aufgabenerfüllung	trifft immer zu	trifft zum Teil zu	trifft selten zu
Bei der Erstellung meines Textes beachte ich:			
• den Kontext, den Adressaten und den Schreibanlass • die Textsortenmerkmale • eine klare Struktur und zielführende Argumentation • das Belegen von Aussagen durch Zitate / Beispiele	☐ ☐ ☐ ☐	☐ ☐ ☐ ☐	☐ ☐ ☐ ☐

Ausdrucksvermögen	trifft immer zu	trifft zum Teil zu	trifft selten zu
Mein Text ist wie folgt formuliert:			
• selbständig und losgelöst vom Ausgangstext • mit thematischem Wortschatz • mit funktionalem Wortschatz (z. B. Konnektoren etc.) • entsprechend dem vorgegebenen Register / Sprachstil	☐ ☐ ☐ ☐	☐ ☐ ☐ ☐	☐ ☐ ☐ ☐

Sprachrichtigkeit	trifft immer zu	trifft zum Teil zu	trifft selten zu
Ich beherrsche:			
• den Wortschatz • die Grammatik • die Orthographie	☐ ☐ ☐	☐ ☐ ☐	☐ ☐ ☐

Sprachmittlung

Folgende Aspekte werden grundsätzlich in einer Sprachmittlung erwartet.

Sprachmittlung	trifft immer zu	trifft zum Teil zu	trifft selten zu
In meinem Sprachmittlungstext setze ich klar um:			
• die Auswahl relevanter Informationen • die Einbettung in den Kommunikationskontext • meine Rolle / Perspektive • den Adressatenbezug • die Textsortenmerkmale des Zieltextes • das Erklären kulturspezifischer Begriffe	☐ ☐ ☐ ☐ ☐ ☐	☐ ☐ ☐ ☐ ☐ ☐	☐ ☐ ☐ ☐ ☐ ☐

Tipps für die Prüfung

In der schriftlichen Abiturprüfung erwarten Sie zwei unterschiedliche Aufgabenteile.
Zum einen die Textarbeit anhand eines englischsprachigen Ausgangstexts, zum anderen eine Sprachmittlungsaufgabe anhand eines deutschsprachigen Ausgangstexts.

Für die Bearbeitung haben Sie im Grundkurs 180 Min. Zeit. Dies ist eine vergleichsweise lange Arbeitszeit, allerdings ist die zu bearbeitende Menge ebenfalls entsprechend groß. Arbeiten Sie deshalb entsprechend zügig.

Beachten Sie, dass Sie in der Textaufgabe (*comprehension*, *analysis* und *evaluation*) und der Sprachmittlungsaufgabe Inhalte auswählen und sammeln, diese anschließend gliedern, eine Struktur entwerfen, eine Reinschrift anfertigen und abschließend noch Korrektur lesen. All diese Schritte benötigen Zeit!

Hinzu kommt, dass Ihnen zwei Evaluations-Aufgaben vorgeschlagen werden, aus der Sie eine Aufgabe auswählen müssen. Entscheiden Sie sich zügig für eine der beiden Aufgaben, um nicht zu viel Zeit zu verlieren.

Um sich rasch für eine der Evaluationsaufgaben zu entscheiden, ist es hilfreich, sich an folgenden Kriterien zu orientieren:

Vorrangig ist der geforderte Inhalt ausschlaggebend. Zu welchen Aspekten und Fragen, die die Aufgabenstellung fordert, haben Sie sich bereits mehr Gedanken gemacht bzw. mehr Hintergrundwissen? Überdies kann auch das geforderte Textformat Ihre Wahl beeinflussen. In der Evaluations-Aufgabe haben Sie die Wahl eine persönliche Stellungnahme (*comment*) zu schreiben oder die Textvorlage(n) kreativ fortzuführen (*re-creation of text*), indem Sie beispielsweise einen Tagebucheintrag, eine Rede oder ein Interview entwerfen. Üben Sie während Ihrer Vorbereitung Inhalte für beide Textarten zu sammeln und die Texte zu verfassen.

Formulieren Sie außerdem Ihre Entwürfe nicht aus, und schreiben diese anschließend in Reinschrift ab. Hierfür ist die Zeit zu knapp. Stattdessen sammeln Sie die Inhalte und strukturieren diese in Stichpunkten und fertigen anschließend gleich die Reinschrift an.

Zudem schlagen Sie während des Schreibens nicht jedes unbekannte Wort im Wörterbuch nach. Versuchen Sie auch schwierige Begriffe in eigenen Worten auszudrücken. Auch das spart Zeit!

Bereiten Sie sich gezielt auf das Abitur vor.
Originalaufgaben und simulierte Abiturprüfungen mit unterstützenden Übungen
in dem Abschnitt „Erste Schritte" und Erwartungshorizonte helfen Ihnen dabei.

Einfach ausprobieren

Übungs-Abi 1: Prospects of young adults today

Klausurteil: Leseverstehen und Schreiben integriert

Excerpt from the *Joy Luck Club*

My mother believed you could be anything you wanted to be in America. You could open a restaurant. You could work for the government and get good retirement. You could buy a house with almost no money down. You could become rich. You could become instantly famous. "Of course, you can be a prodigy, too," my mother
5 told me when I was nine. "You can be best anything. What does Auntie Lindo know? Her daughter, she is only best tricky."

America was where all my mother's hopes lay. She had come to San Francisco in 1949 after losing everything in China: her mother and father, her home, her first husband, and two daughters, twin baby girls. But she never looked back with
10 regret. Things could get better in so many ways. We didn't immediately pick the right kind of prodigy. […]

Every night after dinner my mother and I would sit at the Formica topped kitchen table. She would present new tests, taking her examples from stories of amazing children that she read in *Ripley's Believe It or Not* or *Good Housekeeping*,
15 *Reader's digest*, or any of a dozen other magazines she kept in a pile in our bathroom. My mother got these magazines from people whose houses she cleaned. And since she cleaned many houses each week, we had a great assortment. She would look through them all, searching for stories about remarkable children. […]

One night I had to look at a page from the Bible for three minutes and then
20 report everything I could remember. "Now Jehoshaphat had riches and honor in abundance and … that's all I remember, Ma," I said. And after seeing, once again, my mother's disappointed face, something inside me began to die. I hated the tests, the raised hopes and failed expectations. Before going to bed that night I looked in the mirror above the bathroom sink, and I saw only my face staring back – and
25 understood that it would always be this ordinary face – I began to cry. Such a sad, ugly girl! I made high-pitched noises like a crazed animal, trying to scratch out the face in the mirror. And then I saw what seemed to be the prodigy side of me […]. The girl staring back at me was angry, powerful. She and I were the same. I had new thoughts, willful thoughts – or rather, thoughts filled with lots of won'ts. I won't let
30 her change me, I promised myself. I won't be what I'm not.

(414 words)

Excerpt from: Amy Tan, *The Joy Luck Club*, 1989

[4] **prodigy** child genius, a young and extremely talented person
[12] **Formica** a hard plastic material used to cover tables and furniture

1 Comprehension

12 VP *Sum up the mother's behaviour towards her daughter and the effect it has on her.*

2 Analysis

16 VP *Analyse the atmosphere which the author creates in the novel excerpt. Focus on the narrative perspective and the choice of words.*

3 Evaluation

Choose one of the following tasks:

14 VP **a)** *Comment on the question of whether parents should constantly interfere in their children's education to improve their skills.*

— Tip

→ The tasks in *Erste Schritte* will help you to complete Tasks 1–3.

14 VP **b)** *Re-creation of text:* Write the girl's diary entry on the evening when she realised that she did not want her mother to change her.

> **Tip**
> Remember to write the diary entry from the girl's perspective.

Klausurteil: Sprachmittlung isoliert

4 Mediation

Your American high school friend is doing a project on 'Social mobility and equality of opportunity among young people today'. Your friend asks you about how young people in Germany assess their chances of climbing the social ladder.

18 VP Write an email to your friend informing him/her about personal and external factors which are crucial for a successful career and upward social mobility according to this article.

> **Tip**
> → The mediation task in *Erste Schritte* will help you to prepare for writing your mediation text.

> **Tip**
> Be careful to choose only the information asked for.

Der McDonald's Ausbildungsflash 2014

Die positive ökonomische Entwicklung in Deutschland sowie die gute Situation auf dem Ausbildungs- und Arbeitsmarkt führen dazu, dass die Mehrheit der jungen Erwachsenen weiterhin mit großem Optimismus in die eigene Zukunft blickt. 77 Prozent der 15- bis 24-Jährigen sehen der eigenen beruflichen Zukunft
5 mit Hoffnungen entgegen, nur 13 Prozent mit Befürchtungen. Somit sehen die unter 25-Jährigen ihrer eigenen beruflichen Zukunft mit noch größerem Optimismus entgegen als vor einem Jahr. Damals bewerteten 71 Prozent der jungen Erwachsenen ihre Zukunftsaussichten positiv.
　　Besonders hoffnungsvoll blicken die Auszubildenden in die Zukunft. 86 Prozent
10 von ihnen sehen ihrer beruflichen Zukunft mit Hoffnungen entgegen, vor einem Jahr waren es mit 75 Prozent noch deutlich weniger.
Auch Schüler und junge Berufstätige schätzen ihre Zukunftsaussichten heute signifikant positiver ein als 2013. Lediglich bei den Studenten hat es keine Veränderungen gegeben: Wie im Vorjahr sehen 78 Prozent von ihnen der eigenen
15 beruflichen Zukunft mit Hoffnungen entgegen.
　　Die positive Grundhaltung der jungen Generation zeigt sich jedoch nicht nur in den optimistischen Erwartungen bezüglich der eigenen beruflichen Zukunft, sondern auch in der Beurteilung der sozialen Durchlässigkeit unserer Gesellschaft. Weiterhin schätzen die unter 25-Jährigen die Aufstiegschancen in Deutschland
20 überwiegend positiv ein. Sechs von zehn jungen Erwachsenen sind überzeugt, dass die Aufstiegschancen eines Arbeiterkindes bei entsprechen dem Einsatz und Willen gut oder sogar sehr gut sind; nur rund jeder Dritte hält die Chancen auf einen sozialen Aufstieg für weniger oder gar nicht gut.
　　Bemerkenswert ist, dass auch die unteren Sozialschichten die Aufstiegs-
25 chancen eines Arbeiterkindes aktuell nur wenig schlechter einschätzen als die mittleren oder höheren sozialen Schichten. Noch vor einem Jahr gab es in den unteren sozialen Schichten einen deutlich ausgeprägteren Statusfatalismus. 2013 hielten 40 Prozent der jungen Erwachsenen aus der Unterschicht die Aufstiegschancen in Deutschland für gut oder sehr gut, heute sind es 49 Prozent. […]
30 　　Zu den wichtigsten Erwartungen junger Menschen an einen Beruf zählen gute Erfolgs- und Zukunftschancen. 43 Prozent der unter 25-Jährigen legen bei der Berufswahl ganz besonderen Wert auf einen Beruf, der Erfolg verspricht […]

(330 Wörter)
Der McDonald's Ausbildungsflash, 2014

Erste Schritte

Übungen

Comprehension
Underline keywords for the mother's behaviour and its consequences.

Analysis
a) Focus on the personal pronouns and find out from which perspective the story is told.

_____

b) To help you with Task 2 Analysis, note down the atmosphere which is created in the different parts of the text.

Lines	Atmosphere
1–6	
7–11	
12 ff.	
17 ff.	
end	

Tip
→ To help you prepare for answering Task 1–3, do the task(s) on this page.

Evaluation

a) *Think about pro and con arguments when parents want the very best for their children. Think about your own experiences. First take notes then structure your arguments and then write your text.*

b) *Take notes first and check if they fit the girl's character and the plot.*

Mediation

a) *Read the task carefully again and complete what the task asks for.*

1. Context: _____
   _____

2. Information asked for: _____
   _____
   _____

3. My role: _____

4. My addressee: _____

5. Kind of text I write: _____

b) *Note down in one sentence what the article is about.*

_____
_____
_____

c) *Mark the information from the article which is relevant to write your mediation text and note it down in English.*

External factors crucial for a successful career and social upward mobility:

l. 1: positive development of the economy /

ll. 1–2: _____
_____
_____
_____
_____

Personal factors crucial for a successful career and upward social mobility:

_____
_____
_____
_____
_____

Tip
→ To help you prepare for writing your mediation text in Task 4, do the task(s) on this page.

Lösungsvorschläge

Comprehension
mother believed you could be anything • be a prodigy • Every night new tests • something inside me began to die • hated the tests • Such a sad, ugly girl! • angry • powerful • new thoughts, willful thoughts • I won't let her change me • etc.

Analysis
a) It is a first-person narrator since the author uses personal and possessive pronouns like "my" and "I".

b) ll. 1–6: hopeful, confident, looking forward, numerous opportunities, …;
ll. 7–11: terrible loss, despair, loneliness, …;
ll. 12 ff.: doughtful, pointless, the reader feels critical towards the teaching methods …;
ll. 17 ff.: sad, disappointed, breakdown, refusal, violent, crazy, despair, …;
end: realistic, strong, calm, independent, …

Evaluation
Cf. proposed solutions for the Evaluation in the *Erwartungshorizonte*.

Mediation
a) 1. Context: school project on social mobility
2. Information asked for: how young people in Germany assess their chances of climbing the social ladder / personal and external factors which are crucial for a successful career and upward social mobility according to this article
3. My role: a friend from Germany / student at a secondary school
4. My addressee: friend in the US in high school
5. Kind of text I write: personal email / informal language

b) The text is about how young people in Germany assess the possibilities of succeeding in their job and moving upwards in society.

c) External factors crucial for a successful career and social upward mobility:
l. 1: positive development of the economy
ll. 1–2: a lot of job offers and a decreasing unemployment rate
ll. 16 ff.: equal opportunities for people to climb the social ladder
ll. 24 ff.: the social class that somebody belongs to
ll. 30 ff.: job with good prospects for the future and the possibility of building a successful career
Personal factors crucial for a successful career and upward social mobility:
ll. 21 ff.: motivation to work hard and put a lot of effort into their work

Erwartungshorizonte

1 Comprehension

12 VP *Sum up the mother's behaviour towards her daughter and the effect it has on her.*

In Task 1 you summarise how the mother treats her daughter in the excerpt. Focus on the mother's expectations of her daughter and her daughter's feelings towards her mother.

Task support

Für diese Aufgabe werden insgesamt 12 Punkte auf den Inhalt vergeben.

Form und Umfang meiner Antwort:
Sum up …: Informieren Sie den Leser über das Verhalten und die Erziehungsmethoden der Mutter gegenüber ihrer Tochter. Gehen Sie dabei auch darauf ein, welche Reaktionen diese bei der Tochter hervorrufen.
Formulieren Sie Ihre Antwort in eigenen Worten und geben Sie nur wieder, was Sie dem Text entnehmen können.

Mögliche inhaltliche Aspekte:
- Her mother wants her to become a prodigy.
- Every night her daughter has to do exercises.
- At first she does not want to disappoint her mother but later she changes her mind.
- She realises that she cannot fulfil her mother's dreams. She collapses and finally changes her attitude completely.
- She decides not to do what her mother wants her to do any longer.

Proposed solution:
In the excerpt from Amy Tan "The Joy Luck Club" published in 1989, the main character tells the reader how she suffers from the hard challenges which her mother confronts her with.
The girl's mother is firmly convinced that anything is possible in America and that anybody can become rich in the US. Therefore, she wants to turn her daughter into an exceptionally talented young woman. Every night, the girl has to do difficult tasks with her mother. She does the exercises because she wants to please her mother, but she hates them because she can never seem to fulfil her mother's expectations. One night, she has a mental breakdown, unable to cope with the daily pressure to succeed. While the girl is looking into a mirror, she begins to realise that she does not want to be a person she is not. She has thoughts of her own instead and promises herself that she will not accept her mother telling her what to do anymore. *(159 words)*

> **Tip**
> → Introduce shortly the text your refer to.

2 Analysis

16 VP *Analyse the atmosphere which the author creates in the novel excerpt. Focus on the narrative perspective and the choice of words.*

In this task you should examine the atmosphere which the author creates and how the reader perceives this atmosphere. In order to examine the atmosphere, focus on the content and the language in the different paragraphs. To analyse how the reader perceives the atmosphere, focus on the narrative point of view.

Task support

Für diese Aufgabe werden insgesamt 16 Punkte auf den Inhalt vergeben.

Form und Umfang meiner Antwort:
Analyse …: Arbeiten Sie aus dem Text heraus, welche Emotionen und Stimmungen für den Leser erzeugt werden und erklären Sie, anhand von Belegen im Text, wie die verwendete Sprache und die Erzählperspektive dazu beitragen.

Mögliche inhaltliche Aspekte:
- The reader can understand the main character well because it is a first-person narrator.
- The narrator talks about the past and can therefore provide the reader with background information.
- According to the mother, her daughter has a lot of great prospects in the US.
- The mother's character is presented as very dominant. She had to suffer a lot and is very rigid in the upbringing of her daughter.
- The mother puts her daughter under pressure. She has to work on confusing exercises which are almost impossible to solve.
- The reader feels sympathy for the daughter and can well understand her refusal to practise anymore.
- The author uses direct speech to create suspense.
- The author uses emotive language associated with fear and the behavior of animals to show the girl's distress and pain.
- At the turning point the atmosphere is tense and rebellious. The daughter feels "angry" and "powerful".
- After the turning point, the reader's attention is drawn to the internal feelings and thoughts of the protagonist. The atmosphere is calm and intimate.

Proposed solution:
The author employs a first-person narrative perspective and chooses the language carefully to create an anxious and tense atmosphere.
In general, it is very easy for the reader to sense the atmosphere and understand the main character since the story is told from a first-person point of view. The narrator tells the reader about events in the past, foreshadowing the main character's current situation.
In the beginning of the excerpt, the main character describes her mother's high hopes for their new life in America. She repeatedly stresses what "you could [do]" in America, making America sound like a place of boundless opportunities. Her mother enumerates many opportunities and ends her list with the possibility of becoming rich and famous or even a prodigy (l. 4). This creates a rather promising atmosphere concerning the future of the protagonist. But at the same time, the reader recognises what a burden the mother's high hopes can be on the daughter. Following the mother's wishes for their new life in California, the narrator compares her mother's hopes for the future with the past. In a short flashback she tells the reader in concise language how her mother lost everything in China and what made her decide to emigrate to California. She lost her "mother and father, her home, her first husband, and two daughters" (ll. 8–9), which gives the reader an impression of her mother's desperation and willpower to start a new life. The narrator states clearly that her mother puts all her hope for a better future

> **Tip**
> Introduce your analysis by mentioning the main feature of your answer.

> **Tip**
> To support your findings, explain them and give examples from the text.

in her daughter. She wants her to be a prodigy. However, the reader learns that the mother just forces her daughter to become a prodigy and that her plans are bound to fail when the narrator mentions e.g. "we didn't immediately pick the right kind of prodigy" (ll. 10–11). The impression that her mother chooses a prodigy at random for her daughter is reinforced when you read about the teaching methods. Her mother refers to exceptional people she reads about in magazines like "Good Housekeeping".

The narrator uses direct speech to create suspense and to show vividly how pointless and tiring the training sessions were, especially when she describes a scene in which she had to memorise a scene from the Bible (ll. 19 ff.). This training session finally introduces the decisive turning point in the main character's development. The girl starts to rise up against her mother and the narrator uses short sentences and words associated with pain and animals like "sad", "ugly", "high-pitched noises", "crazed animal" and "scratch out the face" (ll. 26 ff.). Her rebellious behavior reflects her internal anger and distress. The reader's attention is drawn from the external plot to what's going on inside the protagonist. The reader is reassured that the protagonist has found her real 'prodigy'. She can be "powerful" and "angry" (l. 28). The atmosphere is calm and very personal while the narrator repeats her decision: "I had new thoughts […] I won't let her change me, I promised myself. I won't be what I'm not" (ll. 29–30).

(513 words)

> **Tip**
> Do not just list narrative techniques but explain their effects on the reader.

3 Evaluation

14 VP a) *Comment on the question of whether parents should constantly interfere in their children's education to improve their skills.*

Refer to the novel excerpt in which the girl is forced to do learning tasks just because her mother wants her to become a prodigy.
In your answer you may support or argue against the statement in the task.
You may take an impartial postion as well.

Task support

Für diese Aufgabe werden insgesamt 14 Punkte auf den Inhalt vergeben.

Form und Umfang meiner Antwort:
Comment …: Beziehen Sie sich für die Bearbeitung dieser Aufgabe auf die Handlung des Texts und Ihre eigenen Erfahrungen und erläutern Sie Ihre Ansicht anhand mehrerer, unterstützender Argumente.
Stützen Sie Ihre Argumentation durch eine überzeugende Strukturierung Ihrer Argumente und verfassen Sie den Text in formaler Sprache.

Mögliche Inhalte und Struktur meiner Antwort:
- *Introduction:* Parents should always support their children's education.
- *Main part:*
  - Amy Tan's excerpt describes an obviously bad example of how a mother tries to support her child.
  - Above all, the parents support their children in helping them with their homework and showing them the importance of education.
  - Parents can help their children not to fear failing school exams.
  - Parents should accept that every child has different, individual skills.
- *Conclusion:* (Summary of the arguments.)

Proposed solution:
In the novel excerpt from "The Joy Luck Club", a mother hopes to discover that her nine-year-old daughter is a prodigy and forces her to take special tests to discover her special talent. It is questionable whether this is a good idea. Supporting children in their education is worthwhile if it parents are constructive and supportive, but it can be damaging if their expectations are unreasonably high.

The girl in the novel extract is unhappy with the situation. On the one hand, she does not want to disappoint her mother. On the other hand, she hates the tests because it is impossible for her to pass them. As a result the girl becomes seriously frustrated and refuses to continue learning with her mother. The story is a painful example of how a parent can fail to support his or her child.

Nevertheless, parents should take an active role in the education of their children. Children learn so much at an early age just by observing their parents. Later on, parents can contribute to their children's education by helping them with their homework or assuaging the fear of failure. Parents who get involved and show interest in school matters show their children that it is important to do their best at school in order to be successful later in life.

However, parents should avoid pressuring their children too severely and they should not expect their children to fulfil their wishes. Every child has got different skills and capabilities and deserves to be supported regardless of whether they can fulfil their parents' dreams.

For my part, I think my parents have behaved correctly towards me. I am far from being an excellent pupil but my parents leave me alone as long as things are going right for me. But when I neglect school matters, my parents talk to me and we try to find a possible solution.

All in all, parents should care about their children's education. But that should not go beyond being a helping hand or having talks when grades at school deteriorate.

(343 words)

> **Tip**
> Refer critically to the novel excerpt in your comment.

b) *Re-creation of text: Write the girl's diary entry on the evening when she realised that she did not want her mother to change her. (14 P.)*

In this diary entry you have to present the girl's mood and emotions by referring to the excerpt from the novel. Imagine how she might feel after her experience in front of the mirror and write your text from her point of view. Use informal language as it is a personal diary entry.

Task support

Für diese Aufgabe werden insgesamt 14 Punkte auf den Inhalt vergeben.

Form und Umfang meiner Antwort:
Write a diary entry … : Schreiben Sie einen Tagebucheintrag aus Sicht der Protagonistin und knüpfen Sie dabei an die geschilderte Situation in dem Romanauszug an.
Achten Sie darauf, dass Sie den Tagebucheintrag aus der Perspektive der Protagonistin schreiben und in der 1. Person Singular in informeller Sprache verfassen.

Mögliche inhaltliche Aspekte:
- the task you had to do today
- your mother's high expectations and how you disappointed her
- you have to be part of your mother's plans and your mother does not accept your wishes
- you are afraid of hurting your mother if you refuse to continue your tasks in the evening

Proposed solution:

21st May 2017:
The torture continues. Last night I had to take some silly tests that my mother found in a magazine about housekeeping. When my mother chose a page in the Bible at random and told me to remember everything I could, I couldn't stand it anymore and just gave up. I know my mother dreams of a great future for me but training with her is just useless! She got angry and reminded me of my unlimited opportunities to become a prodigy and that I could become rich and famous if I just worked hard enough.
I hate the way she's always treating me. OK, on the one hand I know that she's got my best interests at heart but on the other hand I won't be what I'm not. I'm still a child and that's why I've got other interests like meeting my friends from school or playing with them in the afternoon. But my extra lessons with my mother in the evening make it impossible to meet them.
I think the prodigy side of me is just to accept myself for what I am. My mother's never asked me what I'm interested in and it's obvious that she's trying to make me fulfil her dreams, not mine. The time's come to have a talk with her so that something can really change in the future. But now I'm worried about how she might react. Will she get furious with me? Or will she understand me? I don't want to disappoint her either.
I hope I'll be able to sleep tonight because there are so many things that are on my mind. …

(276 words)

Tip
The girl's thoughts and feelings are an essential part of the diary entry.

4 Mediation

Your American high school friend is doing a project on 'Social mobility and equality of opportunity among young people today'. Your friend asks you about how young people in Germany assess their chances of climbing the social ladder.

18 VP *Write an email to your friend informing him/her about personal and external factors which are crucial for a successful career and upward social mobility according to this article.*

Read the German article carefully and write an email to your friend. Differentiate between important and unimportant information to fulfil the task. Do not get confused by the many numbers and statistics in the German text. Instead, focus on the factors which are considered to be important when it comes to the possibility of upward social mobility. Find and structure them and write your email.

Task support

Für diese Aufgabe werden insgesamt 18 Punkte auf den Inhalt vergeben.

Form und Umfang meiner Antwort:
Write an email ...: Verfassen Sie eine E-Mail an einen Freund in den USA. Beachten Sie die spezifischen Textsortenmerkmale einer E-Mail (Anrede, Schlussformel, ...) und formulieren Sie diese in informeller Sprache.
Achten Sie darauf, dass Ihre E-Mail alle wichtigen inhaltlichen Aspekte umfasst.

Mögliche inhaltliche Aspekte:
Factors, crucial for a successful career and social upward mobility:
- economic growth
- education
- the opportunities for people looking for an apprenticeship, on the job training, and / or employment
- equal opportunities and the possibility for upward social mobility
- the kind of work and possibilities for a career
- one's own social class
- motivation and willingness to climb the social ladder

Proposed solution:
Hi Leslie,
In your last email you told me about your class project and asked me what factors are important to young German people to do well in their job and to climb the social ladder. I did some research and found an interesting article about young people in Germany.
According to the article, the career prospects depend, of course, on external circumstances like the development of the economy and the situation on the labour market. For young people it's also important if you can take on more responsibility in the kind of job that you're doing. This also depends on the kind of training you had. That's why people with an apprenticeship, which usually lasts for two to three years, are quite optimistic about their future.
Of course, your personal character traits matter too. You should be motivated to climb the social ladder. In general, Germans believe in equality of opportunity in society, but at the same time working class people are not as optimistic about their chances as members of the middle class. So you see, equality of opportunity is also a necessity for a career.
I hope I could help you with these facts. Let me know if you have any questions!

Bye,
Julius

(204 words)

> **Tip**
> Structure the personal and external factors in one paragraph each.

Übungs-Abi 2: **The US and the American Dream**

Klausurteil: Leseverstehen und Schreiben integriert

The American Dream has become a burden for most

As wages stagnate and costs rise, US workers recognise the guiding ideal of this nation for the delusional myth it is.

The final chapter of America's Promise, a high-school textbook on American history, ends with a rallying cry to national mythology. "The history of the United
5 States is one of challenges faced, problems resolved, and crises overcome," it states. "Throughout their history Americans have remained an optimistic people, carrying this optimism into the new century. The full promise of America has yet to be realised. This is the real promise of America; the ability to dream of a better world to come."
10 Such are the assumptions beamed from the torch of Lady Liberty, coursing through the veins of the nation's political culture and imbibed with mothers' milk. Their nation, many will tell you, is not just a land mass but an ideal – a shining city on the hill beckoning a bright new tomorrow and a dazzling dawn for all those who want it badly enough. Such devout optimism, even (and at times particu-
15 larly) in the midst of adversity makes America, in equal parts, both exciting and delusional. According to Gallup, since 1977 people have consistently believed their financial situation will improve next year even when previous years have consistently been worse.

But when President Barack Obama was planning his run for a second term his
20 pollsters noticed a profound shift in the national mood. The optimism was largely gone – and with it both the excitement and the delusion. The time-honoured rhetorical appeals to a life of relentless progress, upward mobility and personal reinvention didn't work the way they used to.

"The language around the American Dream wasn't carrying the same reso-
25 nance," Joel Benenson, one of Obama's key pollsters, told the *Washington Post*. "Some of the symbols of achieving the American Dream were becoming burdens – owning that house with the big mortgage was expensive, owning two cars and more debts; having your kid go to college. The cost and burden of taking out those loans was making a lot of Americans ambivalent. They weren't sure a college
30 education was worth it."

This wasn't just about the recession – though of course that didn't help – but a far more protracted, profound and painful descent in expectations and aspirations that has been taking place for several decades. For underpinning that faith in a better tomorrow was an understanding that inequality in wealth would be tolerat-
35 ed so long as it was coupled with a guarantee of equality of opportunity. In recent years they have seen both heading in the wrong direction – the gap between rich and poor has grown even as possibilities for economic and social advancement have stalled.

(444 words)
Gary Younge, *The Guardian*, 2013

Tip
→ *Grundwissen*
The US and the American Dream

[2] **delusional** believing in false realities
[10] **to beam** to shine brightly
[11] **to imbibe** to drink / consume
[12] **shining city on the hill** reference to the Bible
[16] **Gallup** a company which conducts opinion polls
[20] **pollster** a person who conducts opinion polls
[27] **mortgage** money lent by a bank
[32] **protracted** lasting for a long time
[38] **to stall** stop running / working (usually used for an engine)

Tip
The source gives you information about the text type.

1 Comprehension

12 VP — Outline the author's perception of the ambivalence in American society regarding the American Dream.

2 Analysis

16 VP — Analyse how the author presents his view. Focus on the line of argument, the use of language and stylistic devices in this article.

3 Evaluation

Choose one of the following tasks:

14 VP — a) "Some of the symbols of achieving the American Dream were becoming burdens" (l. 26). Comment on this quote referring to examples from the text and work done in class.

14 VP — b) Re-creation of text: A British friend has dropped out of school after year ten and started working as an unskilled labourer in a factory. Now he intends to emigrate to the USA, where he thinks he could be better off financially. Write a personal letter to him in order to make him think more deeply on the question of whether he should emigrate to the USA or rather stay in his home country. Refer to the article and work done in class.

> **Tip**
> → The tasks in *Erste Schritte* will help you to complete Tasks 1–3.

> **Tip**
> Focus on your role, the addressee and the form of the text.

Klausurteil: Sprachmittlung isoliert

4 Mediation

Together with your partner school in Portland, Oregon, USA, you are working on an international project called "from rags to riches around the globe". Your part of the project is to find German people whose dreams in different areas of life have come true and whose stories could serve as rolemodels for others to become ambitious and motivated to make the most of their talents.
You have found the following article about one such success story in the weekly newspaper Die Zeit.

18 VP — Write an informative and formal blog entry for your partner school's course website which outlines the personal characteristics that were necessary for the author to achieve success, as well as the conclusions he draws from his own life in his current job.

> **Tip**
> → The mediation task in *Erste Schritte* will help you to prepare for writing your mediation text.

Rüdiger Grube, Manager

Ich stamme von einem Bauernhof im Alten Land in der Nähe von Hamburg und habe sehr lange in ganz einfachen Verhältnissen gelebt. Mein Bruder und ich mussten von Anfang an auf dem Hof mit anpacken. Meine Eltern hatten sich leider bereits getrennt, als ich gerade fünf Jahre alt war. Meine Mutter hatte uns allein
5 großgezogen und brauchte jede Hilfe. Schule war immer nur lästige Pflicht. Meine Begeisterung für das Lernen habe ich erst spät entdeckt, als Teenager. Damals träumte ich davon Pilot zu werden. Als meine Tante davon erfuhr, lachte sie mich aus und sagte mir am Mittagstisch: „Dazu brauchst du Abitur. Das schaffst du nie."

Dieser Satz ist lange ein Ansporn für mich gewesen, eigentlich bis heute. Nach neun Jahren Hauptschule wechselte ich auf die Realschule und machte dann eine Lehre zum Metallflugzeugbauer beim Hamburger Flugzeugbau Blohm+Voss. Damals arbeiteten 60.000 Menschen für das Unternehmen. Während meiner Ausbildungszeit habe ich für die Betriebszeitung einen Artikel über das Spenden von Organen geschrieben. Helen Blohm, die Frau des Inhabers, las den Artikel und lud mich zu sich ins „feine Blankenese" ein. Die Blohms hatten ein behindertes Kind und waren deswegen von meinem Artikel angetan. Helen Blohm fragte mich nach meinen Zukunftsplänen. Ich antwortete, dass ich gerne Pilot werden wollte oder ein Flugzeugbaustudium aufnehmen würde, mir aber das Geld dazu fehle. Wenige Tage später rief mich ihr Mann, mein oberster Chef, an und fragte, ob ich mit 300 D-Mark jeden Monat auskommen würde für mein Studium. Das war für mich der Start in eine neue Welt.

[…] Dank meines Lebenswegs weiß ich, dass man jungen Menschen eine Chance geben muss, unabhängig davon, wo sie herkommen.

[…] Das ist mit der Grund, weswegen wir bei der Deutschen Bahn als eines der ersten Unternehmen in Deutschland alle Bewerber auf Ausbildungsplätze zu Onlinetests einladen, egal welche Schulnoten sie haben. Im vergangenen Jahr, 2014, haben wir auf diesem Weg etwa 3.700 Menschen eingestellt.

(314 Wörter)
Marco Maurer, *Die Zeit*, 2015

Tip

If necessary, explain concepts and terms which are unique to the German language.

Erste Schritte

Übungen

Comprehension
Read the text and underline information about the American Dream and about living standards in the US.

Analysis
Part of Task 2 requires you to focus on the line of argument in the text. To help you with this, complete the following table.

Paragraph	Main argument of the paragraph	How does it relate to the American Dream?
ll. 1–9	The American Dream is the ability to dream of a better world.	conforms to the American Dream but has yet to be fully realised

Tip
→ To help you prepare for answering Task 1–3, do the task(s) on this page.

Evaluation
a) *To collect ideas, note down pros and cons related to the statement.*

b) *Complete a mind map with "Possible challenges in the US" at its centre.*

Mediation
a) *Read the task carefully again and complete what the task asks for.*

1. Context: _____

   _____

2. Information asked for: _____

   _____

   _____

3. My role: _____

4. My addressee: _____

5. Kind of text I write: _____

b) *Note down the relevant information for your text.*

Characteristics necessary for success:

_____
_____
_____
_____
_____
_____
_____
_____
_____

Conclusions used in Grube's job:

_____
_____
_____
_____
_____

Tip
→ To help you prepare for writing your mediation text in Task 4, do the task(s) on this page.

Lösungsvorschläge

Comprehension
delusional myth • the ability to dream of a better world to come • The optimism was largely gone • ideal • the symbols of achieving the American Dream were becoming burdens • etc.

Analysis

ll. 1–9	The American Dream is the ability to dream of a better world.	conforms to the American Dream but has yet to be fully realised
ll. 10–18	There is widespread optimism among US citizens, even in hard times.	conforms to the American Dream in terms of being optimistic for the future
ll. 19–30	Public opinion in America has changed. Many people can't afford the American Dream anymore.	the American Dream is perceived as a "burden" → does not conform to the American Dream
ll. 31–38	The American Dream is losing believers because opportunities for social progress are dwindling.	people can't achieve the American Dream any more → does not conform to the American Dream

Evaluation
Cf. proposed solutions for the Evaluation in the *Erwartungshorizonte*.

Mediation
a) 1. Context: international project called "from rags to riches around the globe"; your part of the project is to find German people whose dreams in different areas of life have come true • 2. Information asked for: to find German people whose dreams in different areas of life have come true and whose stories could serve as role models for others • 3. My role: student • 4. My addressee: international students • 5. Kind of text I write: formal blog

b) Characteristics necessary for success:
Has been used to hard work since his childhood • had a dream / ambition • learned and studied a lot to achieve his dream • did not stop learning after school • did not give up in difficult times
Conclusions in his job:
gives every applicant a chance whatever his / her education is • the company invites applicants to take tests, regardless of their marks

Erwartungshorizonte

1 Comprehension

12 VP *Outline the author's perception of the ambivalence in American society regarding the American Dream.*

Read the text carefully and write down the factors leading to the American people's ambivalence today. Write a well-structured text. You are not allowed to give any comments or analysis or add any additional information in this task. Just concentrate on the facts given in the text and leave out any unimportant details.

Task support

Für diese Aufgabe werden insgesamt 12 Punkte auf den Inhalt vergeben.

Form und Umfang meiner Antwort:
Outline ...: Skizzieren Sie in Ihrer Antwort die Hauptmerkmale oder zugrundeliegenden Merkmale des gefragten Inhalts.
Beziehen Sie einzelne, wichtige Beispiele aus dem Text in Ihre Antwort mit ein und formulieren Sie Ihre Antwort möglichst in eigenen Worten.

Mögliche inhaltliche Aspekte:
- The idea of equal opportunity and the possibility of climbing the social ladder if you work for it is an integral part of the American Dream.
- Today, the concept of the American Dream doesn't work in the way it should anymore. Even if you work hard, you stay poor.
- At school the concept of the American Dream is still taught, as it is part of a textbook on history.
- Current economic and social developments (see examples in the text) make the American people doubt their constantly optimistic view that everything will become better in the future.
- America's middle class, who used to believe in equal opportunities, is now shrinking and becoming poorer.

Proposed solution:
In the article "The American Dream has become a burden for most", Gary Younge deals with the ambivalence between the myth of the American Dream and the harsh realities which the American people have to accept.
The characteristics of the American Dream have constantly been the guiding ideal of the nation and its people. Students are exposed to the concept quite early, and learn from textbooks on American history that America is a country that has often been confronted with problems, but has always succeeded in solving them in the course of time.
The myth of a whole nation is based on the concept of never-ending optimism that leads to constant progress, upward mobility and self-fulfillment. The political culture of the country follows this idea as well.
Unfortunately, reality for most Americans looks very different from the proclaimed ideals, and this has contributed to a shift in the national mood. Owning a house and two cars and sending children to college come with a big price tag, as mortgages have to be repaid and debts for the cars and education have to be paid off.

Tip
Mention the source you refer to at the beginning of your answer.

Tip
First outline the myth of the American Dream. Then contrast it with the harsh reality.

The American Dream has consequently become a heavy burden for most Americans these days.
The gap between rich and poor has grown too, and the dream of equal opportunity seems to have disappeared. In contrast to this, American society is developing into a rigid class system and the middle class is getting poorer.

(238 words)

2 Analysis

16 VP *Analyse how the author presents his view. Focus on the line of argument, the use of language and stylistic devices in this article.*

Analysing means that you have to put the material of the text into a broader context by showing that you can use the necessary skills you have acquired in your English lessons. The task tells you exactly what you are supposed to analyse: Here it is the line of argument of the text, the use of language and the stylistic devices. Note that you have to analyse all three parts with regard to the author's persuasive strategy: "to present his view". Write a well-structured text and focus on each part separately.

Task support

Für diese Aufgabe werden insgesamt 16 Punkte auf den Inhalt vergeben.

Form und Umfang meiner Antwort:
Analyse …: Beschreiben und erklären Sie in Ihrer Antwort, woran Sie in dem Artikel die Einstellung des Autors erkennen und wie er diese dem Leser mitteilt. Beziehen Sie sich auf stets auf Beispiele oder Zitate, um Ihre Erkenntnisse zu belegen.
Formulieren Sie Ihre Antwort möglichst in eigenen Worten.

Mögliche inhaltliche Aspekte:
- Line of argument: The text begins with the myth, continues with the difficulties in achieving this dream and ends with the fact that inequality has increased in American society.
- Paragraphs 1 and 2 contain lots of imagery and stylistic devices (alliteration, repetition, metaphor etc.).
- From paragraph 3 onwards the author emphasises the economic and social decline and refers to reliable sources (statistics, key pollster).
- The author ends with impressive first-hand experience to support his view.

Mögliche zusätzliche Aspekte:
- Paragraphs 1 and 2 contain references to the Bible.
- From paragraph 3 onwards the language is more subtle.

Proposed solution:
The author starts by giving some information about the concept of the American Dream itself in the first two paragraphs. He begins by describing the American Dream in a very impressive way by using parallelisms in l. 5 ("challenges faced, problems resolved, and crises overcome") and repetitions in ll. 6–9 ("promise", "optimistic"). He continues by portraying the American Dream in an exaggerated way, making clear that it is far from reality. He uses some high-flown words such

Tip
Do not just list rethorical devices but explain their effects on the audience.

as "a bright new tomorrow" (l. 13), "devout optimism" (l. 14) or an alliteration in "dazzling dawn" (l. 13). He also employs several metaphors, like in "assumptions beamed from the torch of Lady Liberty […] coursing through the veins of the nation's political culture and imbibed with mothers' milk" (ll. 10–11) to point out a concept that is omnipresent in the US, however far from reality it may be. To show that the concept of the American Dream is similar to religious symbolism, the author refers to the Bible when he calls America the "shining city on the hill" (l. 12). In contrast to the beginning, the author uses less imagery in the following paragraphs when he describes the actual living conditions in the US. From the third paragraph onwards, he starts giving a critical review of the concept by emphasising that the optimism for a better future was largely gone when President Barack Obama was planning his run for a second term, as some of the symbols of the American Dream were suddenly becoming burdens (l. 26).

From the third paragraph onwards he offers proof of his view that the American Dream has become a burden for most Americans by comparing the ideals of the American Dream with the harsh realities the Americans face in their daily lives. Fulfilling some dreams means going into debt and trust in equal opportunity has disappeared as the gap between rich and poor has increased dramatically. To underline his critical view of the American Dream and its decline, he uses an alliteration, "protracted, profound and painful descent" (l. 32). Additionally, he builds credibility for his text by mentioning the findings of the research institute Gallup (l. 16) and by citing one of Obama's key pollsters views (ll. 25–30).

So the structure of the text starts from the exaggerated description of the myth of the American Dream and ends with the fact that social inequality has been increasing in the US.

(406 words)

> **Tip**
> To support your findings, explain them and give examples from the text.

3 Evaluation

14 VP **a)** *"Some of the symbols of achieving the American Dream were becoming burdens" (l. 26). Comment on this quote referring to examples from the text and to work done in class.*

In this task you have to decide whether you agree or disagree with the statement and give reasons for your decision. Take care that you do not contradict yourself and that you link the sentences in a way that makes your comment more vivid and demanding.

Task support

Für diese Aufgabe werden insgesamt 14 Punkte auf den Inhalt vergeben.

Form und Umfang meiner Antwort:
Comment on …: Erstellen Sie einen strukturierten Text, in dem Sie verschiedene Argumente ausführen, um Ihre Meinung dem Leser mitzuteilen.
Beziehen Sie sich für die Bearbeitung dieser Aufgabe auf die Aussage des Texts und auf Ihr bisher erworbenes Wissen.
Abhängig von Ihren Informationen, wägen Sie ab, für welche These Sie argumentieren werden und erläutern Sie Ihre Ansicht anhand mehrerer Argumente.

Übungs-Abi 2: The US and the American Dream

Mögliche inhaltliche Aspekte: und Struktur meiner Antwort:
- *Introduction:*
  - *The American Dream has been a continuing ideal for a lot of people.*
  - *State your opinion on the topic.*
- *Arguments:*
  - *You enjoy freedom and can fulfil your potential in the US.*
  - *The economic recession is only temporary.*
  - *Other important aspects like freedom of speech or the right to privacy are also part of the American Dream.*
- *(Summarise your opinion.)*

Proposed solution:
It is widely known that the American Dream is a concept that a whole nation is based on. The American Dream has been the guiding ideal of the American people for centuries and at the same time it continues to attract immigrants from many different parts the world. That is the reason why I disagree with the statement and don't believe that the American Dream will become a discontinued model in the future.

Maybe individual expectations have to adapt to the current situation, but as the state does not interfere in most areas of life, in contrast to many European countries, the individual still has the opportunity to make the most of his life according to his own abilities and skills. Sooner or later, economic prosperity will replace recession again. Historically, there have always been bad times as well as good times. Therefore, people shouldn't be too pessimistic about a certain situation in a clearly defined period of time, for example the recession which was brought on by the mortgage crisis.

Moreover, the concept is not based on one characteristic only. It comprises, for example, the freedom of speech, the freedom of religion and liberty as well. Therefore America will always be a dreamland for many immigrants who want to make their fortune there. They do not have to be afraid of being persecuted there because of their religious or political convictions, for example.

To sum up, I think, referring to the American Dream as a discontinued model is farfetched. Granted, it is an ideal and therefore disconnected from real world conditions, but it is based on convictions that no one would seriously call into question. Considering the living conditions in so many other countries, America continues to be a country where dreams can come true.

(296 words)

— **Tip**
Begin your text by stating the question you are going to discuss.

— **Tip**
Start with the weakest argument and end with the strongest.

14 VP **b)** *Re-creation of text: A British friend has dropped out of school after year ten and started working as an unskilled labourer in a factory. Now he intends to emigrate to the USA, where he thinks he could be better off financially.*
Write a personal letter to him in order to make him think more deeply on the question of whether he should emigrate to the USA or rather stay in his home country. Refer to the article and work done in class.

In this personal letter to a friend of yours, you have to present your advice in a coherent and well-structured way by referring to the article and paying attention to the task given. Where language is concerned, you are also allowed to use informal language, as it is a private / personal letter.

Task support

Für diese Aufgabe werden insgesamt 14 Punkte auf den Inhalt vergeben.

Form und Umfang meiner Antwort:
Write a personal letter …: Schreiben Sie einen persönlichen Brief an einen Freund, in dem Sie ihm Ihre Meinung und Ratschläge mitteilen.
Beziehen Sie sich für die Bearbeitung dieser Aufgabe auf die Informationen aus dem Text und auf Ihr bisher erworbenes Wissen.

Mögliche Inhalte und Struktur meiner Antwort:
- (Refer to the reason for writing.)
- Possible arguments:
  - Only a few people make it from 'rags to riches'.
  - Living the American Dream is very expensive – maybe too expensive.
  - A lot of wages are very low in the US.
  - The middle class is shrinking.
  - You need a lot of information before emigrating.
- (Close your e-mail summarising your opinion / giving an outlook / …)

Proposed solution:

Dear Liam,

I know that you're thinking of emigrating to the USA, as you think you might be financially better off there. But please don't forget that you don't have good school or job qualifications. The reality of living in the United States will fall short of your expectations. Maybe you're thinking of all the stories about people who have climbed the social ladder from 'rags to riches' and became millionaires in the end. But these people are just a few lucky ones in a difficult working world. In America the money doesn't come for free either, unfortunately. You have to work really hard as well, and there is much less social security than in Britain. In the newspapers you can often read about the difficulties people have in making their American Dream come true. For a lot of people, this dream has become a huge problem because their debts for education, a house and a car are constantly increasing. At the same time, a lot of wages, especially for unskilled workers, are actually too low to live on and many people have to go to food banks even though they have a job. That's the reason why the middle class in the US is shrinking while the gap between rich and poor is growing. Considering this social development, the American Dream can also turn into an 'American nightmare'. Additionally, you don't know anyone there. There will be no family members and friends who could immediately support you when you are in need of money, for example. You're my friend and I really don't want to stop you from following your dreams, but first try to get more information from the American embassy in your country about job opportunities, housing and how to get a work permit. Then please think about your idea again before you make a decision.

Good luck, whatever you decide!
Jannik

(313 words)

Tip
Begin your letter by mentioning the reason for writing.

4 Mediation

18 VP

Together with your partner school in Portland, Oregon, USA, you are working on an international project called "from rags to riches around the globe".
Your part of the project is to find German people whose dreams in different areas of life have come true and whose stories could serve as rolemodels for others to become ambitious and motivated to make the most of their talents.
You have found the following article about one such success story in the weekly newspaper Die Zeit.

Write an informative and formal blog entry for your partner school's course website which outlines the personal characteristics that were necessary for the author to achieve success, as well as the conclusions he draws from his own life in his current job.

In this task you should first create a short introduction including information about Rüdiger Grube as well as the type of publication. Then write a well-structured text by referring to the task given.
Note that you are asked to write an informative and formal blog entry and therefore pay attention to its special characteristics too.
Add information where necessary (e.g., *Deutsche Bahn*).

Task support

Für diese Aufgabe werden insgesamt 18 Punkte auf den Inhalt vergeben.

Form und Umfang meiner Antwort:
Write an informative formal blog entry …: Schreiben Sie einen informativen – d.h. ohne eine persönliche Stellungnahme – Blog-Eintrag.
Beachten Sie die spezifischen Merkmale für die Textsorte Blog (z.B. klare Strukturierung durch Paragraphen, klare Ansprache der Adressaten, Einladung zu weiteren Kommentaren am Ende etc.).

Mögliche inhaltliche Aspekte:
- *Deutsche Bahn is the German national rail company*
- *Rüdiger Grube, top manager of Deutsche Bahn*
- *has been used to hard work since his childhood*
- *grew up on a farm*
- *had to help his mother*
- *was eager to learn and put a lot of effort into his education and professional training*
- *worked as a mechanic for an airplane construction company*
- *followed his dream and started to study*
- *was helped by people who recognised his potential*
- *gives a chance to everybody, no matter what their grades are*
- *introduced online tests so that everybody can prove their abilities*

Proposed solution:

From rags to riches around the globe – a German story

Today I found an article in the German weekly newspaper "Die Zeit" reporting about a man who made it right to the top of the "Deutsche Bahn" which is our German national rail company, although his childhood wasn't easy and his career started small.

Here is his story:
Rüdiger Grube grew up on a farm and has been used to hard work since his childhood. He was only five years old when his parents got divorced and their mother needed his and his brother's help because she had to run the farm alone. At first, school was just some kind of annoying chore for him. He did not start enjoying learning until he was a teenager.
After going to the simplest kind of secondary school for nine years, he changed to intermediate secondary school and later he completed a traineeship as an airframe mechanic.
After that, with the help of kind people who recognised his motivation, he managed to get a place studying aircraft construction, which had always been his dream.
As the director of the German national rail company, all that finally inspired him to give young people a chance, regardless of where they come from.
Today all applicants for jobs at the German rail company are invited to do online tests, whatever their marks were at school.

You're welcome to comment on my blog entry or add a success story you know anything about.

(245 words)

> **Tip**
> Explain important German terms / names.

> **Tip**
> Invite readers to post further comments.

Übungs-Abi 3: **The media**

Klausurteil: Leseverstehen und Schreiben integriert

When the media misrepresents black men, the effects are felt in the real world

In a 2011 study, Media Representations & Impact on the Lives of Black Men and Boys, conducted by The Opportunity Agenda, negative mass media portrayals were strongly linked with lower life expectations among black men. These portrayals, constantly reinforced in print media, on television, the internet, fiction shows,
5 print advertising and video games, shape public views of and attitudes toward men of color. They not only help create barriers to advancement within our society, but also "make these positions seem natural and inevitable". […]

The Opportunity Agenda study also shows that these media distortions are multi-faceted, especially relative to real-world facts. For example, there is an
10 overall under-representation of black men as 'talking head' experts, users of luxury items in print ads and as reliable and relatable characters with fully developed backgrounds in fiction shows and films. Overwhelming evidence exists of exaggerated associations of African-American men to drug-related crime, unemployment and poverty. "The idle black male on the street corner is not the 'true face' of pov-
15 erty in America, but is the dominant one in the world as depicted by the media", according to the study's executive summary. Too many stories associate black men with intractable problems.

Men of color held in esteem by the media, while entirely worthy of praise, too often personify a circumscribed spectrum of human qualities. Prowess in sports,
20 physical achievement in general and musicality are emphasised inordinately. Common role models depicted by the media such as rap or hip-hop stars and basketball players imply limited life choices. When is the last time you have seen a black college professor, doctor, lawyer or scientist selling a product? Many important dynamics that affect black lives, such as a history of economic disadvantage
25 and a prevailing anti-black bias in society, don't often make it to the presses or the screens. […]

Not only does the media's reluctance to provide more balanced perspectives of our African-American male population worsen cultural division among all people, it enables judges to hand out harsher sentences, companies to deny jobs, banks to
30 decline loans and the police to shoot indiscriminately. The mass media is certainly aware of its vast power to shape popular ideas, opinions and attitudes. They should become equally cognizant of their role as a mechanism of social change for the better of all. […]

All media can and should choose words, images and news angles that give a
35 fuller, more nuanced narrative of African-American men, as well as black history, culture and life in America, as a whole. People of color are individuals, not types.

(422 words)
Leigh Donaldson, *The Guardian*, 2015

Tip
→ *Grundwissen*
The US and the American Dream

[8] **distortion** act of giving a false impression
[10] **talking head** *(infml)* presenter
[32] **cognizant of** aware of

Klausurteil

1 Comprehension

12 VP — Describe how black men are represented in the mass media and how this presentation affects their lives according to the author.

Tip
→ **The tasks in Erste Schritte** will help you to complete Tasks 1–3.

2 Analysis

16 VP — Analyse the language, the stylistic devices and the line of argument the author uses to convince the reader of his view.

3 Evaluation

Choose one of the following tasks:

14 VP — a) "The mass media is certainly aware of its vast power to shape popular ideas, opinions and attitudes." (ll. 30 ff.). Comment on the statement.

14 VP — b) The next issue of your school's magazine will be published in cooperation with your American partner school. The magazine's topic is about "Global challenges of ethnic diversity and the role of the mass media". Your job is to interview an Afro-American editor of a US quality paper, Mr. Hamilton. Both of you have read the article "When the media misrepresents black men, the effects are felt in the real world".

You want to talk about how the editor and his colleagues deal with the responsibility of shaping public opinion. Write a script of the interview.

Tip
Focus on your perspective(s), the addressee and the form of the text.

Klausurteil: Sprachmittlung isoliert

4 Mediation

The Opportunity Agenda is an American non-governmental organisation which is dedicated to overcoming racial prejudices and expanding equal opportunities to people in the US. Your American friend's parents, Mr and Mrs Arnold, work for this organisation and ask you whether there are similar projects in Germany. Your class has participated in the project "Wenn Bilder meine Sprache wären" and you want to inform Mr and Mrs Arnold about it.

18 VP — Write a formal email to Mr and Mrs Arnold, employees of The Opportunity Agenda, in which you describe the aims of the German project.

Tip
The mediation task in Erste Schritte will help you to prepare for writing your mediation text.

Tip
Focus on your addresse, the characteristics of your text type and relevant information.

Islam und Muslime in den Medien

Welche Macht Worte haben können, zeigt das Projekt „Wenn Bilder meine Sprache wären" der Türkischen Gemeinde Deutschlands (TGD). Darin setzen sich Jugendliche mit Migrationshintergrund kritisch mit Medienberichten über das muslimische Leben in Deutschland auseinander und erarbeiten Vorschläge
5 für eine sensiblere und ausgewogenere Berichterstattung. […]
    Darf der stellvertretende Chefredakteur einer großen deutschen Boulevard-Zeitung den Islam in einem Kommentar pauschal als Integrationshindernis bezeichnen und undifferenziert Negativ-Beispiele wie „Ehrenmorde" und „Zwangsheiraten" als Begründung anführen? Fünf junge Männer und Frauen mit
10 Migrationshintergrund, die sich in einer Arbeitsgruppe des Medienanalyse-Workshops der TGD in Stuttgart mit diesem Artikel befassen, sind sich einig: Diese Art der Berichterstattung überschreitet aus ihrer Sicht die Grenzen der Meinungs-

freiheit und fördert Vorbehalte gegen Muslime. Dass sich die Chefredakteurin des Blattes noch am Tag der Veröffentlichung für den Kommentar entschuldigte, reicht den jungen Leuten nicht aus. Ihrer Meinung nach hätten arbeitsrechtliche Konsequenzen folgen müssen.

Stereotypen in Medienberichten
Ähnlich kritisch bewerteten die beiden anderen Arbeitsgruppen des Workshops Berichte über die Scharia-Polizei in Wuppertal und einen Motorradclub, der durch kriminelle Mitglieder mit Migrationshintergrund Schlagzeilen machte. Auch hier wurde aus Sicht der Jugendlichen durch diskriminierende Wortwahl, einseitige Darstellung und Verwendung von Stereotypen ein negatives Bild vom Islam und den Muslimen in Deutschland gezeichnet. „Wir haben beobachtet, dass bei Jugendlichen mit Migrationshintergrund eine große Verunsicherung gegenüber den Medien herrscht. Sie fühlen sich nicht verstanden und kritisieren die Art der Berichterstattung, aber ohne Gegenbeispiele zu nennen", erklärt Projektleiterin Deniz Kauffmann. „In den Workshops wollen wir sie dahingehend stärken, dass sie sich mit den Phänomenen Muslimfeindlichkeit, religiöser Extremismus und Antisemitismus auseinandersetzen und Alternativen für eine kultursensible Darstellung erarbeiten." Auf der anderen Seite sollen Journalisten für ihre Verantwortung als Multiplikatoren sensibilisiert werden. „Vielen Journalisten ist gar nicht bewusst, dass sie mit gewissen Formulierungen Menschen verletzen und ausgrenzen", weiß die stellvertretende Bundesgeschäftsführerin der TGD.

(299 Wörter)
Bundesamt für Migration und Flüchtlinge, 2014

— Tip
If necessary, explain concepts and terms which are unique to the German language.

Erste Schritte

Übungen

Comprehension
Underline the effects of misrepresentation of black men in the media in the text.

Analysis
a) *To focus on the line of argument, examine the structure and how the author supports his arguments. Underline all sources (reports, examples, (personal) experiences, studies, quotes, etc.) the author refers to in the text.*

b) *Note down rhetorical devices and their effect on the reader from the text.*

l./ ll.	Rhetorical device	Effect

Tip
→ To help you prepare for answering Task 1–3, do the task(s) on this page.

Übungs-Abi 3: The media

Evaluation

a) *To gather information for your comment, brainstorm ideas in favour and against the statement and note them down.*

b) *Brainstorm ideas for the editor's argument explaining possible reasons for misrepresentation and what his newspaper does to convey only impartial information.*

Mediation

a) *Imagine a friend of yours has to do the same task. Briefly reformulate the task in your own words and tell him/her what to do.*

_____

_____

_____

_____

> **Tip**
> → To help you prepare for writing your mediation text in Task 4, do the task(s) on this page.

b) *Explain or paraphrase the German words and phrases in English.*

1. Türkische Gemeinde Deutschland: _____

_____

_____

2. Jugendliche mit Migrationshintergrund:

_____

_____

_____

3. ausgewogene Berichterstattung: _____

_____

4. diskriminierende Wortwahl: _____

_____

5. Muslimfeindlichkeit: _____

_____

6. Antisemitismus: _____

_____

7. kultursensible Darstellung: _____

_____

_____

_____

> **Tip**
> Look up keywords and phrases in a dictionary for help.

Lösungsvorschläge

Comprehension
lower life expectations • create barriers to advancement • under-representation of black men • exaggerated associations of African-American men to drug-related crime, unemployment and poverty • personify a circumscribed spectrum of human qualities • imply limited life choices • worsen cultural division • enables judges to hand out harsher sentences • etc.

Analysis
a) ll.1 ff.: 2011 study by The Opportunity Agenda • ll.14 ff.: quote, "The idle black (…) by the media" • ll.22 ff.: rhetorical question, "When is the (…) selling a product?" • ll.29 ff: examples, "judges to hand (…) to shoot indiscriminately".

b) ll.4–5: enumeration ("print media (…) and video games") – to stress the many kinds of media • l.14: metaphor ("not the true face of poverty") – to stress what poverty does not look like • ll.22 ff.: rhetorical question/direct address – to make the reader agree with the author • l.22 ff.: enumeration ("black college professor, doctor, lawyer or scientist") – to show how many black men and jobs there are, which are not shown.

Evaluation
Cf. proposed solutions for the Evaluation in the *Erwartungshorizonte*.

Mediation
a) Write a formal email to your American friend's parents who work for *The Opportunity Agenda*. Tell them about the aims of the project.

b) 1. Türkische Gemeinde Deutschland: German-Turkish organisation dedicated to improving intercultural understanding • an organisation founded by Turkish immigrants in Germany which supports equality • etc.

2. Jugendliche mit Migrationshintergrund: Young people from immigrant backgrounds • young, first and second generation immigrants • young people who immigrated from abroad or whose parents had immigrated • etc.

3. Ausgewogene Berichterstattung: objective reports • unbiased reporters • fair representation in the news • adequate information • etc.

4. Diskriminierende Wortwahl: insulting/discriminating/offending language • etc.

5. Muslimfeindlichkeit: hostility/discrimination/prejudices against Muslims • etc.

6. Antisemitismus: hostility/discrimination/prejudices against Jewish people • etc.

7. Kultursensible Darstellung: considerate representation of the different cultures • considerate report paying attention to the values of different cultures • thoughtful representation taking into account the values of different cultures • etc.

Erwartungshorizonte

1 Comprehension

12 VP *Describe how black men are represented in the mass media and how this presentation affects their lives according to the author.*

Describe briefly which stories are mainly written in the media about black men that lead to negative public perception and which ones convey a more positive perception of them and include the effects that can be derived from the stereotypes of black men as published in the media.
Focus on the information asked for and write a well-structured text.

Task support

Für diese Aufgabe werden insgesamt 12 Punkte auf den Inhalt vergeben.

Form und Umfang meiner Antwort:
Describe …: In Ihrer Antwort müssen Sie die wichtigsten Inhalte des Textauszugs wiedergeben.
Nennen Sie die Aussagen des Texts zur verzerrten Darstellung von Afro-Amerikanern in den Medien und deren gesellschaftliche Folgen.
Strukturieren Sie Ihren Text angemessen und achten Sie darauf, dass Sie nur Aussagen wiedergeben, die im Originaltext stehen und keine eigenen Ergänzungen oder Interpretationen vornehmen.

Mögliche inhaltliche Aspekte:
- When stories are published about black men in the media, the topics often involve topics such as crime, poverty and unemployment.
- Black men face a negative perception by others in the media.
- Afro-Americans face police arbitrariness and harsh sentences in court.
- Many news consumers consider the black population's inferiority and their discrimination to be normal and justified.
- The media contributes to society's cultural division.
- In contrast to that, respected black men like lawyers, experts and presenters on TV are underrepresented in the mass media.
- In mass media, black men are only role models for other blacks when they have become famous basketball stars or hip-hop singers.
- Short life expectancy among Afro-American men.

Proposed solution:
In this text, published in "The Guardian", the author wants to give proof that predominantly negative reports about black men lead to negative prejudices against them in public.
The more people read such news, the more they take them as proof that black men are overwhelmingly involved in those kinds of crime compared to white people. Additionally, such a misleading perception of Afro-Americans may result in white people mistrusting Afro-Americans and in increasing police arbitrariness towards black men.
The reports to be read in the papers often portray black men as poor, lazy and unemployed or drug dealers who face harsh sentences in court. Furthermore, the

media conveys the impression that the black population's inferiority is normal which would justify their discrimination. In this way, the media contribute to society's cultural division as well.

Besides, trustworthy Afro-American characters such as black TV presenters, doctors or lawyers are hardly ever shown on TV or in advertising. Consequently, imbalanced news reports intensify the misleading impressions of Afro-American men in public which puts them at a disadvantage when finding a job or borrowing money from a bank. The only possibility for black men to be successful seems to be in the sports or music industry because the overwhelming majority of positive, black rolemodels depicted by the media are hip-hop stars or basketball players. As a consequence of the discrimination against black men their life expectancy on average is even shorter than that of white people.

(252 words)

> **Tip**
> Use linking words to structure your text.

2 Analysis

16 VP *Analyse the language, the stylistic devices and the line of argument the author uses to convince the reader of his view.*

Examine how the author tries to persuade the reader of his view. First state the author's view clearly. Then show how this view is supported by the line of argument and the use of language in the article.

Task support

Für diese Aufgabe werden insgesamt 16 Punkte auf den Inhalt vergeben.

Form und Umfang meiner Antwort:
Analyse …: Beschreiben und erklären Sie, wie der Autor seine Meinung dem Leser überzeugend darstellt.
Untersuchen Sie in Ihren Ausführungen die Argumentation (Belege, Beispiele, Gewichtung der Argumente, Einbezug des Lesers etc.) und die Sprache (rhetorische Stilmittel, Adjektive etc.).

Mögliche inhaltliche Aspekte:
- *Line of argument:*
  - The author refers to a reliable source (study by The Opportunity Agenda) and to quotes (police officer, etc.).
  - Common stereotypes are mentioned but clearly disproven.
  - The final argument shows drastic examples of discrimination in everyday life (jobs denied, shot).
  - The article ends with an appeal to the responsibility of the media.

- *Use of language and stylistic devices:*
  - The author uses rhetorical devices like enumerations (ll. 4–5/22 ff.), a metaphor (l. 14) and a rhetorical question (l. 22 ff.).
  - His choice of words supports the fact that Afro-Americans are put at a disadvantage (l. 6: "barriers to advancement", l. 10: "overall underrepresentation", l. 12: "Overwhelming evidence … of exaggerated associations", l: 16: "Too many stories …").

Proposed solution

In order to persuade the reader that black men are misrepresented by the media, the author presents a reliable source in the introduction.
He mentions the findings of a study conducted by The Opportunity Agenda in ll.1 ff. and stresses the far-reaching consequences of misrepresentation in the media by enumerating the different kinds of media (ll.4 ff.).
In addition to referring to reliable sources, his choice of words like "The idle black men on the street corner" reflects the stereotypes of Afro-Americans in the media. But he clearly contradicts this picture when saying that this is "not the true face of poverty" (l.14). Furthermore, he states that "overwhelming evidence exists of exaggerated associations" (l.12) and that "too many stories associate black men with intractable problems" (ll.16 ff.). He stresses repeatedly that men of colour are underrepresented and put at a disadvantage in society (l.6: "barriers of advancement", l.10: "underrepresentation", l.19: "circumscribed spectrum of human qualities", l.22: "limited life choices"). Moreover, he uses a rhetorical question to address the reader directly and to reveal the underrepresentation of Afro-Americans on TV in l.23.
In a following argument, he enumerates further examples ending with the most drastic one of how Afro-Americans are discriminated against because of prejudices. Black men are rejected by companies, refused loans by banks or even shot indiscriminately by the police (l.29 ff.). Now he points out that all this could be changed if the media becomes aware of its responsibility and uses its influence to shape public opinion.
He concludes his line of argument, appealing to the media to paint a more balanced picture of Afro-American men and finishes the article with the simple truth that "people of colour are individuals not types."

(295 words)

> **Tip**
> Mention the author's view which you examine in the introductin of your text.

> **Tip**
> Do not just describe the language but explain their effects on the reader.

3 Evaluation

14 VP **a)** *"The mass media is certainly aware of its vast power to shape popular ideas, opinions and attitudes." (ll.30 ff.). Comment on the statement.*

To introduce your comment on the statement above, you can refer to the examples of unbalanced reports about black men in the article. Then give your opinion using your own knowledge. Based on the article, it is recommended that you argue against the statement i.e. the media is *not* aware of its power to shape popular ideas and attitudes. You may also argue in favour of the statement.

Task support

Für diese Aufgabe werden insgesamt 14 Punkte auf den Inhalt vergeben.

Form und Umfang meiner Antwort:
Comment …: Verknüpfen Sie Ihre eigene Meinung und Ihr eigenes Wissen über die Glaubwürdigkeit der Berichterstattung in den Medien mit dem Bericht über die unausgewogene und einseitige Darstellung von Afro-Amerikanern in den amerikanischen Medien. Greifen Sie in der Einleitung die Fragestellung auf und präzisieren Sie diese und den Kontext, in dem Sie diese kommentieren werden.
Erläutern Sie dann Ihre Ansichten, gestützt durch Argumente und Beispiele und schließen Sie Ihren Kommentar z.B. durch einen Rat ab, einseitige Information zu vermeiden. Achten Sie darauf, Ihren Text in formaler Sprache zu verfassen.

Mögliche Inhalte und Struktur meiner Antwort:
- *Introduction:*
  - According to the report about misrepresentation of black men in the US media, readers are influenced in the wrong way.
  - Media companies are not always aware of its power and responsibility to shape public opinion.
- *Main part:*
  - The media only informs about a limited number of topics.
  - Reporters may be biased towards a certain political party.
  - Reports tend to exaggerate to gain more attention.
- *Conclusion: It is best not to trust one source of information only.*

Proposed solution:
You might wonder whether the mass media is aware of its vast power to shape popular ideas, opinions and attitudes. As Leigh Donaldson in his article published in the British newspaper "The Guardian" shows, American media companies convey a false and biased picture of Afro-American men which influences people's impression of black men in a negative way. Since Afro-American men are frequently presented as lazy or violent in the media, black men experience a lot of disadvantages in society. In my point of view, there are various reasons why media companies might distort information.

Basically, a lot of topics are not dealt with in the media since there are just too many. As a consequence the media chooses a limited number of events and topics. In this way the public for example only gets information about the latest crisis although there are many other crises in the world. For example topics such as migration to the EU are only covered by the media when the reason is a recent event like a ferocious civil war which forces people to flee. But after some time, the media do not pay any attention to the civil war and its victims anymore and they are forgotten by the readers and viewers in Europe. But the suffering and the migration continues even though the media do not report about it anymore.

Additionally, there might be reporters who are members of political parties and could try to influence the people's views by publishing one-sided stories though they should report impartially. Luckily, they are still an exception to the rule in my view but the more often those stories about reporters are made public, the more skeptical the readers are.

In addition to that, publishers may adjust certain events to make them more sensational to the audience and to maximise their profits. Especially today, when the income of media companies depends on the number of clicks on their homepage, journalists are likely to exaggerate. Like the example of misrepresentation of Afro-American men in the US shows, a lot of reports tend to exaggerate when they report about black men associated with crime or poverty.

Fortunately, today's information technology enables us to check whether information is true or not. Since almost every household has access to the internet, you can take advantage of social media. In addition to this, the rise of cable and satellite TV with lots of TV stations from around the world, make it possible to use different sources of information and to avoid information that may be passed on incorrectly either accidently or intentionally. You get a wider perspective by gathering information about the same topic in this way. *(440 words)*

Tip
To introduce your comment, mention the source you refer to.

Tip
Sate the question you are going to discuss at the end of your introduction.

Tip
Give at least three arguments in the main part.

Tip
Conclude your text by giving advice.

Übungs-Abi 3: The media

14 VP **b)** *The next issue of your school's magazine will be published in cooperation with your American partner school. The magazine's topic is about "Global challenges of ethnic diversity and the role of the mass media". Your job is to interview an Afro-American editor of a US quality paper, Mr. Hamilton. Both of you have read the article "When the media misrepresents black men, the effects are felt in the real world".*

You want to talk about how the editor and his colleagues deal with the responsibility of shaping public opinion. Write a script of the interview.

Imagine and write an interview with Mr Hamilton focusing on the topics asked for. Pay attention to your role as a student *and* as an editor for a quality paper. Structure your interview adequately (introduce the topic, express your thankfulness, find a proper ending etc.)

Task support

Für diese Aufgabe werden insgesamt 14 Punkte auf den Inhalt vergeben.

Form und Umfang meiner Antwort:
Write the interview …: Verknüpfen Sie Ihre eigene Meinung und Ihr eigenes Wissen über die verzerrte Darstellung und Reduzierung von Schwarzen auf bestimmte Merkmale und Eigenschaften mit den Informationen, die Sie dem vorangestellten Artikel entnommen haben und schreiben sie darauf aufbauend ein Interview mit dem Redakteur.
Fragen Sie nach den Gründen, warum es zu einer einseitigen Darstellung von Schwarzen in den Medien kommt und wie die Zeitungsredaktion mit ihrer Verantwortung umgeht, die öffentliche Meinung zu prägen.
Achten Sie darauf, dass Sie präzise Fragen stellen und Ihre Fragen gut strukturieren.
Versetzen Sie sich zudem in die Lage Ihres Gesprächspartners und formulieren Sie aus dessen Sicht mögliche Antworten auf Ihre Fragen.
Passen Sie das Sprachregister dem mündlichen, aber höflichen Gespräch an.

Mögliche Inhalte und Struktur meiner Antwort
- *Introduction:*
  - Welcome the interviewee.
  - Refer to the article in the Guardian by Leigh Donaldson.

- *Information asked for by the interviewer:*
  - The editor's opinion on the misrepresentation of black men.
  - The reasons for this misrepresentation.
  - How the editors try to prevent biased information?
  - Why there are so few reliable Afro-American characters on TV?

- *Arguments by the editor:*
  - Only some newspapers provide biased information.
  - Newspapers want to get the readers' attention.
  - Newspapers just reflect reality.
  - The editor does not publish information which he cannot prove.

- *Thank your interviewee for the interview.*

Proposed solution:

Student: Mr Hamilton welcome to this interview and thank you for agreeing to share your thoughts on the misrepresentation of Afro-Americans in the media. In his article published in "The Guardian", Leigh Donaldson expresses his view that black men are still discriminated against in the media. What is your opinion on that?

Editor: I have read the article as well and I can partly agree that this seems to be the fact for some newspapers but we shouldn't lump all papers together.

Student: I think you make it too easy for yourself with such an attitude. In a 2011 study conducted by The Opportunity Agenda, it was said that lots of negative mass media reports on black men were linked with black men's lower life expectations.

Editor: It may be true that some reports are biased. For example, tabloid papers tend to focus on sensational reports. But high quality newspapers, for example, usually offer impartial information in an objective way.

Student: But I think more important than just telling people stories that are not true are the negative consequences in public. Those stories make people believe that certain things are just unavoidable and false information can spread like wildfire.

Editor: Yes, I share your point. That's the reason why we want to be a reliable source of information that only publishes true stories in our newspaper. In case of doubt, we just leave them out.

Student: That's interesting to hear. Besides, more and more one-sided reports about black men are published that focus on African-Americans who deal with drugs, look for work or suffer from bad living conditions. Most reports are just negative ones. What is your attitude towards those reports?

Editor: Well, first of all, I think it is not the editor's fault when things are just fact and we report about them.

Student: Yes, but it is also fact that the media shape ideas, opinions and attitudes. What about your responsibility to publish more balanced reports on blacks?

Editor: When we think a story, an event or whatever is worth reporting we tell it to our readers regardless of whether the person behind it is black or white. Therefore, I think our reports are already quite balanced, especially as about 50% of our editors are African-Americans.

Student: That sounds good. What do you think … why do lots of newspapers not provide a more balanced perspective?

Editor: In my opinion, some newspapers fear the reactions from their mostly white readership and do not want to lose them as loyal subscribers.

Student: Oh, that's an unexpected answer! In order to make it clear… do you blame other papers for passing on biased information intentionally?

Editor: Well, I would not claim that other papers pass on false information. I'd rather say that they choose the kind of information they pass on. And of course, they only publish information which is most likely to get the attention of their readers.
A good newspaper also has to report about contrary opinions and about topics which might not appear very interesting to the reader at first glance. So you could say that there are some black sheep in the newspaper industry and they destroy the other papers' good reputation.

Tip
Give arguments from each point of view.

Tip
Always refer to the preceding statement.

Tip
As interviewer keep in mind your central question(s).

Student: I see. Unfortunately, we are already running out of time. But I have got one last question for you: We often see a white group of experts discussing a topic on TV. Where are the black attendees?

Editor: I can only speculate about it but perhaps for most viewers, they are just not credible enough to take part in discussions with certain topics. As you can see, there are still lots of things to improve. We have to be more courageous in order to change public opinion and prejudices about blacks.

Student: Thank you very much for being here. It's been great talking to you.

(640 words)

> **Tip**
> End the talk by thanking for the interview.

4 Mediation

18 VP

The Opportunity Agenda is an American non-governmental organisation which is dedicated to overcoming racial prejudices and expanding equal opportunities to people in the US. Your American friend's parents, Mr and Mrs Arnold, work for this organisation and ask you whether there are similar projects in Germany. Your class has participated in the project "Wenn Bilder meine Sprache wären" and you want to inform Mr and Mrs Arnold about it.

Write a formal email to Mr and Mrs Arnold, employees of The Opportunity Agenda, in which you describe the aims of the German project.

First collect the relevant information asked for ("aims of the project"), then structure the content. Write a formal email and keep in mind your addressee and the specific structure and features of a formal email.

Task support

Für diese Aufgabe werden insgesamt 18 Punkte auf den Inhalt vergeben.

Form und Umfang meiner Antwort:
Write a formal email to …: Zur Auswahl der relevanten Informationen beachten Sie den Kontext wie z. B. welche Ziele verfolgt *The Opportunity Agenda*, wer verlangt Information, welchen Wissensstand haben die Empfänger Ihrer Nachricht, welche Information wird konkret erfragt etc.
Beachten Sie die Merkmale einer formalen E-Mail wie z. B. die Verwendung formaler Sprache.

Mögliche inhaltliche Aspekte:
- The project has been set up by an organisation founded by Turkish immigrants.
- The project tries to promote intercultural understanding.
- Young immigrants analyse the stereotypes of Muslim immigrants in the German media.
- The participants of the project develop strategies to secure a fair representation of Muslims in the media.
- Journalists should become aware of their responsibility and more considerate when writing about Muslims.
- Young immigrants should be supported in their will to contribute to society.

Proposed solution:

Dear Mr and Mrs Arnold,

Since you dedicate your work to equal opportunities for the people, I am happy to inform you about the aims of the German project "Wenn Bilder meine Sprache wären".
My class participated in the project which is run by the "Türkische Gemeinde Deutschlands" (TGD). The TGD is an organisation which was founded by Turkish immigrants and which works for a better intercultural understanding in Germany. The TGD has set up a programme for young people with an immigration background in which they analyse the representation of Muslim immigrants in the German media and try to find strategies to avoid stereotypes of Muslims in the media.
In small groups, the participants of the project analyse reports and news about immigrants and discuss whether and how much reports create bad stereotypes of immigrants. The founders of the project want young people to discuss racism and religious discrimination, for example against Muslims and Jews. As a result, young people are supported in developing strategies to change the picture of immigrants in the media towards a more considerate representation and taking the values of different cultures into account.
Another aim of the project is to foster the exchange between people working in the media and immigrants. In discussions with the participants, the journalists should become aware of possible stereotypes and of their responsibility as important sources of information.
A lot of young Muslims feel insecure towards the media. Therefore the participants should gain confidence when talking about the media and they should be supported in their will to speak up for a fair representation of minorities in Germany.
I hope this information is useful for your work. Should you have any further questions, please do not hesitate to contact me.

Kind regards,
Nico Baumann

(290 words)

Tip
Start your email with a capital letter: "Since ..."

Tip
Explain important German terms / names.

Übungs-Abi 4: **Global disparities**

Klausurteil: Leseverstehen und Schreiben integriert

Tip
→ *Grundwissen*
Global challenges / The US and the American Dream

Excerpt from *The Tortilla Curtain* by Thomas Coraghessan Boyle

In American author T. C. Boyle's novel The Tortilla Curtain, *América, a 17-year-old, pregnant Mexican immigrant and her husband Candido are camping in a canyon near L.A. They are both illegal in the US. Since Candido was seriously hurt in a car accident, he cannot find work anymore.*
Today, América has found a day job at last. Together with Mary, another day labourer she met this morning, she is cleaning small Buddha-figurines for the entrepreneur Mr Pérez.

[…] América was working. Still working. Though the six hours were up and the fat man was nowhere to be found. Candelario Pérez had said six hours' work, twenty-five dollars, and this was eight hours now and she was wondering, did this mean the fat man would pay her more? Six divided into twenty-five was four
5 dollars and sixteen cents an hour, and so, for two extra hours she should get, what – eight dollars and thirty-two cents more. She glowed with the thought of it. She was earning money, money for food, for Candido and her baby – she, who'd never earned a centavo[10] in her life. She'd worked in her father's house, of course, cooking and cleaning and running errands[11] for her mother, and he gave her an
10 allowance[11] each week, but it was nothing like this, nothing like earning a wage from a stranger – and a gringo[13], no less. Candido would be surprised. Of course he would have guessed by now that she was working, but wait till he saw her tonight, coming down that trail into the canyon with all the groceries she could carry, with meat and eggs and rice and a can of those big sardines, the ones in oil
15 so rich you lick it from the tips of your fingers …
    She thought of that, held the image in her brain till it was imprinted there, and her hands were quick and nimble[19] even after eight hours, and the fumes[19] hardly bothered her. They bothered Mary, though. Bothered her plenty. The big gringa with the ring through her nose hadn't shut up about it since the fat man had led
20 them into this great long beautiful room of his house lined with windows and given them each a pair of yellow latex gloves and the plastic bottles of the corrosive[23]. América didn't understand what the woman was saying, of course, and she tried to block her out too, but the drift of it was inescapable. Mary didn't like the work. Mary didn't need the work. Mary had a house with a roof and four walls and a re-
25 frigerator with food in it. She didn't like the fumes or the fat man or his beautiful house or life on this planet. She tipped back a pint of that liquor she had with her and as the day went on she got slower and slower till practically all she did at the end was sit there and complain.

(410 words)
From: Thomas Coraghessan Boyle, *The Tortilla Curtain*, 1995

[10] **centavo** a monetary unit used in Mexico
[11] **to run an errand** to do a small job
[11] **allowance** *here*: Taschengeld
[13] **gringo / gringa** (*infml*) An American, *here*: US citizen
[19] **nimble** agile
[19] **fumes** strong and sometimes dangerous gas or smell
[23] **corrosive** chemical substance

Klausurteil

1 Comprehension
12 VP — Describe América's and Mary's day job.

2 Analysis
16 VP — Give a characterization of both women and compare their situation as presented in the novel excerpt.

3 Evaluation
Choose one of the following tasks:

14 VP **a)** *"Giving illegal immigrants a working permit would save them from exploitation."* Comment on the statement. Refer to the text as well as to work done in class.

14 VP **b)** Later, the entrepreneur Candelario Pérez's son wonders who the two women were and asks his father about them. In this dialogue his father tells his son how to make big money with illegal immigrants. Write down their dialogue.

Tip
→ The **tasks in *Erste Schritte*** will help you to complete Tasks 1–3.

Tip
Focus on your and the form of the text.

Klausurteil: Sprachmittlung isoliert

4 Mediation
18 VP — The social science courses of your school and of your partner school in Los Angeles do a project on career perspectives of immigrants in Germany and the US. The aim of the project is to create a magazine with authentic stories and articles about teen immigrants and their role in the economy. Your group wants to inform the American partner school about illegal teenage migrants in Germany. You have found the following excerpt from an autobiographical novel.

Write a short report about the main character Ela. Focus on her skills and her difficulties to achieve her career as an illegal immigrant.

Tip
→ **The mediation task in *Erste Schritte*** will help you to prepare for writing your mediation text.

Tip
Focus on your addressee, the characteristics of your text type and relevant information.

Auszug aus *Plötzlich war ich Schatten* von Ela Aslan

Edith und Margret Willmann haben für mich eine Maßnahme gefunden, mit der illegale Jugendliche wie ich auf eine Ausbildung vorbereitet werden. Ein Jahr Schule und gleichzeitig ein Nähkurs. Ich habe heute den halben Tag vor einer Nähmaschine gesessen und gelernt, wie man eine gerade Naht näht.
5   *Was ist aus meinem Traum vom Architekturstudium geworden?* Unwillig wische ich diesen Gedanken beiseite, für Selbstmitleid ist jetzt keine Zeit. Wenn ich diese Maßnahme durchziehe, habe ich wenigstens etwas in der Hand. Als Illegale kann ich mich nirgendwo um einen Ausbildungsplatz bewerben, das verbieten die deutschen Gesetze. Und wieder auf die normale Schule? Bestimmt habe ich viel
10 zu viel Stoff verpasst, das hole ich nie nach. Noch dazu auf Deutsch, das kann ich mir abschminken. […]
    Völlig selbstverständlich holt Maike mir eine Cola und stellt sie vor mir auf die Theke „Ela, erzähl, wie gefällt dir die Ausbildungsmaßnahme? Hast du Spaß am Nähen? Und hast du nette Mitschüler?" Verlegen schaue ich auf meine Hände;
15 nervös rolle ich meinen Strohhalm auf der Theke hin und her. Ich würde so gern mal jemandem erzählen, wie ich mich fühle. Und Maike mag ich, ich glaube, ihr kann man vertrauen. Aber wenn ich Maike jetzt erzähle, dass ich am liebsten wieder zur Schule gehen würde, um dann später Architektur in Istanbul zu studieren, würde sie mich bestimmt für total bekloppt halten. Wer bin ich denn?

Tip
If necessary, explain concepts and terms which are unique to the German language.

„Es ist ganz okay."
Maike betrachtet mich einen Moment, dann wechselt sie das Thema. „Du sprichst immer besser Deutsch, was macht ihr denn momentan im Unterricht?"
Ich erzähle ihr vom Deutschunterricht. Und von Mathe. Dass ich den Stoff schon kenne. Irgendwann lass ich fallen, dass ich früher in der Türkei Nachhilfe in Mathe gegeben habe. Maike schaut mich so ermutigend und interessiert an, dass ich ihr immer mehr erzähle. Dass ich Mathe immer toll fand. Und dass ich Klassenbeste war. Dass ich sogar eine Urkunde vom Bürgermeister gekriegt habe.
„Ela, ganz ehrlich, ich habe das Gefühl, dass du mit dem Nähen nicht halb so viel anfangen kannst wie mit dem Lernen."
Ertappt schaue ich auf den Boden.

(340 Wörter)
Ela Aslan, *Plötzlich war ich Schatten*, 2012

Erste Schritte

Übungen

Comprehension
To describe the kind of work the women are doing, note down the following information: What are they doing? What are the working conditions?

Analysis
To compare América's and Mary's character, complete the table with information about them as mentioned in the excerpt.

América	Mary
ll. 5 ff., looks forward to getting paid → the hourly wage is a lot of money to her (indirect characterization)	l. 19, tall, white American, ring through her nose (direct characterization)
ll. 6–7, thinks about Candido and her baby → takes care of her husband, thinks about her future (indirect)	

Tip
→ To help you prepare for answering Task 1–3, do the task(s) on this page.

Tip
Look for direct (e.g. appearance) and indirect (e.g. feelings) characterization.

Evaluation

a) *Brainstorm information about working and living conditions of illegal immigrants.*

b) *Brainstorm ideas about the father's and his son's attitudes to employing illegal immigrants.*

Mediation

To help you to prepare for writing your mediation text in Task 4, do the following tasks.

a) *Read the task carefully again and complete what the task asks for.*

1. Context: _____

   _____

2. Information asked for: _____

   _____

3. My role: _____

4. My addressee: _____

5. Kind of text I write: _____

b) *State shortly in one or two sentences the obstacles which hinder Ela from becoming an architect.*

_____

_____

_____

_____

c) *Skim through the text and mark the relevant information for your review.*

> **Tip**
> → To help you prepare for writing your mediation text in Task 4, do the task(s) on this page.

Lösungsvorschläge

Comprehension
What are they doing? A day job; clean small dirty Buddha statues; use corrosives; work with their hands; etc.
What are the working conditions? No fixed working time; no fixed salary; breathe a lot of fumes; work in their employer's home; etc.

Analysis

América	Mary
l. 5 ff., looks forward to getting paid → the hourly wage is a lot of money to her, she is very poor (indirect characterization)	l. 19, tall, white American, ring through her nose (direct characterization)
l. 6–7, thinks about Candido and her baby → takes care of her husband, thinks about her future (indirect)	l. 19, she keeps on talking → very talkative (indirect characterization)
l. 6, looks forward to her first paycheck → is very proud of her work (indirect)	l. 23, unmotivated to work (direct)
ll. 13 ff., wants to buy food → suffers from hunger, (indirect)	l. 24, lives in a house (direct)
ll. 17 ff., very industrious → likes her work, is very motivated (indirect)	ll. 26 ff., drinks liquor during work → suffers from a drinking problem (indirect)
l. 20, admires Mr Pérez's house → is poor, dreams of a house (indirect)	l. 28, just sits there and complains → unhappy with her life (indirect)
l. 23, tries to ignore Mary → does not like her, maybe she is even envious of her (indirect)	does a badly paid day job → has no regular income (indirect)

Evaluation
Cf. proposed solutions for the Evaluation in the *Erwartungshorizonte*.

Mediation
a) 1. Context: to create a magazine about teen immigrants • 2. Information asked for: information about Ela, an illegal immigrant who has difficulties establishing a career • 3. My role: participant of a project • 4. My addressee: students from L.A. • 5. Kind of text I write: short report

b) Ela has to catch up with a lot of classes and she has to learn German. In addition to this, she is not allowed to choose a course of study or job path but has to take a course which she does not like.

c) Z. 2–3, „Ein Jahr Schule … gleichzeitig ein Nähkurs." • Z. 5, „Was ist aus … vom Architekturstudium geworden?" • Z. 7–9, „Als Illegale kann … die deutschen Gesetze." • Z. 9–11, „Und wieder auf … ich mir abschminken." • Z. 16, „ich glaube, ihr kann man vertrauen." • Z. 17–19, „am liebsten wieder … in Istanbul zu studieren" • Z. 26, „Dass ich Mathe … ich Klassenbeste war."

Erwartungshorizonte

1 Comprehension

12 VP *Describe América's and Mary's day job.*

Describe América's and Mary's day job as presented in the extract. Focus on what kind of work it is, the workplace, etc.

Task support

Für diese Aufgabe werden insgesamt 12 Punkte auf den Inhalt vergeben.

Form und Umfang meiner Antwort:
Describe ... : Beschreiben Sie die Art der Arbeit, die América und Mary verrichten. Formulieren Sie Ihre Antwort in eigenen Worten und geben Sie nur wieder, was Sie dem Text entnehmen können.

Mögliche inhaltliche Aspekte:
- *It is a day job with insecure working conditions, e.g. no fixed working hours.*
- *The women clean small Buddha-statues using chemicals.*
- *The two women are on their own.*
- *It is simple and monotonous work.*
- *They work in the home of their employer.*

Proposed solution:
In the excerpt from Thomas C. Boyle's novel "The Tortilla Curtain" published in 1995, the main character América, a 17-year old, pregnant Mexican immigrant informs the reader about her day job at Mr Pérez's house.
She and Mary, another American day labourer, are busy cleaning small Buddha-figurines at Mr Perez's home. They work in the home of their employer. It is a beautiful and big house to live in and the women work alone in one of the rooms. The work is simple and monotonous because they are just cleaning all the time but América likes doing it as she is proud to earn her own money. The women have to clean small statues with their hands using bad smelling corrosives.
The job is a typical day job because Mary and América are employed for just one day and will get paid that evening in cash. There are no fixed working conditions since the women do not know how long they have to work. In addition to this, their pay is just the result of a spoken agreement with their employer. All in all their working conditions are pretty insecure.

(190 words)

> **Tip**
> Mention the source you refer to at the beginning of your answer.

2 Analysis

16 VP *Give a characterization of both women and compare their situation as presented in the novel excerpt.*

Explain how América and Mary are characterized and compare them. Focus on similarities and differences between their characters and living conditions. Finish your analysis with a precise résumé of the comparison of the two women.

Erwartungshorizonte 61

Task support

Für diese Aufgabe werden insgesamt 16 Punkte auf den Inhalt vergeben.

Form und Umfang meiner Antwort:

Give a characterization ... and compare ...: Vergleichen Sie die Charaktere von Mary und América.
Achten Sie dazu auf Gemeinsamkeiten und Unterschiede und gruppieren diese. Mögliche Gruppierungen wären Lebensstandard, Arbeitsmotivation, Zukunftspläne, Lebenszufriedenheit etc.
Schließen Sie Ihren Text in einem aussagekräftigen Resümee ab.
Belegen Sie Ihr Aussagen anhand des Textes und formulieren Sie Ihre Antwort in eigenen Worten. Als grundsätzliche Zeitform verwenden Sie das Präsens.

Mögliche inhaltliche Aspekte:

- América is a 17-year old, pregnant, illegal Mexican immigrant who is camping with her husband in a canyon outside of L.A.
- In contrast to América, Mary is unhappy to work.
- In comparison to América, Mary can earn money easily and has a high living standard.
- The prospects of a house and a regular income motivate América to work even harder.
- América is optimistic about her life and future while Mary is deeply unsatisfied.
- In conclusion, América has relatively bad prospects in the US but she is much more optimistic and motivated than Mary.

Mögliche zusätzliche Aspekte:

- Mary suffers from a drinking problem.

Proposed solution:

In this excerpt from "The Tortilla Curtain" by T. C. Boyle we read about América, who is a 17-year old, pregnant, illegal Mexican immigrant who is camping with her husband in a canyon outside of L.A. She is in urgent need of money as her husband cannot work anymore after a bad car accident.

América and Mary are described as quite different characters. They both work for Mr Pérez today but while América is happy to work, Mary seems to be very unmotivated. Mary does not concentrate on her work, instead she continually talks to América and grumbles about the work until she finally just sits there and makes a fuss over it (l. 28).

Moreover, Mary is a US citizen while América is an illegal immigrant. This makes a huge difference for América. Since she is illegal, it is difficult for her to find a job and earn money whereas it is much easier for Mary to find work. As a consequence, the living conditions of the two women are very different. América lives in a camp in a canyon and cannot even afford to buy food regularly. Mary, in comparison, has a house and always has enough money to buy food (l. 24). In spite of this inequality or maybe exactly because of it, América is highly motivated to work and earn money.

Furthermore, the two women differ in their attitude to their life. América looks forward to the baby she will have and has plans for her future (l. 7). She dreams of a house, maybe similar to the one of Mr Pérez (l. 20). Mary, in comparison,

---

Tip
Category 1 to compare: work ethic.

Tip
Category 2 to compare: living standars.

Tip
Category 3 to compare: attitude to their lives.

does not seem to have any dreams. Obviously, she has taken this day job only out of sheer necessity to earn just enough money to live on since she actually does not like the work (l.23). Besides, Mary seems to be disappointed with her life and appears to have an addiction to alcohol since she carries a bottle of liquor with her (l.26).

In conclusion, it can be said that Mary and América are two completely different characters. In contrast to Mary, América is put at a huge disadvantage considering her legal status and her future prospects in the US, but still América is looking forward to her future. In comparison, Mary has everything which América longs for but still she seems to be deeply unsatisfied with her life.

(400 words)

> **Tip**
> Conclusion: Major findings of the comparison.

3 Evaluation

14 VP **a)** *"Giving illegal immigrants a working permit would save them from exploitation." Comment on the statement. Refer to the text as well as to work done in class.*

In this task you have to decide whether you agree or disagree with the statement and give reasons for your decision. Refer to América's situation in the novel extract and what you know about the current situation of undocumented immigrants from work done in class.
Take care not to contradict yourself and give proof of your point of view in your answer. Write a well-structured text.

Task support

Für diese Aufgabe werden insgesamt 14 Punkte auf den Inhalt vergeben.

Form und Umfang meiner Antwort:
Comment on …: Beziehen Sie sich in Ihrer Antwort auf den Romanauszug und liefern Sie mehrere unterstützende Argumente für Ihre Ansicht in dem Sie Ihr bisher erworbenen Wissen mit einbeziehen.
Strukturieren Sie Ihre Argumente angemessen und verfassen Sie den Text in formaler Sprache.

Mögliche inhaltliche Aspekte: und Struktur meiner Antwort
- *Introduction: There are about 2.5 million undocumented immigrants in California.*
- *Main part:*
  - *As an illegal immigrant, América has to trust her employer who can treat her unfairly.*
  - *Illegal immigrants hide from the public in order to avoid police attention.*
  - *Employers exploit their illegal status by paying them less money or even withholding money from them.*
  - *A legal working permit would save immigrants from exploitation because they could defend themselves against unfair working conditions.*
- *(Personal conclusion / outlook)*

Proposed solution:
According to recent research, there are more than 2.5 million illegal immigrants in California. In his famous book "Tortilla Curtain", T. C. Boyle describes a day job of América, an illegal Mexican immigrant. Like many other illegal Hispanic immigrants in California, she is in danger of being exploited. The scene describes very clearly how easy it is for employers to exploit illegal or undocumented immigrants and what a difference it could make if she could work legally in the US.
In the scene, América is just modest and happy to be offered a day job at a rich man's house. She surely knows that the only way to survive as an illegal Mexican immigrant is to earn some money to buy food for herself, the baby she is expecting and her husband who cannot work anymore. Therefore she is willing to do a really good job. Nevertheless, it is questionable if she will be paid the money she deserves. She has been working hard and for two hours longer than was originally agreed upon. It is unsure whether her employer will pay her the overtime or any money at all. It can be expected that her employer might reproach her for not being quick enough to do the job in the six hours they agreed to before.
América's situation illustrates the fate of a lot of illegal immigrants in the US. Undocumented immigrants are always afraid of being deported back to their home countries in case they are found by the police. Consequently, they have to hide in order not to come to the police's attention. This paves the way for unscrupulous employers who can take advantage of their illegal status. They know that illegal immigrants need money urgently and that they are unprotected. As a result, they usually pay them less money or even withhold money from them when their work is done. Therefore, legal working permits would save undocumented people from exploitation in the US. The advantages of a legal working permit for immigrants are perfectly obvious: Immigrants could apply for all kinds of jobs and would not have to depend on occasional day jobs. They would not have to work for unfair wages. If treated badly, they could demand legal protection.
All in all, it can be said that measures which legitimize undocumented workers are a good step in the right direction. Besides, people other than immigrants would profit too. Legal immigrants would be able to pay taxes which all Americans can benefit from. But declarations of intent are not enough to change the situation for the better. Governments and the people have to follow their words with action.
(445 words)

Tip
State the topic you are going to discuss at the end of your introduction.

Tip
Start with the weakest argument and end with the strongest.

Tip
Conclude your text by giving an outlook / a personal resumee.

14 VP **b)** *Later, the entrepreneur Candelario Pérez's son wonders who the two women were and asks his father about them. In this dialogue his father tells his son how to make big money with illegal immigrants. Write down their dialogue.*

In this task you are asked to imagine a dialogue between the entrepreneur and his son. Imagine what they might say from their point of view about illegal workers. Include the father's explanation why he employs illegal immigrants. You may decide what the son's attitude is like.

Task support

Für diese Aufgabe werden insgesamt 14 Punkte auf den Inhalt vergeben.

Form und Umfang meiner Antwort:
Write down their dialogue …: Versetzen Sie sich in die Lage des Unternehmers Candelario Pérez und seines Sohns.
Entwickeln Sie einen Dialog, indem der Sohn sich nach den Arbeiterinnen erkundigt und der Vater ihm seine eigennützigen Gründe für die Beschäftigung von illegalen Arbeitern erklärt.
Verwenden Sie gesprochene Sprache und als Zeitform das Präsens.

Mögliche Inhalte und Struktur meiner Antwort
- Illegal immigrants are cheap and hard-working.
- You earn more money than with regular employees.
- The father does not care about fairness.
- You can also earn money by paying higher wages.
- It is exploitation.

Proposed solution:
Son: Hi dad, who were those two women in our house today?
Father: Oh, I don't know their names actually. I just hired them today to clean the Buddha-figurines. I found a buyer for them and I will sell them tomorrow.
Son: So the women won't come again, will they?
Father: No, they are just cheap day labourers looking for some money to earn.
Son: Wouldn't it be better to employ people regularly?
Father: No, why? If I employed people regularly they would be much more expensive. Those day labourers don't ask for much. If one asks for too much money, you just ask the man standing next to him and often he is willing to work for less. They work illegally and they need the money. It's how I run my business. I pay my employees very little and mark up the price of the product as much as possible. That's the principle of my business and that's how you make money in this world.
Son: This doesn't sound fair to me.
Father: I don't care if it's not fair. All I care about is the money in my wallet.
Son: Couldn't you also earn money with legal employees?
Father: Yes I could but my profit margin would be much less. Illegal immigrants are hard-working and cheap. So why pay more?
Son: Well, I see. It's good for business but bad for the people in our house. It's like exploitation, isn't it?

(240 words)

> **Tip**
> Think about a good question / statement to start your dialogue.

4 Mediation

The social science courses of your school and of your partner school in Los Angeles do a project on career perspectives of immigrants in Germany and the US.
The aim of the project is to create a magazine with authentic stories and articles about teen immigrants and their role in the economy. Your group wants to inform the American partner school about illegal teenage migrants in Germany.
You have found the following excerpt from an autobiographical novel.

18 VP *Write a short report about the main character Ela. Focus on her skills and her difficulties to achieve her career as an illegal immigrant.*

In your report, describe the main character Ela and the obstacles which make it hard for her to fulfil her dreams. Choose the relevant information from the novel excerpt carefully. Introduce your report by briefly referring to your source.

Task support

Für diese Aufgabe werden insgesamt 18 Punkte auf den Inhalt vergeben.

Form und Umfang meiner Antwort:
Write a short report ...: Schreiben Sie einen kurzen Report, ausgehend von den Informationen in dem Romanauszug.
Beschreiben Sie darin die Schwierigkeiten der autobiografischen Hauptdarstellerin ihre persönlichen Ziele zu verfolgen.
Beachten Sie den Wissenstand ihrer amerikanischen Adressaten und erklären sie gegebenenfalls bestimmte Inhalte wie z. B. den Titel.
Beachten Sie die formalen Merkmale eines Reports.

Mögliche inhaltliche Aspekte:
- *does not know whom to trust since she is illegal*
- *would like to study architecture in Istanbul (since she is excellent at maths)*
- *cannot choose on-the-job training since she is illegal*
- *has to do the kind of training which she is offered*
- *has been missing a lot of lessons at school*
- *cannot speak or understand German well*

Proposed solution:

It is like a life in the shadows
In the autobiographical novel "Plötzlich war ich Schatten", which means "my life in the shadows", the main character Ela, who is an illegal immigrant, tells the reader about her difficulties to achieve her dreams in Germany. In an excerpt she describes her feelings about her education and her future.
In general Ela is afraid to trust the people around her, which makes it difficult for her to integrate. Since she is illegal in Germany, she always thinks twice before she talks with somebody about her personal situation.
In her book she also describes her future plans. Ela actually had a plan for her career. She wanted to study architecture in Istanbul. However, she has realized that this is almost impossible even though she is extremely skilled in mathematics.
The reason is because as an illegal immigrant she cannot choose her education. Ela's only option to make money seems to be to join a special training program that will teach her how to sew. She does not like the training but it is her path to education. Ela often wishes that she could go to school again and prepare to become an architect, but even if she was allowed to do so, she doubts that she could finish her schooling successfully. In addition to legal obstacles, she would have to catch up on a lot of classes at school and she still has to learn German. This excerpt shows how difficult it is for skilled and motivated young people to achieve their career goals when their status in the country is illegal. They have very few opportunities open to them.

(280 words)

Tip
Explain the German title.

Tip
Give the information asked for. Do not give your personal opinion in a mediaton task.

Übungs-Abi 5: **Rising nation India**

Klausurteil: Leseverstehen und Schreiben integriert

Controversy over the Dharavi Redevelopment Project

By 8 am, Dharavi is already noisy. Tea stalls already clinking, leather-making and embroidery and plastic-crushing machines already cranking through their long daily grind. Dharavi, the most well-known informal settlement in Mumbai, stands in a category of its own, and challenges the very notion of a slum. Its maze of
5 matchbox buildings contains thousands of micro-industries, which collectively turn over $650m annually and provide affordable housing to the city's working class. Over decades, Dharavi's residents – its potters, garment-makers, welders and recyclers from all over India – have transformed what was a marshy outpost into a thriving entrepreneurial community.
10 But Dharavi is no longer in the boondocks. Massive northwards growth in the peninsula city of Mumbai over the last two decades has engulfed Dharavi's humble plot of 525 acres. Today, Dharavi stands on a goldmine: a slice of land in the heart of the megapolis with the highest land prices in India. Its coveted position sits at the intersection of two main train lines, and is just a stone's throw
15 from a new business district, the Bandra-Kurla Complex. Not surprisingly, Dharavi has caught the attention of sharkish developers.
  Under the government-led Dharavi Redevelopment Project, developers will provide the people living there – who can prove residency since 2000 – a new, 300 sq ft house for free. In return, authorities have allowed the builders to go higher
20 (increasing the floor space index in Dharavi from 1.33 to 4), thereby concentrating residents into tower blocks and freeing up space for luxury high rises that will reap huge returns. The plan has created a storm of controversy.
  Everyone agrees that Dharavi needs better working and living conditions. The settlement may have organically achieved the low-rise, mixed-use commu-
25 nity of many urban planners' dreams, but it is not without its problems. Years of government neglect have left Dharavi's hygiene and safety levels grossly inadequate. There are queues for everything, including toilet blocks, municipal water taps and healthcare clinics. The 300,000 or so residents – there has been no official count and studies suggest it could be double that – squeeze into an area just one-
30 third bigger than Hyde Park.
  The new plan to redevelop Dharavi increases that density to inhumane proportions. Although the tower-block buildings offer amenities such as toilets, they also threaten to destroy the fabric of a community in which homes, roofs and outdoor spaces transform into places of work and social interaction – the only way
35 many of the micro-enterprises can operate. Dharavi's design is not an accident; it responds to the social ties and economic needs of the community.

(422 words)
Carlin Carr, *The Guardian*, 2015

Tip
→ **Grundwissen**
India / Global challenges

[3] **grind** hard work, toil
[10] **in the boondocks** far away, in an isolated place

1 Comprehension
12 VP — Outline Dharavi's location in Mumbai and the Dharavi Redevelopment Project.

2 Analysis
16 VP — Analyse the picture the author presents of the current settlement in Dharavi and her attitude to the Dharavi Redevelopment Project. Focus on her use of language, argumentative techniques and rhetorical devices.

3 Evaluation
Choose one of the following tasks:

14 VP — a) Discuss the advantages and disadvantages of the Dharavi Redevelopment Project for its inhabitants.

14 VP — b) Re-creation of text: Imagine you are running a small business in Dharavi. Write a letter to the mayor of Mumbai, Mrs Ambekar, referring to the Dharavi Redevelopment Project.

> **Tip**
> → The tasks in *Erste Schritte* will help you to complete Tasks 1–3.

> **Tip**
> → Focus on your role, the addressee and the form of the text.

Klausurteil: Sprachmittlung isoliert

4 Mediation
Your Indian friend's geography class has set up a blog about redevelopment projects in big cities. On their blog, the students want to publish examples of development plans in other cities. Your friend asked you to add a blog post about a German city on the blog. You have found the following article and decide to post it.

18 VP — Write a formal report for the blog in which you inform the Indian students objectively about the project in Essen and about the reasons for it.

> **Tip**
> → The mediation task in *Erste Schritte* will help you to prepare your mediation text.

Wie ein Immobilienkonzern einen Stadtteil umbaut

Das Eltingviertel hat einen schlechten Ruf – zumindest bei den Essenern, die überhaupt wissen, dass es existiert. Eine Handvoll Straßenzüge, die im Stadtzentrum liegen, eingequetscht zwischen Fußgängerzone, dem Konzern-Gelände von RWE und der Grünen Mitte. […]

5   Für die Bewohner des Viertels soll sich nun alles ändern. In diesen Wochen beginnt im Eltingviertel ein Experiment: Ein sozial schwaches Quartier, voll mit schönen, aber ramponierten Altbauten, wird in einer konzertierten Aktion erneuert.
    Selbst wenn es im Rest von Essen Anzeichen für einen kleinen Aufschwung gibt: Ruhrgebietsstädte leiden unter Arbeitslosigkeit, Schulden und Leerstand.
10 Dass das Eltingviertel eine Art Generalprobe für die Problemzonen einer ganzen Region sein soll, machte Nordrhein-Westfalens Bauminister Michael Groschek bei der „Innovation City"-Vorstellung im April klar: „Wir wollen das, was hier passiert, ins ganze Land hinaustragen."
    Durchgeführt wird das Experiment von der Deutschen Annington. Dem größten
15 deutschen Wohnungsunternehmen gehören hier 1400 Wohnungen, mehr als 40 Prozent des Wohnraumes. Die Annington hat sie vor einigen Jahren auf einen Schlag dem Energiekonzern RWE abgekauft. Jetzt hat sie einen Masterplan für die Gegend entwickelt, zusammen mit Innovation City, einem Unternehmen für Stadtentwicklung, und der Stadt Essen.

> **Tip**
> If necessary, explain concepts and terms which are unique to German.

20 9,3 Millionen Euro gibt die Annington allein für die erste Bauphase aus. In zehn Jahren soll das Eltingviertel ein „lebendiges Quartier" mit energetisch sanierten Altbauten sein, in dem laut Annington „sozial Benachteiligte, Studenten und Rentner" zusammenleben. Auch wenn die Planer das nicht zugeben: Besserverdienende Mieter wären natürlich auch nicht schlecht. [...]

25 Ute Hennemann sitzt im Innenhof eines der Karrees. Sie lebt seit 38 Jahren hier und sagt: „Gemacht werden muss was. Das ist nicht mehr das Viertel, das es mal war." Sie zeigt auf die abgenutzte Grasfläche vor sich. „Da war mal ein Spielplatz, den haben sie irgendwann abgerissen." Einen neuen will jetzt die Annington bauen, außerdem Geschäfte und Cafés ins Viertel holen. Hennemann und vielen
30 anderen Mietern will sie einen Balkon an die Wohnung bauen. Noch aber ist Hennemann skeptisch: „Ich bin mal gespannt, was passiert."

(320 Wörter)
Jannis Brühl, *Süddeutsche Zeitung*, 2015

Erste Schritte

Übungen

Comprehension
Note down the possible advantages of the Redevelopment Plan for the people in Dharavi.

Tip
→ To help you prepare for Tasks 1–3, do the tasks on this page.

Analysis
To analyse the author's view, collect positive aspects of the current situation and possible threats by the redevelopment project.

Positive aspects of life in Dharavi right now: _____

Possible threats by the redevelopment project: _____

Evaluation

a) *Brainstorm positive and negative aspects of the situation right now and in a newly built district.*

b) *Brainstorm information about your possible work, income, family and plans for the future.*

Mediation

a) *Read the task again carefully and complete what the task requires.*

1. Context: _____

2. Information asked for: _____

3. My role: _____

4. My addressee: _____

5. Kind of text I will write: _____

Tip
→ To help you prepare your mediation text in Task 4, do the tasks on this page.

b) *Explain or paraphrase the German words and phrases in English.*

1. Viertel: _____

2. einen schlechten Ruf haben: _____

3. Ruhrgebietsstädte: _____

4. ein sozial schwaches Quartier: _____

5. Masterplan: _____

6. energetisch sanieren: _____

7. lebendiges Quartier: _____

8. Geschäfte und Cafés ins Viertel holen: _____

Tip
Look up keywords and phrases in a dictionary if necessary.

Lösungsvorschläge

Comprehension
new and solid apartments, better hygiene standards, higher living standards, apartments for free, new offices and apartments in the middle of Mumbai, etc.

Analysis
Positive aspects of life in Dharavi right now: there are many micro-industries, a lot of people have jobs, a lot of people live there, it is not as expensive as in other parts of Mumbai, people from the working class can afford to live there, the community has been working well, etc.

Possible threats by the redevelopment project: a lot of people will lose their homes, shop owners and craftsmen will lose customers, the new apartments will be too expensive for working class people, the construction company will not offer cheap apartments, the population density in the tower blocks will be unbearable for its inhabitants, etc.

Evaluation
Cf. proposed solutions for the Evaluation in the *Erwartungshorizonte*.

Mediation
a) 1. Context: request for a blog post about redevelopment projects in big cities in Germany • 2. Information asked for: general information about the project and information about the expectations of the different people involved • 3. My role: German student • 4. My addressee: Indian students • 5. Kind of text I will write: report for a blog

b) 1. Viertel: district • neighbourhood • community • area • quarter • part of town • etc.
2. einen schlechten Ruf haben: to have a bad reputation • to be infamous for • etc.
3. Ruhrgebietsstädte: former industrial cities in the Ruhr area / in North Rhine-Westphalia
4. ein sozial schwaches Quartier: a district in which a lot of residents suffer from unemployment or have a very low income • an area where most of the inhabitants are very poor and earn very little • etc.
5. Masterplan: an example of how to … for other … • a master plan • etc.
6. energetisch sanieren: to modernise in order to use less energy • etc.
7. lebendiges Quartier: lively community • busy neighbourhood • etc.
8. Geschäfte und Cafés ins Viertel holen: to make it a desirable place for shops and cafés • to attract cafés and stores • etc.

Erwartungshorizonte

1 Comprehension

12 VP *Outline Dharavi's location in Mumbai and the Dharavi Redevelopment Project.*

Describe Dharavi and its surrounding districts and the aims of the Dharavi Redevelopment Project.

Task support

Für diese Aufgabe werden insgesamt 12 Punkte auf den Inhalt vergeben.

Form und Umfang meiner Antwort:
Outline ...: Es ist empfehlenswert, Ihre Antwort mit einer Beschreibung der besonderen Lage Dharavis zu beginnen. Was macht die Lage für Immobilieninvestoren besonders interessant?
Präsentieren Sie anschließend den Plan zum Abriss des Slums und zum Neubau von Wohn- und Bürogebäuden.
Gehen Sie dabei auf die Ziele der Projektplaner ein und wie diese umgesetzt werden sollen.
Formulieren Sie Ihren Text grundsätzlich im Präsens und in eigenen Worten.

> **Tip**
> For further information on the different *Operatoren*, go to page 10.

Mögliche inhaltliche Aspekte:
- Dharavi is situated in a very desirable place to live and work since it is part of the city centre and close to a new business district and two main train lines.
- The Dharavi Redevelopment Project is organised by the city and private construction companies.
- The construction companies want to build apartments and luxury homes.
- If an inhabitant can prove that he/she has lived in Dharavi since 2000, he/she will be offered an apartment for free.
- The city wants to improve the living and working conditions.

Proposed solution:
Dharavi is in the middle of Mumbai, next to a new business district and close to two main train lines of the city. Therefore, it is a very desirable place to live and work and the new apartments and offices could be sold at high prices.
The Dharavi Redevelopment Project is organised by the city of Mumbai and private construction companies. Their aim is to tear down the slums and to build new tower blocks with new apartments and luxurious homes. As compensation for destroying the homes of the current residents, the organisers of the project will offer new 300-sq-ft houses to them for free. However, only some of the inhabitants will get an apartment for free. In order to be entitled to an apartment, you have to prove that you have lived in Dharavi since 2000.
By replacing the run-down huts with new tower blocks, the managers of the project want to improve the working and living conditions in the area. Right now, the hygiene standards are very poor in Dharavi since, for example, there are not enough toilets for the large number of people living there.

> **Tip**
> As a basic rule, write your text in the present tense.

(200 words)

2 Analysis

16 VP *Analyse the picture the author presents of the current settlement in Dharavi and her attitude to the Dharavi Redevelopment Project. Focus on her use of language, argumentative techniques and rhetorical devices.*

First, state Carr's view on the redevelopment project. Next, examine the language and the arguments she uses to present her attitude to the reader.

Task support

Für diese Aufgabe werden insgesamt 16 Punkte auf den Inhalt vergeben.

Form und Umfang meiner Antwort:
Analyse …: Beschreiben Sie die Einstellung der Autorin gegenüber dem Immobilienprojekt und erläutern Sie, wie sich diese in ihrer Sprache und ihren Argumenten widerspiegelt.
Achten Sie z. B. auf ihre Wortwahl, wenn Sie das Leben in Dharavi oder die Interessen der Investoren beschreibt.
Belegen Sie Ihre Aussagen anhand des Textes und verfassen Sie Ihre Antwort in der Regel in der Zeitform des Präsens.

Mögliche inhaltliche Aspekte:
- The author opposes the Dharavi Redevelopment Plan. For her, the existing buildings and public places have a lot of advantages for the inhabitants.
- She emphasises the economic importance of the slum and calls it a "thriving entrepreneurial community" (l. 9).
- She refers to statistics (l. 6, "$650 m") and examples (l. 7, "potters, garment-makers, …") to describe the economic activities.
- She uses metaphors to show that Dharavi is an expensive landmark (l. 12, "goldmine").
- She admits that the living conditions have to be improved and explains the reasons for it (l. 26, "Years of government neglect"; l. 28, "300,000 residents").
- She compares Dharavi's size with Hyde Park to show how densely it is inhabited.
- Her choice of words shows that she disapproves of the project (l. 16, "sharkish developers"; l. 22, "reap huge returns"; l. 31, "inhumane proportions").

Proposed solution:
In her article, the author describes the living and working conditions in Dharavi. In her opinion, the current community and economy work well and the Dharavi Redevelopment Project poses a dangerous threat to its inhabitants.
The author starts her article by describing the beginning of a day in Dharavi. She clearly refutes the common stereotype of a run-down slum by listing some of the many economic activities and by referring to surprisingly high economic figures. She points out that there are innumerous small businesses (l. 5, "thousands of micro-industries"), which turn over 650 m dollar each year (l. 6). The author enumerates the different kinds of craftsmen like potters or garment-makers (l. 7), showing that the district offers employment to a lot of people. The author finishes the first paragraph by stressing that the slum has become a "thriving entrepreneurial community" (l. 9).
In addition to the inhabitants' economic productivity, the author continues that Dharavi is neither an isolated nor remote place. Dharavi is in the middle of

> **Tip**
> Introduce your analysis by describing Carr's view.

Mumbai surrounded by shops and office towers and close to two main train lines. The author writes that Dharavi "stands on a goldmine" (l. 12). As this metaphor shows, Dharavi is a desirable place to live and to work since the city centre can be reached quickly from there.

However, the author does not deny that the living conditions such as hygiene standards have to be improved. People have to queue for toilets, fresh water and a doctor (ll. 27 ff.). She also explains the reasons for these problems. First, the community has been constantly neglected by the government and, second, Dharavi is densely populated because at least 300,000 residents live there. To make it easier for the reader to imagine its population, she refers to Hyde Park as an example of an area with almost the same size as the slum (ll. 28 – 30). Although life in Dharavi is not comfortable, the author emphasises that the community and the economy work well in Dharavi, whereas the redevelopment plan will destroy this community. She refers to the Dharavi Redevelopment Plan as a plan of "sharkish developers" (l. 16) who want "to reap huge returns" (l. 22) by increasing the number of people in a tower block "to inhumane proportions" (l. 31). As the author's choice of words proves, she strongly criticises the project since it would not improve the living conditions of its current inhabitants but only allow the construction companies to sell expensive apartments and offices and to earn a lot of money.

(450 words)

> **Tip**
> Do not just describe the language but explain their effects on the reader.

3 Evaluation

14 VP **a)** *Discuss the advantages and disadvantages of the Dharavi Redevelopment Project for its inhabitants.*

Discuss several positive and negative arguments of the redevelopment project and support them by giving reasons. Refer to information from the text and knowledge which you have gained in class.

Task support

Für diese Aufgabe werden insgesamt 14 Punkte auf den Inhalt vergeben.

Form und Umfang meiner Antwort:
Discuss …: Stellen Sie zu Beginn des Textes das Projekt und Ihre Fragestellung kurz vor. Erläutern Sie anschließend mehrere Argumente für und wider das Immobilienprojekt. Schließen Sie Ihren Text mit einem Ausblick oder einer pointierten Zusammenfassung Ihrer Erläuterungen ab. Verfassen Sie den Text in formeller Sprache und beziehen Sie sich auf die Information aus dem Text und Ihr eigenes Wissen.

Mögliche Inhalte und Struktur meiner Antwort:
- *Introduction:* (Draw the reader's attention to the project and reformulate the question.)
- *Main part:*
  - Living conditions will improve.
  - Some of its inhabitants will get apartments for free in the new buildings.
  - A lot of its inhabitants might be refused an apartment and lose their homes.
  - Most of the people will lose their business and work.
  - Only a few residents might find a job in the new district.
- *Conclusion:* Actually, only a minority of the inhabitants might benefit from the project.

Erwartungshorizonte | **75**

Proposed solution:
Finally there is a Redevelopment Project for one of India's biggest slums. Dharavi should be modernised and its residents might soon live in solid apartments with regular access to fresh water and electricity. However, some people are afraid that the inhabitants of Dharavi might also lose their homes and property. Is it possible that the Redevelopment Project might not actually help its inhabitants?
First, the project aims at improving the living and working conditions of the people in Dharavi. The new tower blocks can provide the people with better homes. There will be more toilets, a better sewage system and access to clean drinking water for all residents. The construction company will also build roads and provide the buildings with electricity and each household will have access to the internet. As a result, the working conditions will become much more efficient.
In the past, the inhabitants of slums were often driven away when new houses were built. This time, there is a plan to take care of Dharavi's inhabitants. Every inhabitant is offered a 300 sq ft house for free if he/she can prove that he/she has been living there since 2000. As a consequence, people who have been living in Dharavi for several years can stay and even move to a modernised home.
So far, the project might sound like a good deal for its inhabitants. But as the plan says, it requires you to prove that you have lived there since 2000. A lot of the slum's inhabitants might not have the necessary documents proving that they have lived there since 2000. Therefore, a lot of residents might be refused a new home.
Even if you get an apartment, you are very likely to lose your income. Most of the people in Dharavi have a small business and depend on the customers in the streets. As can be expected, there will not be many customers left once all the people have moved away who were not provided with a new apartment for free. In addition to this, these small entrepreneurs cannot buy or rent an expensive store in the newly built tower blocks and it is unlikely that a lot of craftsmen like potters or garment-makers and small shopkeepers will find employment in one of the newly built office towers. So even if some people might get a new apartment, they would not have an income anymore to make ends meet.
In conclusion, the majority of the inhabitants will not profit from the redevelopment plan. A lot of inhabitants will have to look for a new home and most of the small entrepreneurs will have to find a new place to earn their living.

(450 words)

> **Tip**
> Reformulate the question you are going to discuss at the end of your introduction.

> **Tip**
> Conclude your text by summarising your opinion.

14 VP **b)** *Re-creation of text: Imagine you are running a small business in Dharavi. Write a letter to the mayor of Mumbai, Mrs Ambekar, referring to the Dharavi Redevelopment Project.*

Write a letter to the mayor of Mumbai. Present your situation and express your fears concerning the project. Refer to Carr's article and to work done in class. Use formal language in your letter.

Task support

Für diese Aufgabe werden insgesamt 14 Punkte auf den Inhalt vergeben.

Form und Umfang meiner Antwort:
Write a letter … : Versetzen Sie sich in die Lage eines Kleinunternehmers in Dharavi und stellen Sie Ihre Bedenken und Ängste bezüglich des Stadtentwicklungsprojekts dar.

Ausgehend von Ihren Sorgen, vermitteln Sie der Politikerin deutlich Ihr Anliegen bzw. Ihre Forderung.
Formulieren Sie den Brief in der 1. Person und in formeller Sprache.
Achten Sie auf einen formal angemessenen Aufbau Ihres Briefs (Betreff, Anrede, Grund des Schreibens etc.).

Mögliche Inhalte und Struktur meiner Antwort:
- *Introduction: (Introduce yourself and present your reason for writing.)*
- Main part:
  - *My wife and I moved to Dharavi in 2000.*
  - *We started a small business as garment-makers.*
  - *Our business grew steadily.*
  - *Today we employ two workers.*
  - *Like most entrepreneurs we will lose our business if the project is enforced.*
  - *Please reconsider and change or stop the project.*
- *Conclusion: (Make a proposal/Reformulate your appeal.)*

Proposed solution:

Re: The impact of the Dharavi Redevelopment Project on small enterprises

Dear Mrs Ambekar,

As an entrepreneur who runs a small business in Dharavi, I ask you for your support to reconsider the Dharavi Redevelopment Project.
I am a garment-maker and father of three children. My wife and I moved to Dharavi in 2000. Therefore, we might be allowed to stay in Dharavi but we still will lose our business. My wife and I have built our business from scratch. At the beginning there were just the two of us in our shop. After years of hard work, our business grew and we used the money to build a new house with a bigger shop for our business. At this time, we also started to employ our first part-time employee. Today, we employ two full-time workers and our business is growing steadily. Now my wife and I have read about the Redevelopment Project and it comes as a real shock to us. Like most of the other entrepreneurs in Dharavi, we are deeply concerned about the plans. Most of my customers and business partners will have to leave Dharavi and I am afraid that I will not find many new customers among the inhabitants of the newly built tower blocks. Like other craftsmen and shopkeepers, I need the lively streets of Dharavi to find customers. If the Redevelopment Project is enforced, my wife and I will lose our business and our family and the families of our employees will sooner or later have to move somewhere else to earn a living again. Therefore, I appeal to you to reconsider the project and stop or at least change it.
Of course, the inhabitants welcome an improvement of the sewage system and better roads, but in order to do this it is not necessary to destroy and rebuild the whole district. It would be much better to modernise the existing houses and to just build some important buildings like schools or hospitals. Such a project would support much more people than the Dharavi Redevelopment Project and it would be much cheaper. Please decide in favour of the people of Dharavi.

Yours sincerely,
Ranbir D–

(350 words)

> **Tip**
> State your reason for writing at the beginning of your letter.

Erwartungshorizonte

4 Mediation

Your Indian friend's geography class has set up a blog about redevelopment projects in big cities. On their blog, the students want to publish examples of development plans in other cities. Your friend asked you to add a blog post about a German city on the blog. You have found the following article and decide to post it.

18 VP *Write a formal report for the blog in which you inform the Indian students objectively about the project in Essen and about the reasons for it.*

Read the article carefully and write a report aimed at Indian students. Include general information about the district *Eltingviertel* and information about the hopes and expectations of the people involved in the project.

Task support

Für diese Aufgabe werden insgesamt 18 Punkte auf den Inhalt vergeben.

Form und Umfang meiner Antwort:
Write a formal report ... : Verfassen Sie einen formalen Artikel, in dem Sie indische Schüler über das Stadtentwicklungsprogramm Eltingviertel in Essen informieren. Beachten Sie hierzu das Hintergrundwissen Ihrer Adressaten.

Mögliche inhaltliche Aspekte:
- The area has a reputation for unemployment and poor housing.
- The project should be an example of how to modernise a run-down area.
- Almost half of the buildings are owned by Deutsche Annington and will be sold or rented by the company.
- Different people (old, young, rich, poor, etc.) should live together in the district.
- The inhabitants hope that their apartments will be modernised (heating, balcony).

Proposed solution:

Redeveloping the centre of Essen
The city of Essen is going to present an example of how to redevelop a neglected city district with poor housing. Together with the construction company *Deutsche Annington*, the city of Essen will try to modernise the district *Eltingviertel*.
Like many other cities in this region of Germany, Essen once was an important industrial centre. Today, parts of Essen's city such as the *Eltingviertel* suffer from unemployment, debts and abandoned buildings. Unfortunately, this area has a bad reputation and it is infamous for its old run-down buildings.
Now the city of Essen and *Deutsche Annington* have presented a plan to modernise the district. Almost half of the apartments are owned by *Deutsche Annington* and should be renovated by the company. The people responsible for the plan hope that different kinds of people like students or retired people will live together in the new neighbourhood. There will also be relatively cheap apartments for people with low incomes and of course more luxurious apartments which can be rented or sold at high prizes.
The current residents hope that their apartments will be modernised. For example, the construction company promised to build balconies and to improve the heating in order to use less energy. In addition to this, a lot of inhabitants hope that the face of their neighbourhood will change. Old, run-down playgrounds should be rebuilt and shops and cafes should move there.   (220 words)

— Tip
Explain important German terms/names.

— Tip
Give the information asked for. Do not give your personal opinion in a mediaton task.

Übungs-Abi 6: The US and global security

Klausurteil: Leseverstehen und Schreiben integriert

Statement by the President on ISIL

My fellow Americans, tonight I want to speak to you about what the United States will do with our friends and allies to degrade and ultimately destroy the terrorist group known as ISIL.

As Commander-in-Chief, my highest priority is the security of the American people. Over the last several years, we have consistently taken the fight to terrorists who threaten our country. […]

We can't erase every trace of evil from the world, and small groups of killers have the capacity to do great harm. That was the case before 9/11, and that remains true today. And that's why we must remain vigilant as threats emerge. At this moment, the greatest threats come from the Middle East and North Africa, where radical groups exploit grievances for their own gain. And one of those groups is ISIL – which calls itself the "Islamic State."

Now let's make two things clear: ISIL is not "Islamic." No religion condones the killing of innocents. And the vast majority of ISILs victims have been Muslim. And ISIL is certainly not a state. It was formerly al Qaeda's affiliate in Iraq, and has taken advantage of sectarian strife and Syria's civil war to gain territory on both sides of the Iraq-Syrian border. It is recognized by no government, nor by the people it subjugates. ISIL is a terrorist organization, pure and simple. And it has no vision other than the slaughter of all who stand in its way.

In a region that has known so much bloodshed, these terrorists are unique in their brutality. They execute captured prisoners. They kill children. They enslave, rape, and force women into marriage. […]

Abroad, American leadership is the one constant in an uncertain world. It is America that has the capacity and the will to mobilize the world against terrorists. It is America that has rallied the world against Russian aggression […]. It is America that helped remove and destroy Syria's declared chemical weapons so that they can't pose a threat to the Syrian people or the world again. And it is America that is helping Muslim communities around the world not just in the fight against terrorism, but in the fight for opportunity, and tolerance, and a more hopeful future.

America, our endless blessings bestow an enduring burden. But as Americans, we welcome our responsibility to lead. From Europe to Asia, from the far reaches of Africa to war-torn capitals of the Middle East, we stand for freedom, for justice, for dignity. These are values that have guided our nation since its founding. […]

May God bless our troops, and may God bless the United States of America.

(435 Wörter)
Barack Obama, September 10, 2014

Tip
→ **Grundwissen**
Global challenges / The US and the American Dream

9 **vigilant** alert, attentive, watchful
15 **al Qaeda** terrorist organization which was responsible for the attacks on 9/11
29 **Ebola** a dangerous, infectious disease
34 **to bestow** to present (to) / to give (to)

1 Comprehension

12 VP — Outline the role of America in the context of ISIL according to Obama's speech.

2 Analysis

16 VP — Analyse how Obama presents his view. Focus on his line of argument, his choice of words and rhetorical devices.

3 Evaluation

Choose one of the following tasks:

14 VP — a) According to Obama "It is America that has the capacity and the will to mobilize the world against terrorists." (ll. 24–25). Discuss this statement.

14 VP — b) Re-creation of text: Obama's daughter Malia is very proud of her father's speech, especially how he views Islam and wants to support communities which are threatened by terrorism. Write her diary entry in the evening after the speech.

Tip → The Tasks in *Erste Schritte* will help you to complete Tasks 1–3.

Tip — Focus on your perspective, the addressee and the form of the text.

Klausurteil: Sprachmittlung isoliert

4 Mediation

On the last day of your stay with your American host family you discuss Obama's statement on ISIL. Your host parents ask you whether there are similar problems in Germany. You are not sure, so once you are back in Germany you research the topic on the internet. After reading the following article in a German newspaper dealing with the threat of terrorism in Germany due to immense and continuing immigration of civil war refugees from the Middle East, you decide to send an email to your host parents in the US.

18 VP — Write an informal email to your host parents informing them about how dangerous the situation in Germany is assessed by safety experts.

Tip — The mediation task in *Erste Schritte* will help you to prepare for writing your mediation text.

Tip — Focus on your addressee, the characteristics of your text type and relevant information.

Analyse: «Abstrakte Terrorgefahr» in Deutschland

Wie groß ist die Terrorgefahr in Deutschland? Sicherheitsexperten bereitet es Sorgen, dass sich nach der Euphorie der ersten Wochen unter den Flüchtlingen Frust breit machen könnte.

Berlin/Istanbul (dpa) – Der junge Mann trägt Sonnenbrille, sein Gesicht sieht freundlich aus, auf seinem T-Shirt steht groß „Thank you". Seit Tagen kursiert dieses Foto bei Twitter. Der junge Mann, heißt es, sei ein Flüchtling auf dem Weg nach Deutschland.

5 Daneben ist ein zweites Bild geheftet worden. Auch hier ist ein junger Mann zu sehen. Aber er trägt Uniform und einen Munitionsgürtel, in der rechten Hand hält er ein Schnellfeuergewehr. Das Foto dieses Kämpfers der IS-Terrormiliz soll vor zwei Jahren aufgenommen worden sein – und angeblich denselben Mann zeigen wie das erste Bild.

10 Überprüfen lässt sich diese Behauptung nicht. Trotzdem tragen solche Bilder zu der Sorge bei, mit der Flucht von Zehntausenden aus Syrien und dem Irak könnten sich Extremisten in den Strom Richtung Deutschland gemischt haben. […]

15 Belege für Dschihadisten unter den Flüchtlingen gibt es allerdings bisher nicht.

Tip — If necessary, explain concepts and terms which are unique to the German language.

Trotzdem macht sich Hans-Georg Maaßen, Präsident des Bundesamts für Verfassungsschutz (BfV) keine Illusionen: "Wir müssen zumindest davon ausgehen, dass unter den vielen Flüchtlingen auch solche sein können, die Kampferfahrung haben", [...]

Zwar sind seither Tausende Kriegsflüchtlinge aus Syrien zusätzlich gekommen, doch die Sicherheitslage in Deutschland hat sich nach Informationen der Deutschen Presse-Agentur in der Zwischenzeit nicht verändert. Es gebe keine konkreten Hinweise darauf, dass unter den Frauen und Männern, die in der Bundesrepublik Schutz suchen, solche sind, die in Deutschland Terror und Gewalt verbreiten wollen. [...]

Sorgen bereitet Sicherheitsexperten auch, dass sich nach der Euphorie der ersten Wochen unter den Flüchtlingen Frust breit machen könnte. "Einige könnten sich irgendwann in die Islamisten-Szene integrieren", fürchtet Maaßen. Der Verfassungsschutz in Nordrhein-Westfalen hat bereits registriert, dass extremistische Salafisten versuchen, Kontakt zu muslimischen Flüchtlingen aufzubauen. Auch die Behörden in Bayern melden Versuche von Salafisten, Flüchtlinge anzuwerben.

Flächendeckend seien solche Aktivitäten in Deutschland aber noch nicht festgestellt worden, eine zentrale Steuerung sei ebenfalls nicht erkennbar, sagen Verfassungsschützer. Auch die Logik spreche dagegen, dass Werbeaktionen islamistischer Extremisten unter Flüchtlingen auf ein allzu großes Echo stoßen: Immerhin seien die Menschen eben erst vor dem IS-Terror geflohen. Da würden sie mit Salafisten wohl eher nichts zu tun haben wollen.

(330 Wörter)
Süddeutsche Zeitung, 2015

Erste Schritte

Übungen

Comprehension
Create two mindmaps to collect the important information for task 1. Write "Threat of ISIL" and "America's role" in their centre.

Analysis
Note down the rhetorical devices in the text and their effect on the audience.

Rhetorical device	Effect on the audience

Tip
→ To help you prepare for answering Task 1–3, do the task(s) on this page.

Evaluation

a) *Brainstorm ideas for arguments in favour of and against Obama's statement.*

b) *Brainstorm reasons why Obama's attitude towards the Muslim world makes his daughter proud.*

Mediation

Paraphrase and/or explain these German words and phrases in English.

1. Präsident des Bundesamts für Verfassungsschutz: _____

2. Abstrakte Gefahr: _____

3. Deutsche Presse Agentur: _____

4. Frust macht sich breit: _____

5. extremistische Salafisten: _____

6. Nordrhein-Westfalen und Bayern: _____

7. Verfassungsschützer: _____

8. Auf ein großes Echo stoßen: _____

Tip
→ To help you prepare for writing your mediation text in Task 4, do the task(s) on this page.

Lösungsvorschläge

Comprehension
Mindmap 1 "Threat of ISIL": greatest threats from Middle East and North Africa • ISIL not "Islamic" • recognized by no government, nor people • no vision other than slaughter • unique in their brutality • etc.
Mindmap 2 "America's role": security of the American people • American leadership is the one constant • capacity and will to mobilize the world • rallied world against Russian aggression • helping Muslims • destroyed chemical weapons • fight for opportunity, tolerance and hopeful future • etc.

Analysis
direct address of the audience: supports the feeling of national unity • repetition (ll. 13 ff., "no"): shows the weakness of terrorists • anaphora (ll. 21 ff., "They execute …"): emphasizes the numerous crimes and the cruelty • metaphor (ll. 25 ff., "America"): conveys the image of America as an active actor or person you can turn to • anaphora (ll. 25 ff., "It is America that …"): shows America's power • alliteration (l. 31, "endless blessings bestow an enduring burden"): shows the endless character of America's task

Evaluation
Cf. proposed solutions for the Evaluation in the *Erwartungshorizonte*.

Mediation
1. Präsident des Bundesamts für Verfassungsschutz: the president of the Office for the Protection of the Constitution • a leading state official who is responsible for monitoring possible terrorist threats • the head of a security department whose employees surveil possible threats by terrorists • etc.
2. Abstrakte Gefahr: no imminent danger but you have to stay vigilant • there might be terrorists but there is no proof of them • etc.
3. Deutsche Presse Agentur: a big German news agency • an important German company gathering news • etc.
4. Frust macht sich breit: to become increasingly disappointed • etc.
5. extremistische Salafisten: radical Salafists • radical Islamists • fundamentalist Muslim groups • etc.
6. Nordrhein-Westfalen und Bayern: regions / federal states in west- and south Germany • the federal state North Rhine-Westphalia and Bavaria • etc.
7. Verfassungsschützer: security officers who specialize in the defense against terrorism • security agents who are responsible for the prevention of terrorism • employees of the Office for the Protection of the Constitution • etc.
8. Auf ein großes Echo stoßen: to succeed in capturing somebody's attention • to get a lot of attention for • to experience a huge support for • to be met with approval • etc.

Erwartungshorizonte

1 Comprehension

12 VP *Outline the role of America in the context of ISIL according to Obama's speech.*

Briefly describe the terrorist group calling itself the "Islamic State" and the threat they pose to their victims. In addition to this, mention the role that America has played in fighting against terror and the success it has achieved in the past. Do not forget to include the biblical reference that imposes the duty on America to support oppressed people in the world. (Leave out less important details of the speech like the reference to 9/11 or the relations to al Qaeda.)
Focus on the information requested and write a compact and concise summary.

Task support

Für diese Aufgabe werden insgesamt 12 Punkte auf den Inhalt vergeben.

Form und Umfang meiner Antwort:
Outline …: Fassen Sie in Ihrer Antwort die wichtigsten Inhalte des Auszugs der Rede zusammen. Der Umfang der Wortanzahl Ihres Textes soll deutlich unter der Wortanzahl des Originaltextes liegen.
Formulieren Sie Ihre Antwort in der Regel im *simple present* und verwenden Sie formale Sprache.
Strukturieren Sie Ihren Text sinngemäß und geben Sie nur Inhalte wieder, die Sie dem Originaltext entnehmen können.
Sie dürfen weder Informationen ergänzen, noch Ihre eigene Meinung wiedergeben, noch das Gelesene interpretieren.

Mögliche inhaltliche Aspekte:
- ISIL is a terrorist organization that threatens the world.
- Even though ISIL calls itself "Islamic state", it is not state.
- The ideology of ISIL is not based on religion/It has nothing to do with Islam.
- The terror organization is terribly violent in oppressing innocent people.
- America is willing to meet the challenge to defend freedom, equality, justice and dignity in the world.
- America has received endless blessings and therefore feels obliged to do God's will by helping oppressed people in the world.
- From the American perspective, America has been the leading power in the fight against terrorism.
- ISIL's main area of operations is in the Middle East and in North Africa.

Proposed solution:
According to Barack Obama's speech in September 2014, the cruel acts of terror that the terrorist group ISIL has been committing in Iraq and Syria call for America to protect the people from this threat.
He points out that the members of ISIL are a serious danger to the people in America as well to the people in the Middle East and North Africa. Even though ISIL calls itself "Islamic State" and pretends to be a state, it is nothing but a terrorist organization. Obama calls the terrorists "killers" as there is no religious justification in the Islamic religion to oppress or kill people. Moreover, he enumerates some of their brutal crimes and points out that the terrorists violate Islam.

Tip
Use the simple present to write your answer.

In reaction to these acts of terrorism, Obama outlines America's past success in fighting aggressors and its role as the main protagonist in defending oppressed minorities in the world. He emphasizes that America will make a concentrated effort to defeating ISIL once and for all. He adds that America is supporting Muslim groups in their struggle for safety, freedom and hopeful prospects for their future. In the last part of his speech, he finally makes clear that it is America's duty to help oppressed people in the world and to restore freedom, justice and dignity to them. It is part of their national values and of God's promise to the American people to live peacefully and free. Therefore America has to fulfil God's will and protect people from terrorism, even in distant parts of the world.

(260 words)

> **Tip**
> Use your own words to summarize the speech.

2 Analysis

16 VP *Analyse how Obama presents his view. Focus on his line of argument, his choice of words and rhetorical devices.*

In Task 2 you should examine how Obama tries to persuade the reader of his optimistic view on America's role in the fight against terrorism. Examine the line of argument (contrast of America vs. the terrorists, etc.), the choice of words (feelings, etc.) and the rhetorical devices in his speech and their effect on the listener.

Task support

Für diese Aufgabe werden insgesamt 16 Punkte auf den Inhalt vergeben.

Form und Umfang meiner Antwort:
Analyse how …: Beschreiben und erklären Sie, wie der Redner das Publikum in der Ansicht bestärkt, dass Amerika dem sogenannten 'Islamischen Staat' moralisch und langfristig überlegen ist.
Untersuchen Sie hierzu, die Struktur der Argumente über Amerika und über die Terrororganisation, die Wortwahl und die Verwendung rhetorischer Stilmittel. Formulieren Sie Ihre Schlussfolgerungen eigenständig und belegen Sie diese mit Informationen und Zitaten aus dem Text.

Mögliche inhaltliche Aspekte:
- *Obama addresses the audience directly to support the feeling of national unity.*
- *Line of argument: He starts with the description of ISIL and closes with the praise of the American values. He contrasts the terrorists' cruelty with American values. Obama*
  - *describes the crimes of ISIL in the first half of his speech;*
  - *draws the attention to America and successful military interventions in the past;*
  - *says that it is America's task to defend human rights in the world;*
  - *praises American values and their importance in restoring peace.*
- *Use of repetition ("our"/"they") to co ntrast America's unity against the terrorists.*
- *Use of metaphor (ll. 25ff., "America") to convey the image of America as a person you can rely on.*

- *Use of anaphora to emphasize the numerous crimes and the cruelty (ll. 21 ff., "They execute …").*
- *Use of anaphora to show America's power (ll. 25 ff., "It is America that …").*
- *Use of alliteration (l. 31, "endless blessings bestow an enduring burden") to show the endless character of America's task.*

Mögliche zusätzliche Aspekte:
- *America is supported by friends and allies – ISIL is neither a state nor does it have any government or support from its people.*
- *Structure: President Obama begins by giving a realistic view of global terrorism to gain credibility right from the start.*
- *Use of emotive language to show the terrorists' despicable motifs (l. 19, "slaughter").*

Proposed solution:
In his speech Obama sharply contrasts the terrible crimes of the terrorist organization ISIL with the USA, which has put much effort in maintaining peace and freedom in the world. The line of argument and the language to describe the terrorists and the US support the contradiction between ISIL and America.

Right from the beginning when President Obama introduces the topic of his speech, he addresses his audience directly (l. 1, "My fellow Americans"). He further strengthens the feeling of national unity and importance of the topic by speaking repeatedly in the first-person and including the audience. Thus he also clearly contrasts the terrorists with America by using the personal pronoun "we" when talking about the US and "they" when referring to ISIL. Further he reminds his listeners that "we have […] taken the fight to terrorists" (ll. 5 – 6).

Obama continues to state clearly that the people in the US have to be vigilant in defending themselves against terrorism. By taking this realistic point of view, he shows how serious the topic is and gains credibility.

He then goes on revealing ISIL's lies about being Islamic or a state. Obama stresses that ISIL is just a group of terrorists by repeating what it is "not" (ll. 13 ff., "ISIL is not Islamic" etc.). Instead, he lists their numerous crimes and stresses their brutality by using an anaphora (They execute … They kill …" ll. 21 – 22) and uses words associated with uncontrollable and aggressive feelings to show the organization's true motifs (l. 19, "slaughter").

Having stated ISIL's infamy for brutality clearly, Obama goes on to refer to the US and its role as a defender of basic human rights in the second half of his speech. The US stands for universal values and is supported by allies and friends in contrast to ISIL which has no allies.

Obama emphasizes America's successful military interventions in the past and its power by using an anaphora ("It is America …", ll. 25 ff.). America is most capable of bringing peace, freedom, justice and dignity to different parts of the world and stresses the endless character of this task with the alliteration "our endless blessings bestow an enduring burden" (l. 31).

At the same time he uses "America" as a metaphor for a person who takes care of people all around the world.

Obama ends his speech by asking God to protect the American people and their troops.

(405 words)

Tip
Introduce your analysis by mentioning the main feature of your answer.

Tip
Always prove your statements with examples from the text.

Tip
Do not just list rhetorical devices but explain their effects on the listener.

3 Evaluation

14 VP **a)** *According to Obama "It is America that has the capacity and the will to mobilize the world against terrorists." (ll. 24–25). Discuss this statement.*

Relate the content of Obama's speech to the president's statement. Your answer should include your background knowledge about America's role as a peacekeeper in global politics. Do not forget to mention that its role is based on its values and belief that America should bring peace, freedom, dignity and justice to the people in the world. It is up to you if you agree or disagree with the statement but give arguments for both views.

Task support

Für diese Aufgabe werden insgesamt 14 Punkte auf den Inhalt vergeben.

Form und Umfang meiner Antwort:
Discuss …: Erstellen Sie einen zusammenhängenden Text mit Pro- und Kontra-Argumenten und diskutieren Sie dabei die vorgegebene Aussage, dass die USA am besten geeignet ist, bei der Bekämpfung des Terrorismus eine führende Rolle unter den Staaten einzunehmen.
Achten Sie bei Ihrer Antwort darauf, dass Sie Pro- und Kontra-Argumente schlüssig strukturieren und gewichten und Ihre eigene Einschätzung abschließend dem Leser mitteilen.

Mögliche Inhalte und Struktur meiner Antwort:
- Introduction: Reasons for/characteristics of America's role as a global power.
- Pro: America has proven to be successful in being a superpower.
- Pro: It is part of the American mentality to spread freedom and peace to the world.
- Contra: Other states do not fully support US foreign policy since it often does not lead to peace but follows the interests of the US.
- Contra: Recent conflicts prove that the US was not capable of restoring peace.
- Resume: It is difficult for the US to mobilize the world since other nations regard their strategy critically.

Proposed solution:
In the 20th century, America has become the world's most powerful nation and it has been using its military and economic strength to continuously influence international politics. So far American politicians have been happy to accept the role of a global superpower for two reasons. First, America has been successful in keeping its powerful position and, second, it represents part of the American Dream, which is to spread freedom and democracy around the world. However, confronted with international terrorism, there are doubts if the US will continue to be able to lead the world, especially in the fight against terrorism.
America's religious conviction is based on the principle that all people are created equal and that they can practice their religion freely, like the first settlers who fled their home countries due to religious and political persecution. Therefore the willingness to get involved in conflicts abroad and to free people from oppression is widespread among US citizens. As Obama says, it is a continuous burden that America carries in the name of God. America has always made intensive efforts to help people in the world who suffer from oppression and violence. Like the con-

— **Tip**
Begin your text by stating the question you are going to discuss.

— **Tip**
To discuss the topic present arguments in favour and against the statement.

flict in Syria shows, the violation of basic human rights has often caused the US to form an international alliance and put (military) pressure on countries which oppress its people.

Nevertheless, America's military role in the world has often been seen as illegal interference in another country's internal affairs. America has been reproached for furthering its own interests in several regions with the consequence that critics doubt the selflessness and human ideals of the US government.

Additionally, America has frequently been involved in wars, as in Afghanistan, Syria and other conflicts, but has not been successful in achieving its goals. After their military retreat from Afghanistan, for example, the situation for the civilian population deteriorated and there have been more suicide attacks than ever before. Therefore America seems to have realized that they are only able to defeat terrorist groups such as ISIL by working together with allies. International partners seem to be necessary because they can take responsibility for different military actions too.

On the whole, I think it is difficult for America to mobilize the world against terrorism. More and more nations are critical of its military influence in some regions of the world. US military actions have proven ineffectual in fighting terrorism effectively. In my opinion a lot of countries cooperate with the US, but in light of recent failures, these countries are much more likely to think twice about following the US into another armed conflict.

(433 words)

Tip
End with your strongest argument.

Tip
Conclude your text by giving your personal resumee.

14 VP **b)** *Re-creation of text: Obama's daughter Malia is very proud of her father's speech, especially how he views Islam and wants to support communities which are threatened by terrorism. Write her diary entry in the evening after the speech.*

In this task you are asked to write a diary entry of the president's daughter Malia. Express your pride about how your father presented Islam and Muslims in the context of the fight against terrorism in his speech. Refer to the speech and your knowledge from class.

Task support

Für diese Aufgabe werden insgesamt 14 Punkte auf den Inhalt vergeben.

Form und Umfang meiner Antwort:
Write her diary entry …: Erstellen Sie einen Tagebucheintrag aus Sicht der Tochter des Präsidenten.
Berichten Sie, wie stolz Sie auf Ihren Vater sind und das Bild dass er vom Islam in seiner Rede zeichnete.
Zentral in der Rede Obamas ist z. B. die klare Trennung von Islam und Terror.
Verfassen Sie den Eintrag in informeller Sprache.

Mögliche Inhalte und Struktur meiner Antwort:
- Introduce the topic of your entry.
- State your pride clearly.
- The terrorists do not represent Islam. Muslims also appreciate freedom, peace and equality.
- Most of the victims are Muslims.
- America is going to support Muslims in their fight against terrorism.
- It is part of the American identity to protect people from religious persecution.
- He regards the Muslims as his allies.

Proposed solution:

11th April 2017

Dad gave a very important speech today. He talked about ISIL, dangerous terrorists in the Middle East and North Africa and actually all around the world. There were a lot of listeners and you could feel that this topic was really serious and that it affected the audience deeply.

I'm very proud of dad for making the point that most Muslims are against terrorism. They actually suffer the most of terrorism since most of the cruel terrorist attacks are committed in North Africa and the Middle East.

A lot of people are afraid of Islam but dad stressed that the terrorists do not represent the Islam religion. Instead he reminded the audience that the Muslim communities appreciate values like freedom and equality and are prepared to defend these values against terrorism.

In addition to this, he made a point that America is willing to support them. This really impressed me. He proved that America's values are still at the core of our international politics. He motivated the audience to help victims of religious persecution, which reminded me of the first settlers in the US.

As dad explained, ISIL is just a terrorist organization. ISIL is not a state nor are they supported by the people. They oppress the people which include all kinds of religious minorities including Muslims.

A lot of people in America are afraid of Muslims and don't trust them. But my dad used his position as president to make it clear that Muslims are our allies against terrorism.

(260 words)

Tip
Give the date at the beginning of your diary entry.

Tip
Write the diary entry from the first-person point of view.

4 Mediation

On the last day of your stay with your American host family you discuss Obama's statement on ISIL. Your host parents ask you whether there are similar problems in Germany. You are not sure, so once you are back in Germany you research the topic on the internet. After reading the following article in a German newspaper dealing with the threat of terrorism in Germany due to immense and continuing immigration of civil war refugees from the Middle East, you decide to send an email to your host parents in the US.

14 VP Write an informal email to your host parents informing them about how dangerous the situation in Germany is assessed by safety experts.

In this task your American host family asks you for information about the situation of security in Germany. Write an informal email to them. Inform them about the source of your information and include information which is relevant to an American audience. Where necessary, explain and paraphrase facts which are unique to Germany.

Task support

Für diese Aufgabe werden insgesamt 18 Punkte auf den Inhalt vergeben.

Form und Umfang meiner Antwort:
Write an informal email …: Verfassen Sie eine informelle, dennoch höfliche E-Mail an Ihre amerikanische Gastfamilie.
Je nachdem wie viele kulturspezifische deutsche Begriffe Sie erklären müssen, kann der Wortumfang Ihres Textes höher ausfallen.

Mögliche inhaltliche Aspekte:
- The source of your information.
- Some people fear that there might be terrorists among the refugees.
- According to the head of the security department (which is in charge of monitoring terrorist threats) there is no proof that there are terrorists among the refugees. However, it is possible and the police have to stay vigilant.
- According to a big German news agency, the number of crimes has not increased since the first refugees came to Germany.
- Radical Muslim organizations have tried to attract new members among the refugees.
- It is rather unlikely that refugees join radical groups since they fled from these groups and refuse them.

Proposed solution:
Hi Carol,
After our talk about Obama's statement on ISIL and the risks of terrorism in Germany, I've found some interesting information about the threat of terrorism here. A highly respected German newspaper has interviewed several sources about the risk of terrorists coming from the Middle East to Germany as refugees.
The head of the security department who is in charge of fighting terrorism warns that there might be terrorists among the refugees. He adds that some refugees might have fought in military conflicts. But he states that there hasn't been any proof that there are terrorists among the refugees. The same fact is supported by a big German news agency. The number of crimes hasn't grown since the first refugees arrived in Germany.
The police has found out that some radical groups in parts of west and south Germany have tried to attract new members among the refugees. But according to several security officers, they won't be very successful. Of course, there might be some immigrants who get so frustrated that they turn to violence, but basically, the refugees oppose these radical groups. They have fled from similar groups and refuse violence and fundamentalism. Like Obama said in his speech, the people in Germany have to stay vigilant too.
I hope to hear from you soon!

Bye,
Linus

(245 words)

Tip
Explain and/or paraphrase content which is unique to Germany.

Tip
Give the information asked for. Do not give your personal opinion in a mediaton task.

Abitur 2014: Visions of the future

Klausurteil: Leseverstehen und Schreiben integriert

Suzanne Collins, *The Hunger Games* (extract)

In the future state of Panem the 74th Hunger Games are about to begin. All inhabitants of District 12 are in the market square, among them the narrator Katniss Everdeen (16) and her sister Primrose (12). Everybody is waiting for the opening ceremony.

[…] the mayor steps up to the podium and begins to read. It's the same story every year. He tells of the history of Panem, the country that rose up out of the ashes of a place that was once called North America. He lists the disasters, the droughts, the storms, the fires, the encroaching seas that swallowed up so much
5 of the land, the brutal war for what little sustenance remained. The result was Panem, a shining Capitol ringed by thirteen districts, which brought peace and prosperity to its citizens. Then came the Dark Days, the uprising of the districts against the Capitol. Twelve were defeated, the thirteenth obliterated. The Treaty of Treason gave us the new laws to guarantee peace and, as our yearly reminder that
10 the Dark Days must never be repeated, it gave us the Hunger Games.
    The rules of the Hunger Games are simple. In punishment for the uprising, each of the twelve districts must provide one girl and one boy, called tributes, to participate. The twenty-four tributes will be imprisoned in a vast outdoor arena that could hold anything from a burning desert to a frozen wasteland. Over a period of
15 several weeks, the competitors must fight to the death. The last tribute standing wins.
    Taking the kids from our districts, forcing them to kill one another while we watch – this is the Capitol's way of reminding us how totally we are at their mercy. How little chance we would stand of surviving another rebellion. Whatever words
20 they use, the real message is clear. "Look how we take your children and sacrifice them and there's nothing you can do. If you lift a finger, we will destroy every last one of you. Just as we did in District Thirteen."
    To make it humiliating as well as torturous, the Capitol requires us to treat the Hunger Games as a festivity, a sporting event […].
25   It's time for the drawing. Effie Trinket says as she always does, "Ladies first!" and crosses to the glass ball with the girls' names. She reaches in, digs her hand deep into the ball, and pulls out a slip of paper. The crowd draws in a collective breath and then you can hear a pin drop, and I'm feeling nauseous and so desperately hoping that it's not me, that it's not me, that it's not me.
30   Effie Trinket crosses back to the podium, smoothes the slip of paper, and reads out the name in a clear voice. And it's not me.
    It's Primrose Everdeen. […]

(420 words)
Excerpt from: Suzanne Collins, *The Hunger Games*, 2008

[2] **Panem** the phrase panem et circenses ("bread and games") describes the policy of giving food and entertainment to the crowds in ancient Rome
[6] **Capitol** *here:* the capital of Panem
[25] **Effie Trinket** she is the hostess of the opening ceremony and the tributes' escort

Tip
Der Textumfang der Abiturprüfung 2014 wurde redaktionell an die Vorgaben gültig seit 2017 angepasst.

1 Comprehension

12 VP — Outline Panem's history. Focus on its development as well as the function and rules of the Hunger Games as officially presented by the Capitol.

2 Analysis

16 VP — Analyse how the narrator's situation and her attitude to Panem and the Hunger Games are presented. Focus on point of view, choice of words and stylistic devices.

3 Evaluation

Choose one of the following tasks:

14 VP — **a)** Discuss the role and the options of an individual like Katniss in a future state like Panem. Refer to the extract as well as work done in class.

14 VP — **b)** Re-creation of text: That night Katniss cannot sleep. She thinks about the day and her decision. In a personal letter to Primrose she expresses her fears and explains the reasons for her decision. Write her letter.

Tip
Katniss' decision: Imagine Katniss volunteered to replace and protect her sister.

Klausurteil: Sprachmittlung isoliert

4 Mediation

As part of an exchange program, you attend a high school in the US for a year. Your class has read The Hunger Games and is organizing a conference to discuss the popularity and ethics of reality TV. As an international guest you are invited to deliver the opening statement to the students. You have found the following interview with professor Angela Keppler and want to use it as a source to talk about the popularity of reality TV series.

18 VP — For the conference, prepare your opening statement by focusing on the reasons why reality TV is popular among the audience. Add information where necessary. Write your speech.

Tip
Die Sprachmittlung wurde nachträglich redaktionell ergänzt. Seit 2017 ist Sprachmittlung Teil der Abiturprüfung.

„Es gibt im Fernsehen keine unverstellte Realität"

Angela Keppler ist Professorin für Medien- und Kommunikationswissenschaft an der Universität Mannheim und forscht über Reality-TV zwischen Fiktion und Dokumentation.

Badische Zeitung (BZ): Frau Keppler, Reality-TV boomt auf allen Kanälen: Von Arte bis RTL II erzielen Casting-Formate, Doku-Soaps und Survival-Shows beste Quoten. Was reizt das Publikum am Echtmenschenfernsehen?

Angela Keppler: Ich glaube, das ist einfach: Die Zuschauer interessieren sich für
5   die Schicksale von Leuten, mit denen sie nichts zu tun haben. Dabei ist es eine entlastete Form der Anteilnahme: Man sieht Probleme, die den eigenen unter Umständen ähneln, kann sie aber aus der Distanz betrachten und muss nicht selber handeln.

BZ: Fast wie im richtigen Leben – aber nur fast. Denn längst ist ja bekannt, dass
10   viele Reality-Serien die Wirklichkeit nur fingieren. Ist echtes Leben im Fernsehen schon wieder zu langweilig?

Keppler: Um Missverständnisse auszuschließen, es gibt im Fernsehen keine unverstellte Realität, jede Fernsehsendung, egal ob fiktional oder dokumentarisch, arbeitet mit fernsehspezifischen Formen der Darstellung: Das heißt, es werden bestimmte Elemente hervorgehoben, andere werden vernachlässigt. Beim Reality-TV gibt es in der Tat einen klaren Trend hin zu immer dominanter werdenden Formen der Inszenierung. Die Grenzen zwischen Dokumentation und Fiktion werden systematisch verwischt […]. Allerdings sehe ich darin auch wieder einen Reiz für die Zuschauer.

BZ: Und welcher ist das?

Keppler: Was ist real? Was inszeniert? Was gescriptet? Was den Protagonisten in den Mund gelegt? Das sind die Fragen, über die mit anderen diskutiert werden kann. Denn dass die Anschlusskommunikation, das Darüberreden, für das Zuschauervergnügen an diesen Formaten genauso konstitutiv ist wie der häufig beschworene Voyeurismus, ist unbestritten. Das hat auch eine Befragung des Internationalen Zentralinstituts für das Jugend- und Bildungsfernsehen ergeben. 75 Prozent der Zuschauer von *Germany's Next Top Model* und 82 Prozent der DSDS-Zuschauer gaben an, dass sie sich am Tag nach den Sendungen mit anderen darüber unterhalten. […]

BZ: Gibt es eigentlich Erkenntnisse darüber, wer Reality-TV anschaut?

Keppler: Aber ja, alle! Reality-TV ist kein Unterschichtfernsehen, wie oft vermutet wird, jedenfalls nicht, was die Zuschauer betrifft! Natürlich gibt es Vorlieben. Castingshows werden zum Beispiel überproportional von weiblichen Jugendlichen gesehen. Und je älter die Zuschauerinnen sind, desto weniger interessieren sie sich für die Sendungen.

(330 Wörter)
Maikka Kost, *Badische Zeitung*, 2012

Erwartungshorizonte

1 Comprehension

12 VP *Outline Panem's history. Focus on its development as well as the function and rules of the Hunger Games as officially presented by the Capitol.*

Briefly describe the development which led to the founding of Panem and the introduction of the Hunger Games. When writing about the Hunger Games, also add the rules and the function of the Hunger Games according to the Capitol.

Task support

Für diese Aufgabe werden insgesamt 12 Punkte auf den Inhalt vergeben.

Form und Umfang meiner Antwort:
Outline … : Skizzieren Sie die Entstehung und Entwicklung des Staates Panem. Beschreiben Sie dabei als Folge des Bürgerkriegs auch die Regeln der Hungerspiele und deren Funktion aus Sicht des Kapitols.
Formulieren Sie Ihre Antwort in eigenen Worten.

Mögliche inhaltliche Aspekte:
- Panem's history:
  - The founding of Panem was preceded by natural catastrophes and a war.
  - The territory which was known as North America became Panem.
  - There was a civil war between the Capitol and 13 districts in Panem.
  - The Capitol won the war and introduced the Hunger Games.
- The function and the rules of the Hunger Games:
  - The Hunger Games should remind the people of the war, oppress the districts and entertain the people.
  - As part of the game, the districts have to send tributes. The tributes have to survive and fight against each other in an enclosed territory. The last tribute surviving wins the game.

Proposed solution:
The novel the "Hunger Games" by Suzanne Collins is set in the utopian state Panem. The state of Panem was established after a lot of natural catastrophes and finally a terrible war had destroyed North America. The territory which was formerly known as North America then became Panem.
Panem consisted of 13 districts and the Capitol. Soon the districts rebelled against the Capitol and in a brutal civil war the Capitol defeated twelve of the districts. The thirteenth district was completely destroyed.
After the conflict, the Capitol introduced the Hunger Games which are described in the novel. The games are held each year to remind the people of the terrible civil war. In addition to this, the Hunger Games are used to stress that the Capitol is superior to the remaining twelve districts and to punish them for their rebellion. The Hunger Games are also presented as a sports festival with the aim to entertain the audience. The rules are the following: Each of the twelve districts has to send a girl and a boy to take part in the games. The tributes have to survive in a large enclosed territory and fight against each other while the audience watches them. The last boy or girl surviving in the territory wins the Hunger Games.

(215 words)

Tip
Use the simple past to describe the *founding* of Panem.

Tip
Use the simple present to describe the protagonist's present.

2 Analysis

16 VP *Analyse how the narrator's situation and her attitude to Panem and the Hunger Games are presented. Focus on point of view, choice of words and stylistic devices.*

Examine from which point of view the story is told and how the narrator presents her situation. Explain her situation in relation to her attitude towards the Hunger Games."

Task support

Für diese Aufgabe werden insgesamt 14 Punkte auf den Inhalt vergeben.

Form und Umfang meiner Antwort:
Analyse …: Untersuchen Sie, wie die Erzählerin ihre Situation darstellt und welche Einstellung gegenüber Panem und den Hungerspielen sie dem Leser vermittelt. Wie unterstützen die Erzählperspektive, der Sprachgebrauch und rhetorische Stilmittel die (positive / negative) Darstellung der Hungerspiele? Stützen Sie Ihre Argumente anhand von Belegen aus dem Textauszug.

Mögliche inhaltliche Aspekte:
- At the beginning, the narrator informs the reader about Panem and the Hunger Games in an objective style.
- From line 17 onwards the tone changes
- The reader is likely to sympathise with the first-person narrator.
- The narrator's life is completely at the mercy of the Capitol. (l. 18)
- Any resistance will be punished (ll. 21–22)
- The narrator uses words related to coercion (ll. 12 ff., "must", "imprisoned") and danger (ll. 14 ff. "kill", "burning desert")
- She calls the games "humiliating" and "torturous" (l. 23)
- In an anaphora she expresses her deepest wish (l. 29 "that it's not me.")

Proposed solution:
In the given excerpt of the novel "The Hunger Games", the main character Katniss describes the scene where the participants are chosen for the Hunger Games and everybody is afraid of becoming one of the tributes.
At the beginning of the excerpt, the narrator reports in an objective and informative style about the opening ceremony of the games and about the emergence of Panem. The opening statement by the mayor is rather boring since it is the "same story every year" (l. 1) and the narrator summarises the mayor's speech about the rise of Panem without any enthusiasm.
However, the narrator's tone changes from line 17 onwards. Now it becomes obvious that the reader is experiencing the plot from Katniss' point of view. She is the first-person narrator as the personal pronouns "we", "our", "I" and "me" prove in the second half of the text. Since the story is told by a first-person narrator it is very easy for the reader to sympathise with Katniss. The reader is very likely to share her feelings and fears, e.g. when Katniss explains that the Capitol takes "the kids from our districts forcing them to kill one another while we watch" (l. 17). Further, the first-person narrator points out that her situation is completely helpless. For example, she uses several words and phrases that express her fear and the oppression of the people in the province by the Capitol. She states that

Tip
Do not just list narrative techniques but explain their effects on the reader.

the Capitol rules over the provinces and that everyone's lives are "totally at their mercy" (l.18). Using a metaphor, Katniss informs the reader that any resistance to the Capitol will be severely punished even if you "lift a finger" (l.21).
Moreover, the first-person narrator states clearly that the people fear the Hunger Games and that it is not a festivity which you look forward to. She uses words which express aspects of coercion and threat. No participant is a volunteer since the games are a "punishment" (l.11) and each province "must" provide a participant (l.12) who will be "imprisoned" (l.13) in a territory. The notion of the severe threat becomes obvious when Katniss explains that the tributes are forced to kill each other (l.15) in a hostile environment like a "burning desert" or "frozen wasteland" (l.14).
In addition to the fear, Katniss also shows the distress and sadness which is caused by the games. She calls the event "humiliating and torturous" (l.23), which reveals the true character of the Hunger Games.
Finally, Katniss expresses all her fears and deepest wish in the drawing ceremony. Using an anaphor she repeats her only hope in this scene which is that "it's not me" (l.29).
To conclude, Katniss' situation is very difficult and pitiful. Her family's, her friends' and her own life are at risk because of the Hunger Games and there is nothing she can do to change this since the Capitol is oppressing them.

(490 words)

> **Tip**
> Always prove your statements with examples from the text.

3 Evaluation

14 VP **a)** *Discuss the role and the options of an individual like Katniss in a future state like Panem. Refer to the extract as well as work done in class.*

Discuss arguments in favour of and against Katniss' capabilities to oppose the Hunger Games and end the oppression of the people in the twelve districts. Think about what an individual in Katniss' situation could do to win support for his/her aim.

Task support

Für diese Aufgabe werden insgesamt 14 Punkte auf den Inhalt vergeben.

Form und Umfang meiner Antwort:
Discuss …: Sammeln Sie ausgehend von dem Romanauszug und von Ihrem im Unterricht erworbenen Wissen mehrere Ideen, die dafür bzw. dagegen sprechen, dass Katniss die Lebensbedingungen ihrer Mitmenschen und ihre eigenen entscheidend beeinflussen kann. Strukturieren Sie Ihre Ideen und erörtern Sie diese in formeller Sprache.

Mögliche Inhalte und Struktur meiner Antwort:
- Introduction: Katniss suffers from the cruel rules of the Hunger Games. Is it possible for her to protect her sister from the Hunger Games?
- Main part:
  - She is an ordinary teenager who is expected to accept the decision.
  - Her options are very little and any resistance will be punished.
  - However, she can trust in her personal qualities.
  - She can persuade the people around her to speak out against the Hunger Games.
  - She might experience a lot of sympathy for her cause.
- End: She has few options right now but she can change this.

Proposed solution:
As presented in the extract, Katniss belongs to an oppressed group of people in the state of Panem. Every year she has to be afraid that she herself or a person she loves might have to take part in the Hunger Games. She lives under constant fear and insecurity because of the people in the Capitol who threaten and control her life. Despite Katniss' difficult situation, would it be possible for her to change her life and escape her misery?

It is unlikely that Katniss can help her sister. The capitol wants to prove its power and supremacy over the people of the districts. Like the family and friends of the other tributes, Katniss is expected to accept that her sister has to take part in the Hunger Games and any resistance by Katniss against the decision of the Capitol would be followed by fierce punishment. In addition to this, she is just an ordinary teenager. Who would listen to her or even speak up for her? Therefore her options are very few and her role is confined to accepting the Capitol's decisions and adapt as well as possible to her environment.

In contrast to accepting the unjust and brutal Hunger Games, Katniss can try to change her life even though she is just a common teenager. She might be poor and unknown among the people of Panem but still she might persuade them to stand up against the Hunger Games. Nobody can deny that she is brave, self-confident and hard-working and she can use these personal qualities, e.g. to organise a campaign against the Hunger Games and the inequality between the Capitol and the twelve districts. There are many people in the districts who have suffered like her from oppression and maybe there are even people in the Capitol who think that the Hunger Games are unfair. Since her sister was chosen, she is also personally affected by the brutality of the Hunger Games and people are likely to feel sympathy for her. It is surely dangerous to organise resistance against the Hunger Games but if she manages to talk to and persuade a lot of people in the districts and even in the Capitol, she might win enough supporters to end the oppression of the districts.

To conclude, Katniss might not have the power or authority right now to influence the Capitol's policy but she can become a powerful heroine who stands up against the oppression of the Capitol. *(415 words)*

Tip
Begin your text by stating the question you are going to discuss.

Tip
To discuss the topic, present arguments in favour and against the statement.

Tip
Conclude your text by giving your personal assessment.

14 VP **b)** *Re-creation of text: That night Katniss cannot sleep. She thinks about the day and her decision. In a personal letter to Primrose she expresses her fears and explains the reasons for her decision. Write her letter.*

In the given solution, the author imagines that Katniss volunteered in place of her sister as a tribute in order to protect her from participation in the Hunger Games. Write a personal letter from Katniss' point of view to her little sister Primrose. Explain why you volunteered and what you are afraid of in the Hunger Games.

Task support

Für diese Aufgabe werden insgesamt 14 Punkte auf den Inhalt vergeben.

Form und Umfang meiner Antwort:
In a personal letter … she expresses …: Versetzen Sie sich in die Situation von Katniss und schreiben Sie einen Brief an Ihre jüngere Schwester am Abend nach der Auswahl der Teilnehmer.
Erklären Sie Ihrer jüngeren Schwester Ihre Entscheidung und teilen Sie ihr Ihre Ängste mit.

Verfassen Sie den Brief in informeller Sprache und beachten Sie die formalen Merkmale eines persönlichen Briefs (Anrede, Einleitung etc.).

Mögliche inhaltliche Aspekte:
- *I wanted to protect you.*
- *You are less experienced than me.*
- *I'm really afraid of the competition and don't know how to react.*
- *The organisers of the Hunger Games can manipulate us.*
- *I've got to make a plan how to survive.*

Proposed solution:

Dear Primrose,

How are you? Please don't worry too much because you are my little sister and I want to protect you.
I still think about this terrible day and I can still feel the shock when I heard your name. At first, I was so shocked that I almost collapsed. But then I imagined you as a participant in the Hunger Games and I couldn't bear it. I couldn't have let you go or even watch you try to survive in a dry desert. All I wanted to do in this moment was to protect you. I'm older and more experienced than you while you wouldn't have had a chance to survive. That is the reason why I volunteered to go in your place.
Of course, I hate this stupid game and at the same time I'm afraid of it. It will definitely be dangerous for me. I'll just try to survive and I hope that I don't have to hurt or even kill somebody. Actually, I don't know what to do when I meet another participant. I can just try to hide and survive or maybe I can persuade the other participants to disobey the rules. But will this plan work? The Capitol is so powerful and can even manipulate us. Anyway, this might be a plan. I hope the other tributes will trust me.
If only this stupid game were abolished and I could see you again!

Love,
Katniss

(240 words)

Tip
The first line begins with a capital letter.

Tip
As a basic rule, write your letter in the present tense.

4 Mediation

As part of an exchange program, you attend a high school in the US for a year. Your class has read The Hunger Games *and is organizing a conference to discuss the popularity and ethics of reality TV. As an international guest you are invited to deliver the opening statement to the students. You have found the following interview with professor Angela Keppler and want to use it as a source to talk about the popularity of reality TV series.*

18 VP   *For the conference, prepare your opening statement by focusing on the reasons why reality TV is popular among the audience. Add information where necessary. Write your speech.*

Write an introductory speech for the conference. In your speech, inform the audience about the ongoing popularity of reality TV series according to Professor Keppler. Since this is a mediation task, talk only about information which is given in the German text and do not add personal comments or facts. Present your speech in spoken but formal language.

Erwartungshorizonte

Task support

Für diese Aufgabe werden insgesamt 18 Punkte auf den Inhalt vergeben.

Form und Umfang meiner Antwort:
Write your speech … : Schreiben Sie eine einleitende Rede, in der Sie sich auf das Interview mit Frau Keppler beziehen.
Nennen Sie in Ihrer Rede die Gründe für die anhaltende Popularität von Reality TV und strukturieren Sie Ihre Rede angemessen, indem Sie z. B. das Thema vorstellen und abschließend Ihren Zuhörern für Ihre Aufmerksamkeit danken und zu weiteren Diskussionen einladen.

Mögliche inhaltliche Aspekte:
- Reality TV is very popular in Europe and the US.
- Professor Keppler, an academic who studies media and communications, provides us with interesting information about the popularity of reality TV.
- People enjoy watching other people dealing with familiar problems from a distant point of view.
- People love to discuss the latest episodes.
- The audience does not mind if reality TV series follow a script because then they can discuss which part of the plot is real and which part follows a script.

Proposed solution:

Dear students,

To begin our discussions about the ethics and popularity of reality TV programs, I want to focus on the reasons for their popularity. As in the US, reality TV series are also very popular in Germany. People simply enjoy watching other people's lives. However, I still wonder why people love watching reality TV programs to such an extent and don't even mind if the plots follow a script.
I read an interview with Professor Keppler, an academic studying media and communications in Germany. In it, I discovered some interesting information about this question. In general, people enjoy watching other people deal with problems which they are familiar with while they are sitting in front of the TV and don't have to deal with the problems themselves. Of course, the interviewer argued that the plots in reality TV programs often follow a script and so the reactions are neither spontaneous nor real. But even scripted reality is interesting to the audience as Professor Keppler explains. For the audience, it can be very exciting to discuss which of the participants' reactions follow a script, and which reactions are actually real. And as most of us know, we love to discuss the latest episodes of reality TV series the next day because it is exciting to talk about the participants' reactions. So even if reality TV series follow a script, this just adds another aspect to discuss which is: Which part of yesterday's episode followed a script and which part was really real?

So you see, reality TV series are still very successful even though they might not be real.

Thank you very much for your attention and I'm looking forward to our discussions.

(280 words)

> **Tip**
> Adress the audience and state the topic of your speech.

Abitur 2015: **Tradition and change in the UK**

Klausurteil: Leseverstehen und Schreiben integriert

Ed Miliband: Speech to the Labour Party Annual Conference

In this extract from his keynote speech the Labour leader Ed Miliband talks about his experiences during the 2013 local election campaign.

And I talked to people about their lives. I remember this town meeting I had in Cleveleys. It was just coming to the end of the meeting and this bloke wandered up. He was incredibly angry. It's a family show so I won't exactly repeat what he said. He was so angry he wouldn't give me his name, but he did tell me his story
5 about how he spent the last ten years looking after his disabled wife, and then another four years looking for a job and not finding one. He was angry about immigration and some people in the crowd booed him. But actually he wasn't prejudiced, he just felt the economy didn't work for him. And then I think about the two market traders I met in Chesterfield, standing by their stalls, out in all
10 weathers, working all hours, and they said look this country just doesn't seem to be rewarding our hard work and effort. There seem to be some people getting something for nothing. This society is losing touch with our values. [...]
   And then I think about this scaffolder I met just around the corner from where I live. I was just coming back from a local café I'd been at. He stopped me in the
15 street, he said to me, "Where's your bodyguard?" I said I don't have one, but that's another story. He told me his story. And what he said to me was "look, I go out, I do the work, I go all around the country, again out in all weathers, I earn a decent wage, but I still can't make ends meet". And he said to me, "Is anyone ever going to do anything about those gas and electric bills that just go up and up, faster
20 than I can earn a living?" He wanted someone to fight for him.
   Now if you listen to these stories – four of millions of the stories of our country – and you have your own, and your friends and family, what do you learn? All of these people love Britain, they embody its great spirit, but they all believe that Britain can do better than this. Today I say to them and millions of others you're
25 right, Britain can do better than this, Britain must do better than this, Britain will do better than this with a government that fights for you.

(399 words)
Ed Miliband, *2013 conference speech,* September 24, 2013

[2] **Cleveleys** town in England
[9] **Chesterfield** town in England

The Royal Baby

Prince George, the first son of William and Kate, Duke and Duchess of Cambridge, was born 22 July, 2013. The cartoon in the form of a banknote was published two days after the birth of the royal baby.

"Your Next Head of State But 2 whether you want it or not, suckers, I Rule You Pay".
In the UK, the V-sign with the back of the hand facing the observer is an insult.

Steve Bell, 2013

1 Comprehension

12 VP Describe the cartoon and the political issues and views presented in both cartoon and speech.

2 Analysis

16 VP Analyse how these issues and views are presented. Consider communicative strategies in the speech, visual and textual features of the cartoon as well as their intended effects.

3 Evaluation

Choose one of the following tasks:

14 VP a) Discuss the message of the cartoon. Refer to work done in class on the British monarchy and modern democracy.

14 VP b) Re-creation of text: As a second generation immigrant you have listened to Miliband's speech. Write a response to his speech in a formal letter to your local Labour MP. Focus on your personal experience and your expectations of a future government.

Klausurteil: Sprachmittlung isoliert

4 Mediation

18 VP *You are a member of a group of international bloggers who maintain a blog aimed at young people in Europe and North America. Your group's next topic which you will blog about will be "How to make a difference". You have found the following article about Sophia Giannakis and her experiences in politics.*
Write a blog entry in which you inform the reader about Sophia's positive experiences as a young politician.

> **Tip**
> Die Sprachmittlung wurde nachträglich redaktionell ergänzt. Seit 2017 ist Sprachmittlung Teil der Abiturprüfung.

Jugendliche setzen sich in der Kommunalpolitik tatkräftig ein

Düsseldorf. So richtig zugetraut hat Sophia Giannakis sich das mit der Politik zuerst nicht. Einen Ruck musste sich die 17-Jährige geben, um bei der Wahl des Düsseldorfer Jugendrats anzutreten. Nun, nach mehr als einem Jahr im Amt der stellvertretenden Sprecherin ist sie begeistert. „Man hat so viele Möglichkeiten,
5 etwas zu verändern", sagt die Abiturientin. „Ich liebe einfach dieses Mitmischen!"
   Mit 30 weiteren gewählten Mitgliedern zwischen elf und 21 Jahren setzt sich Giannakis für die Belange der Jugendlichen ein, hobbymäßig neben der Schule. So funktioniert das in vielen NRW-Kommunen. Etwa alle acht Wochen trifft sich der Jugendrat im Rathaus. Sie tragen Anzüge, im Publikum sitzt eine Schulklasse –
10 wie bei einer richtigen Ratssitzung. Nur, dass das letzte Wort die Erwachsenen haben, die Politiker. Die Jugendräte sind in den Ausschüssen als beratende Mitglieder vertreten. Ihre Ideen leiten sie als Anträge an die Politiker weiter, die dann darüber entscheiden.
   Aktiv und heftig debattiert der Jugendrat drei Stunden lang. Man merkt, sie
15 nehmen ihre Aufgaben ernst. Wie können mehr öffentliche Räume für Graffiti-Maler geschaffen werden? Wie sehen die Ergebnisse der Jugendbefragung aus? Wo haben Jugendliche Probleme?
   Als es ums Thema Geld geht, ist ein Ratsmitglied entgeistert: „Warum gibt es eigentlich Geld für den Kö-Bogen, aber nicht für uns Jugendliche?" Das letzte
20 Wort haben eben die Erwachsenen. Die anderen beruhigen ihn, jetzt sind andere Themen wichtig: Flüchtlinge und öffentliche Verkehrsmittel, Giannakis' Spezialthema. Überfüllte Bahnen zu Schulzeiten und veränderte Nachtfahrpläne beschäftigen die Jugend. Zur Ratssitzung hat sie einen Vertreter der Rheinbahn eingeladen, um dem Problem auf den Grund zu gehen.
25 Nur selten muss Jugendrats-Geschäftsführer Joachim Möntmann, einer der wenigen Erwachsenen im Saal, bei den Jugendlichen eingreifen. „Politik bedeutet Auseinandersetzung. Das machen sie intensiver und respektvoller als Erwachsene", sagt er. Politikverdrossenheit der Jugend, daran glaubt er nicht. „Man muss ihnen nur Raum geben, sich zu engagieren", sagt Möntmann.

(312 Wörter)
Kölner Stadtanzeiger, 2015

Erwartungshorizonte

1 Comprehension

12 VP   *Describe the cartoon and the political issues and views presented in both cartoon and speech.*

You are asked to inform the reader about the general political topics which Ed Miliband talks about. In addition to this, give *some* (not all) examples and / or details of the text.
Do the same when describing the cartoon. Tell the reader what can be seen in the cartoon but do not analyze it in detail – only present the reader the political issue (here the costs of the monarchy) and the cartoonist's view on it.
The task asks you for issues and views presented in *both* materials. Do not forget to mention the issue(s) / view(s) which they have in common.

Task support

Für diese Aufgabe werden insgesamt 12 Punkte auf den Inhalt vergeben.

Form und Umfang meiner Antwort:
Describe … : Beschreiben Sie anhand von Beispielen die geforderten Inhalte und (Haupt-)aussagen der Rede und des Cartoons und vergleichen Sie die zentralen Botschaften abschließend.
Formulieren Sie Ihre Antwort in eigenen Worten.

Mögliche inhaltliche Aspekte:
- Ed Miliband's speech:
  - unemployment
  - shift in the value of hard / manual work
  - low incomes and high living costs
  - need for the government to change things and support the people better
- Cartoon:
  - form of a banknote
  - Baby George on a cloud wearing a crown and shining like the sun
  - offensive (V-sign, text)
  - criticism of high costs for the monarchy

Proposed solution:
In his speech to the Labour Party in 2013, Ed Miliband focuses on the need for the government to listen carefully to the people and to improve living standards for the working class in Great Britain. He refers to various people he has talked to in the streets and to the difficulties they have had with their employment situations and finances.
According to Miliband's experiences, it is difficult for a lot of people to get back into the workforce after a period of unemployment. He also addresses a shift in the value system. Hard work, especially manual work, is not appreciated anymore like it used to be. Often workers earn too little to pay their utility bills even though they have a full time job. It is the government's responsibility to care for these people.
The cartoon which was published two days after the birth of Prince George resembles a banknote and displays the royal baby. George is lying on a cloud and

Tip
The cartoon says "Your Next Head of State But 2", i.e. Prince George is in third position to succeed the throne.

wearing a big crown which reflects beams of light. He is insulting the spectator by showing him the V-sign. The text on the cartoon is likewise very offensive saying "Your Next Head of State But 2 whether (…), I Rule, You Pay."
The artist criticises the monarchy and its expenditures. The British people have to pay for the costs of the royal family even if they disagree with the monarchy. Miliband and the cartoonist both draw attention to a growing gap between the common people and the elite in Britain.

(250 words)

> **Tip**
> Finish your answer by comparing the cartoon and the speech.

2 Analysis

16 VP *Analyse how these issues and views are presented. Consider communicative strategies in the speech, visual and textual features of the cartoon as well as their intended effects.*

When analysing Miliband's speech, it is worthwhile to pay attention to its setting. The speech was delivered by the leader of the Labour party during an election campaign. As can be expected, the speaker tries to rally support for his party. Therefore, focus on Miliband's persuasive strategies to appeal to his listeners' emotions and to win their support.

To analyse the cartoon, take into consideration its form (banknote, style of writing etc.) and compare it with its content. Give reasons for the artist's choice of form, content and symbols.

Task support

Für diese Aufgabe werden insgesamt 16 Punkte auf den Inhalt vergeben.

Form und Umfang meiner Antwort:
Analyse …: Beschreiben und erklären Sie im Detail, mit welchen rhetorischen bzw. visuellen Mitteln Miliband bzw. der Zeichner ihr Publikum auf Missstände hinweisen und für sich gewinnen wollen.
Beziehen Sie sich stets auf Beispiele oder Zitate, um Ihre Erkenntnisse zu belegen. Formulieren Sie Ihre Antwort in eigenen Worten.

Mögliche inhaltliche Aspekte:
- *Ed Miliband's speech:*
  - *A political change is necessary and possible to improve life in Britain.*
  - *Labour understands and supports British people best.*
  - *Miliband uses informal language to prove that he does not belong to the elite.*
  - *He lists several personal experiences to show his understanding of the average living conditions in Britain.*
  - *He enumerates the hard working conditions to show his sympathy.*
  - *He quotes directly to gain authenticity and to make it easier for his audience to identify with the people.*
  - *He addresses the audience directly to appeal to their feelings.*
  - *He generalises their experiences and persuades them that they represent the majority of Britain.*

- Steve Bell's cartoon:
  - The cartoonist criticises the expenditures of the royal family.
  - He uses irony and sarcasm to enrage the spectators and to persuade them that the monarchy exploits British citizens.
  - In the cartoon, form and content contradict each other. On first glance, the banknote looks like a normal banknote but when looking closer, the offence becomes obvious.
  - The symbols contradict each other too. On the hand hand, the crown on a white cloud, on the other hand, the V-sign.

Mögliche zusätzliche Aspekte:
- (Speech:) Miliband ends his reports about people he met with a rhetorical question, which is an appeal for a political change.
- (Cartoon:) The fact that the message is written on a banknote degrades their possessors again because they have to carry it with them.

Proposed solution:
In his speech at the Annual Conference of Labour in 2013, Miliband uses various communicative strategies to show the difficulties of British people earning a living and to present himself and Labour as the correct political party to make a difference.
Miliband refers to several personal experiences to gain credibility and to prove his close relations to the people. He lists some talks with common people, always introducing them with the anaphor "And (then) I …" (ll. 1 ff., 8 ff., 13 ff.) which makes him appear to know about innumerous such stories and which makes it easy to follow as a listener. To distance himself from the elite and demonstrate his familiarity with the troubles of average British citizens, he also uses informal language like "bloke" (l. 2).
Miliband states clearly that the majority of British people are disappointed by their present situation. In his first example he repeats several times that the man he talked to was "angry" (ll. 3 ff.). In addition to this, he adds that he can understand his anger and thus shows his sympathy for the average citizen again. He also tries to arouse the listeners' sympathy by describing the market traders' hard work (ll. 9–10, "standing by their stalls … working all hours).
The last worker Miliband talks about is the most persuasive example. Again, he describes the kind of work a scaffolder does, but this time he quotes him directly using the first-person point of view to describe his work (ll. 16 ff.). This makes it easier for the listeners to identify with the scaffolder. Having caught the sympathy of the listeners, Miliband ends the scaffolder's story with a rhetorical question (ll. 18 ff.) which is actually an appeal for a change in politics.
In the last part of his speech, Miliband addresses the audience directly. He stresses that his listeners, like "millions" (ll. 21 ff.) of other people, share the same experiences. He conveys the impression that they are the majority of Britain and that they can improve their situation with a government that listens to them.
The cartoonist Steve Bell criticises the inequality between common British people and the elite, here the royal family, much harsher than Miliband does.
The cartoonist uses above all irony and sarcasm to enrage and irritate the spectators. On the one hand, the form conveys the impression of a valuable document

Tip
To introduce your analysis, mention the source(s) you refer to.

Tip
To support your findings, explain them and give examples from the text.

Tip
Do not just list rhetorical devices but explain their effects on the audience.

whose content is of high cultural or moral value. The letters are beautifully written like in a great work of literature or in a religious document.

On the other hand, the content is the opposite. The skillfully written text is insulting, which just confirms the inequality by saying "I rule, you pay". Beneath the title "Your Next Head of State" the spectator would expect the portrait of an honourable monarch, but instead, the baby on display is hardly recognizable. However, you can see a white cloud and a radiant crown, but the spectator is irritated by the baby's insulting V-sign sticking out of the cloud. If there is any doubt left about the materialistic and contemptuous character of the baby, its extremely arrogant message becomes obvious when reading the smallest print beneath the title "Your Next Head of State" which says "whether you want it or not, suckers". The reader is left no choice whether to pay or not and is deeply insulted with a pejorative.

All in all, this banknote ridicules and degrades British taxpayers above all because everybody would have to carry the banknote with the offending message in his pocket.

The cartoonist severely criticises the British monarchy. In his view, it is unjust and arrogant to the people who do not support the monarchy.

(600 words)

3 Evaluation

14 VP **a)** *Discuss the message of the cartoon. Refer to work done in class on the British monarchy and modern democracy.*

You can argue in favour or against the British monarchy. You can also decide to stay neutral and leave the decision to the reader. However, it is essential that you give several meaningful arguments for and against the monarchy in the UK.
In the following "proposed answer", the author decided to argue in favour of the monarchy.

Task support

Für diese Aufgabe werden insgesamt 14 Punkte auf den Inhalt vergeben.

Form und Umfang meiner Antwort:
Discuss …: Sammeln Sie mehrere Ideen zu Vor- und Nachteilen der Monarchie im Vereinigten Königreich.
Der Cartoon beispielsweise bietet einige Anknüpfungspunkte, für Gründe gegen die Monarchie.
Um auf Vorteile der Monarchie hinzuweisen, entkräften Sie die Kritik des Cartoons bzw. beziehen Sie Ihr im Unterricht erworbenes Wissen mit ein.
Insgesamt sollten Sie insgesamt mindestens vier Pro- bzw. Contra-Argumente geben.

Erwartungshorizonte

Mögliche Inhalte und Struktur meiner Antwort:
- *Introduction:*
  - *The royal family is very popular (example).*
  - *(Reformulation of the topic to discuss.)*
- *Arguments against the monarchy:*
  - *The monarch has hardly any political functions.*
  - *Costs could be reduced if one person is elected as Head of State.*
- *Arguments in favour of the monarchy:*
  - *The Royals fulfil important functions in business and politics.*
  - *They are important for companies in tourism and the media.*
  - *They strengthen British culture and identity.*
- *(Conclusion with your opinion, outlook or appeal, etc.)*

Proposed solution:

The news about William and Kate expecting a baby was adopted by the media and the public with great joy. British people and people from abroad were looking forward to the birth. Finally, when little George was born, it was celebrated not only by the royal family but also by a lot of British citizens and the newspapers tried to get a picture of the royal baby to please its readership. However, not everybody joined the happiness about the next successor to the throne since it was a sign that the monarchy and its expenditures would prevail for many years to come. So are there actually any reasonable arguments in favour of a monarchy in the 21st century?

Most of the European neighbours of the United Kingdom have abolished monarchy about one hundred years ago. However, the United Kingdom has maintained its monarchy while depriving its monarch of almost all political power. Today, the royal family has only representative functions.

Moreover, a lot of money could be saved by abolishing the monarchy. British taxpayers have to pay for the luxurious lifestyle, housing and security of an entire family. If the United Kingdom would be represented by just one elected person as Head of State, the costs could be certainly reduced.

However, the royal family does not just enjoy luxurious dinners with foreign representatives and consume the money of taxpayers. They are also entrepreneurs who are in charge of their own businesses and of their revenue. They have to think and work like businessmen. When going abroad they represent the United Kingdom and have to fulfil the functions of diplomats. Actually, they do work for Britain.

The media and tourism industry depends heavily on the monarchy. Every year millions of tourists travel to England because of its monarchy. In any travel guide you will find Buckingham Palace among the major attractions.

As surveys show, a huge majority of British people is in favour of keeping the monarchy. The royal family stands for unity and the British identity. They are considered to be part of British culture and their value can hardly be expressed in terms of money.

All in all, taxes could be reduced by abolishing the monarchy, but at the same time we must not underestimate the financial and cultural advantages of the monarchy.

(385 words)

Tip Reformulate the topic which you are going to discuss.

Tip Con-argument 1

Tip Con-argument 2

Tip Pro-argument 1

Tip Pro-argument 2

Tip Pro-argument 3

Tip Conclusion and personal opinion/appeal.

14 VP **b)** *Re-creation of text: As a second generation immigrant you have listened to Miliband's speech. Write a response to his speech in a formal letter to your local Labour MP. Focus on your personal experience and your expectations of a future government.*

Write a formal and polite letter to your local Labour representative in parliament. Remember the topics in Miliband's speech and think about similar experiences you might have had as a second generation immigrant. Finish your letter with an appeal for a future government.

Task support

Für diese Aufgabe werden insgesamt 14 Punkte auf den Inhalt vergeben.

Form und Umfang meiner Antwort:
Write a response ...: Schreiben Sie einen formellen Brief an den Parlamentsabgeordneten für Ihren Wahlbezirk.
Beziehen Sie sich auf die in der Rede genannten Themen und setzen Sie diese in Beziehung mit Ihren eigenen Erfahrungen als Brite mit Immigrationshintergrund. Entwickeln Sie ausgehend von Ihren persönlichen Erfahrungen Forderungen an den Abgeordneten.
Achten Sie auf die Textsortenmerkmale eines formellen Briefs (Adresse, Betreff, Anrede, Schlussformel etc.).

Mögliche Inhalte und Struktur meiner Antwort
- *Introduction: (Refer to the speech.)*
- *Possible arguments:*
  - *parents' experiences of hard work*
  - *high living costs*
  - *difficulty to find a job*
  - *necessity to overcome prejudices*
  - *need to be valued for one's work*
- *End: (Stress your demand.)*

Proposed solution:

David Johnson
11 Green Hill
Watford AB1 23C

Mr. Manicks (MP)
24 Avon Lane
Watford CD4 56X

25th September 2013

Speech to the Labour Party Annual Conference on September 24, 2013

Dear Mr Manicks,

Having listened to Mr Miliband's speech at the Annual Conference, I write to you as the representative of my constituency. I want to draw attention to a huge minority in our society: People with an immigration background.
Mr Miliband referred to a lot of people he met in the streets. I appreciate his willingness to listen to average citizens and their problems. Like Mr Miliband said,

Tip
State the speech you refer to in the title.

Tip
The first line begins with a capital letter.

a lot of people suffer from low-paying work and high living costs. Unfortunately he did not mention the groups of people with an immigration background although this group probably suffers the most from these problems. Most of the people who came to the United Kingdom from former Commonwealth countries have to work hard and do manual work. As we all know, these kinds of jobs are rather badly paid. Like my parents, who came to the UK in 1979, a lot of them are happy to live in this country. They are diligent workers, they try to save money for their future and their children and they are unlikely to complain in a society which regards them as strangers. My parents have never regretted that they came to the UK even though they have experienced all the difficulties Mr Miliband spoke of. Both of them have full time jobs but their pay is low. Like many other immigrants they suffer from poor housing because they cannot afford to move to a more expensive flat. They are glad if they can pay all their bills each month.

I can say that I am better off than my parents. My education is better and I have found a well-paid job. But it was difficult for me. I had to prove my motivation and sometimes I get the impression that some of my customers would value my work more if they did not see my immigration background.

Mr Miliband is right and as a fervent supporter of Labour policy, I ask you to listen to people like my parents and me. We might be a minority in this country but we are a big minority and we want to contribute to this country. Please, do not forget people like me and my parents who work hard and want to be valued for it. Help us reduce prejudices and convince everybody that we are Britain too.

Sincerely,
David J –

(425 words)

> **Tip**
> Outline your expectations for the future at the end.

4 Mediation

18 VP *You are a member of a group of international bloggers who maintain a blog aimed at young people in Europe and North America. Your group's next topic which you will blog about will be "How to make a difference". You have found the following article about Sophia Giannakis and her experiences in politics.*
Write a blog entry in which you inform the reader about Sophia's positive experiences as a young politician.

In this task you should write a blog. First introduce the reason for writing your blog. Then inform the reader about Sophia's positive experiences as a young politician. The style of the blog should be aimed at a young audience, yet formal and informative. Pay attention to the textual features of a blog.

Task support

Für diese Aufgabe werden insgesamt 18 Punkte auf den Inhalt vergeben.

Form und Umfang meiner Antwort:
Write a blog entry …: Schreiben Sie einen informativen – d.h. ohne eine persönliche Stellungnahme – Blog-Eintrag.
Berichten Sie einer jungen, internationalen Leserschaft von Sophias positiven Erfahrungen in der Politik und beachten Sie die spezifischen Merkmale für die Textsorte Blog (z.B. Titel, Datum, klare Strukturierung durch Paragraphen, klare Ansprache der Adressaten, Einladung zu weiteren Kommentaren am Ende etc.).

Mögliche inhaltliche Aspekte:
- *reason for writing*
- *introduction of the example (place, members etc.)*
- *reasons and examples why Sophia likes the work (influence decisions, make young people heard, support interests of young people, etc.)*
- *act like in a real council*
- *teenagers respect each other*

Proposed solution:

How to make a difference in Düsseldorf, Germany
08 November 2016

For our topic "How to make a difference" I've found an interesting example of a group of young people in Düsseldorf, Germany. The city has decided that regular meetings are to be held in the town hall to represent the interests of young people. The members of this meeting are aged 11 to 21 years. Read about Sophia Giannakis, who is one of its members and the reasons why she likes to get engaged. Sophia has been a member for one year now and so far she really loves the work. She can influence political decisions and make life more worthwhile for young people in her city. Together with the other members of the group, they make surveys among young people to find out what they need. Moreover, they help graffiti artists show their art in the city. And they can invite experts to discuss topics. Sophia, for example, has invited an expert for public transport since she's decided to focus above all on this topic.
The members of the youth council act and behave like in the 'real' city council. For example, they wear suits and often have an audience.
In their meetings the young politicians always discuss the topics very seriously and respectfully. Even a city official admits that the young people do this much better than their grown up counterparts.

I'm looking forward to your comments on Sophia's work.

(240 words)

— Tip
As a basic rule, write your text in the present tense.

— Tip
Explain or paraphrase important German terms/names.

— Tip
Do not give your personal opinion in a mediaton task.

— Tip
Invite readers to post comments.

Abitur 2016: **The US and the American Dream**

Klausurteil: Leseverstehen und Schreiben integriert

Valerie Jarrett is a Senior Advisor to President Barack Obama. Her text was first published in the official White House blog.

Valerie Jarrett: *New Citizens and the American Dream*

Yesterday, I had the privilege of speaking at a naturalization ceremony for newly naturalized citizens of the United States of America.

There were over 700 representatives from 92 countries across 6 continents who became Americans. From the Philippines, to Germany, El Salvador, to Peru, to
5 Australia, and every other corner of the globe, they embodied not just the face of the world, but the face of America.

Their presence is a testament to the promise of the American Dream. It's the dream that says no matter who you are, where you came from, what your last name is, what you believe, or who you love, if you come here, and work hard, if you
10 believe in yourself, if you embrace the spirit of limitless possibilities, then in this great country, you can make it if you try.

All Americans have the same dream – receive a good education, have a job, the ability to afford a home, send their kids to college, health care so they don't have [to] worry about going broke if they get sick, or are in an accident, and the ability
15 to retire with a little money in their pocket.

Our newest Americans came here in pursuit of that dream. And in so many ways, they are already woven into the fabric of our great country. They've gone to school here, worked here, been active in our communities, served, and defended our country through active military service, and made our nation stronger, safer,
20 and better.

When the newest Americans stood tall, and faced our American flag, and pledged allegiance to the country they now official[ly] call home, my eyes swelled with tears, knowing that they were accepting both the privilege, and responsibility of citizenship in our great country. And they reminded me of how precious our
25 citizenship is – of how much it is worth, why we should never take it for granted, and why it is worth protecting.

Simply put, they belong here. And they remind us again of the importance of fixing our immigration system, so that aspiring Americans can take the pathway that they have taken, and become full-fledged citizens.
30 That's why President Obama has made immigration reform one of his top priorities this year. Last month, the Senate passed an historic piece of legislation in an overwhelming bipartisan vote. Now it's time for the House to take action. [...]

We owe it to our heritage, to our country's future, and to the next generation, to fix our broken system, today. After all, America's strength has always come from
35 the rich diversity, and core decency of our people.

(420 words)

Valerie Jarrett, *The White House Blog*, 2013

---

[31] **Last month, the Senate passed an historic piece of legislation** *here:* reference to a vote in the Senate on an immigration reform bill

[32] **the House** *here:* reference to the House of Representatives

Tip

Der Textumfang der Abiturprüfung 2016 wurde redaktionell an die Vorgaben gültig seit 2017 angepasst.

1 Comprehension

12 VP Describe Valerie Jarrett's views on immigration and her demands as presented in the official White House blog.

2 Analysis

16 VP Analyse how she tries to convince the reader of her views. Consider structure, communicative strategies and stylistic devices.

3 Evaluation

Choose one of the following tasks:

14 VP **a)** Using your knowledge about the American Dream, discuss Jarrett's claim that "America's strength has always come from the rich diversity, and core decency" (ll. 34 ff.) of the American people.

14 VP **b)** Re-creation of text: Imagine you have just immigrated to the USA and had to wait for your Green Card for a long time. Write a critical letter to Jarrett.

Klausurteil: Sprachmittlung isoliert

4 Mediation

Your class is hosting the exchange students of your partner school in the US. In class you want to discuss the topic of immigration in Germany and the US. As one of the hosts, you are invited to give an informative speech about the recent developments of immigration to Germany. You have found the following article about Carolina López and decide to use her experiences as an example to report to your American guests about the current development of immigration to Germany.

18 VP Prepare a speech in which you talk about Carolina López's reasons for migration and her experiences as an immigrant in Germany. Add information where necessary. Write your speech.

— Tip
Die Sprachmittlung wurde nachträglich redaktionell ergänzt. Seit 2017 ist Sprachmittlung Teil der Abiturprüfung.

Der deutsche Traum

Eine neue Generation von Migranten sucht in der Bundesrepublik eine Zukunft: Hochqualifizierte aus Süd- und Osteuropa. Ohne sie erlahmt die Konjunktur – Deutschland muss lernen, die Zuzügler zu halten.

Ein halbes Jahrhundert nachdem ihr Großvater Juan mit dem Zug von Sevilla nach
5 Deutschland fuhr, löste Carolina López, 28, ein Ticket für den Billigflieger nach Berlin. Es war die Not in Spanien, die sie im Frühsommer 2012 trieb. Denn dort taumelt die Wirtschaft, mehr als jeder Vierte ist arbeitslos, gerade junge Leute finden keinen Job mehr. Carolina López wollte Arbeit und vor allem eine Perspektive.
   Es war auch die Not, die ihren Großvater getrieben hatte, damals, 1961, denn in
10 Spanien konnte er nicht genug verdienen, um seine Familie zu ernähren.
   Wenn Carolina López über ihren Großvater spricht, fallen ihr trotzdem mehr Unterschiede ein als Gemeinsamkeiten. Das Deutschland, das sie aus seinen Erzählungen kennt, gibt es nicht mehr. Der einzige Deutsche, an den Großvater Juan sich erinnert, ist der Vorarbeiter in der Fabrik von Continental in Korbach, der
15 ihn immer anbrüllte. Juan wollte schnell Geld verdienen und kehrte so bald wie möglich nach Spanien zurück.

Carolina López ist nicht von anderen Jungberlinerinnen zu unterscheiden: Ein weites Shirt fällt über ihre Röhrenjeans, die Füße stecken in Skateboard-Latschen. Sie lacht gern und viel, sie nimmt das Leben ernst, aber nicht zu ernst. López hatte bereits während ihres Marketing-Studiums 2009 ein halbes Jahr lang in Berlin gelebt, in einer Wohngemeinschaft in Kreuzberg. Berlin kam ihr freigeistig und international vor, sagt López, so modern, wie sie es aus Spanien nicht kannte. Jetzt ist sie zurück und diesmal will sie bleiben, arbeiten, leben und Berlin zu ihrem Zuhause machen.

Eine neue Generation von Migranten kommt nach Deutschland: die europäischen Krisenflüchtlinge. Sie sind jung, gut ausgebildet, sie sprechen mehrere Sprachen. Zu Hause sehen viele keine Chancen mehr, seit das europäische Finanzsystem zu wanken begann und bald danach der Arbeitsmarkt daheim zusammenbrach. Sie gehen nach Deutschland, wie vor einem halben Jahrhundert ihre Großeltern, auf der Suche nach einer Zukunft.

(330 Wörter)
Sven Becker et al., *Der Spiegel*, 2013

Erwartungshorizonte

1 Comprehension

12 VP *Describe Valerie Jarrett's views on immigration and her demands as presented in the official White House blog.*

Describe the author's views on immigration and her appeal to the House of Representatives (and the reader). Include in your answer the impact which immigration has on American society and the American Dream.

Task support

Für diese Aufgabe werden insgesamt 12 Punkte auf den Inhalt vergeben.

Form und Umfang meiner Antwort:
Describe …: Beschreiben Sie Valerie Jarretts Einstellung gegenüber Immigration und Ihre daraus resultierende Forderung.
Formulieren Sie Ihre Antwort in eigenen Worten und wählen Sie als allgemeine Zeitform das Präsens.

Mögliche inhaltliche Aspekte:
- *Immigrants represent American society.*
- *Immigration proves that the American Dream is still alive.*
- *America's strength depends on the immigrants' work.*
- *She demands reforming the immigration law so that every immigrant has the opportunity to become a US citizen.*
- *A reform is necessary to secure America's strength for future generations.*

Proposed solution:
In her blog Valerie Jarrett outlines her views on immigration to the US and demands a reform to the immigration system.
At a recent naturalization ceremony, there were numerous immigrants who became US citizens. For Valerie Jarrett those immigrants represent the American society and prove that the American Dream is still alive. According to her, immigration has had a crucial impact on the US.
The fact that people have been immigrating to the US shows that values like equal opportunity and liberty are known abroad to be practiced in the US. Immigration is also very important for improving American society. A lot of immigrants contribute to the US by working hard, volunteering in their communities or serving in the military.
For Valerie Jarrett US citizenship is valuable and has to be protected, but at the same time every immigrant who is willing to become a US citizen should have the opportunity to do so. Therefore, she demands that the immigration law be changed. The Senate has already approved of the reform and now she tries to convince the House of Representatives to support Obama's immigration reform too. She concludes that it is necessary to adjust the immigration law to maintain America's strength now and for future generations.

(200 words)

> **Tip**
> Introduce shortly the text your refer to.

2 Analysis

16 VP *Analyse how she tries to convince the reader of her views. Consider structure, communicative strategies and stylistic devices.*

Outline Valerie Jarrett's views and analyze how she expresses them. Focus on the structure, communicative strategies and stylistic devices of the text and explain their effect on the reader.

Task support

Für diese Aufgabe werden insgesamt 16 Punkte auf den Inhalt vergeben.

Form und Umfang meiner Antwort:
Analyse …: Beschreiben und erklären Sie, wie Valerie Jarrett den Leser von der Bedeutung der Immigranten für die USA und der Notwendigkeit einer Reform des Einwanderungsgesetzes überzeugt.
Achten Sie dazu z. B. auf den Aufbau ihrer Argumentation, ihre Sprache, die Adressatenorientierung und rhetorische Stilmittel.
Beziehen Sie sich stets auf Beispiele oder Zitate, um Ihre Erkenntnisse zu belegen.
Formulieren Sie Ihre Antwort in eigenen Worten.

Mögliche inhaltliche Aspekte:
- She calls her invitation a „privilege" (l. 1) which shows that she appreciates the naturalization ceremony.
- She presents high figures to impress the reader (l. 3, "over 700 representatives from 92 countries").
- She uses the metaphor of a "face" (l. 5) to show the different parts of US society.
- She uses the word "testament" (l. 7) and an anaphora (l. 9) to stress that the immigrants prove the existence of the American Dream.
- She lists several examples of the American Dream in everyday life (ll. 12 ff.) to appeal to her readers.
- She uses the metaphor "woven into the fabric of our great country" (l. 17) and lists the immigrants' contributions to communities (l. 17) to point out their importance to society.
- She includes the reader in her thoughts by using the pronouns "our", "we" or "us".
- She refers to her personal emotions (l. 22) to get the readers' sympathy.
- Finally, she expresses her plea to support the immigration reform and thus maintain the American Dream (ll. 30 ff.).

Proposed solution:
In her blog entry, Jarrett tries to convince the reader of the necessity to reform the immigration law in the US in order to make it easier for immigrants to become US citizens.
In the introduction, the author tries to impress the reader by describing her personal experience as a speaker at a naturalization ceremony. She writes that she had the "privilege" (l. 1) of speaking at the ceremony, which shows that she really appreciated the event. Talking about the ceremony, she presents impressive figures. She states that there were more than 700 people from 92 countries and says that the new citizens represent not just the world but also American society. The

Tip
Mention the author's view which you examine in the introduction of your text.

metaphor that America's immigrants make up "the face of America" (l. 5) shows that immigrants are an essential part of American society.

In the next part (ll. 7–11), Jarrett continues to explain that immigrants prove that the American Dream is still alive. She calls their presence a "testament" to the American Dream. Using anaphora (ll. 9 ff., "if you"), she reminds the reader of the many promises which the immigrants embody. For the author, the immigrants are a powerful confirmation that the American Dream still exists.

In the next paragraph (ll. 12–15), the author lists several examples of the American Dream. By doing so, she includes the reader because the examples like having a job, health care or a home (ll. 12–13) matter to immigrants and US citizens as well. Jarrett goes on to emphasize that immigrants play a crucial part in American society (ll. 16–20). She uses the metaphor "woven into the fabric of our great country" (l. 17) to point out that they are an integral part of US society. In addition to this, she lists their contributions to society and concludes that immigrants make the US "stronger, safer and better" (ll. 19–20). In this way the author proves that immigrants do not just share the American Dream but are also necessary to make it possible for everybody. Jarrett also includes the reader in her argument by using the pronouns "our", "we" or "us" (ll. 16 ff.) and stresses that the success of the nation depends on everybody (l. 17 "our great country", l. 19 "our nation").

After this reference to the immigrants' contribution to society, the author expresses her inner feelings. She tells the reader how her eyes "swelled with tears" at the naturalization ceremony and how the new citizens filled her with pride. This section is the most emotional part in which she speaks out in favor of the immigrants and tries to attract the reader's sympathy.

Now the author puts forward her appeal. She demands that the immigration system be reformed and appeals to the members of the House of Representatives to sign the reform. To show the importance of their support, she calls it an "historic piece of legislation" (l. 31) and states that even future generations will benefit from the decision.

(490 words)

> **Tip**
> To support your findings, explain them and give examples from the text.

3 Evaluation

14 VP **a)** Using your knowledge about the American Dream, discuss Jarrett's claim that "America's strength has always come from the rich diversity, and core decency" (ll. 34 ff.) of the American people.

Discuss Valerie Jarrett's statement using the information in her blog entry and your knowledge gained from class discussions. Since you should discuss the quote, mention arguments in favour of and against it. Finish your text with a personal opinion.

Task support

Für diese Aufgabe werden insgesamt 14 Punkte auf den Inhalt vergeben.

Form und Umfang meiner Antwort:
Discuss …: Sammeln Sie mehrere Ideen zu Argumenten, die Mrs Jarretts Aussage stützen bzw. widersprechen.
Beginnen Sie mit schwächeren Argumenten, gefolgt von stärkeren Argumenten, die auch Sie vertreten.
Verfassen Sie den Text in formeller Sprache und beziehen Sie Ihr im Unterricht erworbenes Wissen mit ein.

Mögliche Inhalte und Struktur meiner Antwort:

- Introduction: (Introduce the question you are going to discuss.)

- Contra-arguments:
    - Many famous people who have made it 'from rags to riches' are not decent at all.
    - The economic elite mainly consists of white men and is not diverse.
    - Pro-arguments:
    - People who live the American Dream do not necessarily expect to become millionaires.
    - A diverse workforce is a huge advantage for a company.

- End: (Give your personal conclusion / outlook / advice / etc.)

Proposed solution:

Valerie Jarrett concludes her blog post by stating that "America's strength has always come from the rich diversity, and core decency" (ll. 34 ff.). Thinking about ethnic segregation in many American cities and rich millionaires who show their luxurious life on TV, you might wonder if her final statement is right.

To begin with, a central aspect of the American Dream is the idea of building a career "from rags to riches". Speaking of the American Dream, a lot of people imagine becoming a millionaire and retiring in a luxurious mansion. You cannot call this a decent dream.

Furthermore, the really powerful people who make America strong are mostly white men. Women or people from non-white backgrounds are underrepresented in powerful positions in the economy and in the government. Therefore, diversity does not really exist among the elite.

Nevertheless, America is the most powerful nation in the world and it has been a nation of immigrants since its foundation. Therefore, decency and diversity must have played a crucial part in America's success story.

Of course, not everybody in the US can earn millions of dollars. However, this is not necessary to make the American Dream come true. For most Americans the American promise consists of a home, a regular income, health insurance and a good education for the children. In addition to this, the average immigrant does not expect to become a millionaire in the US but wishes to enjoy freedom and security. Therefore, decency is indeed widespread in American society and a source of America's strength.

Moreover, the leading positions in big companies may be dominated by white men but a company's success depends on each single worker and employee. A lot of companies profit from their diverse workforce. Different people contribute different ideas and skills and this is an advantage for the enterprise. In addition to this, immigrants are known to work hard and thus they support their companies a lot.

In conclusion, I agree with Valerie Jarrett's statement. The US society is diverse and a lot of American people work hard and live decent lives. However, prejudice and segregation threaten the peaceful coexistence and must be reduced.

(360 words)

Tip
Use linking words to structure your arguments.

Tip
To discuss the topic present arguments in favour and against the statement.

Abitur 2016: The US and the American Dream

14 VP **b)** *Re-creation of text: Imagine you have just immigrated to the USA and had to wait for your Green Card for a long time. Write a critical letter to Jarrett.*

Write a critical but polite letter to Ms Jarrett. Imagine your situation as an immigrant in the US concerning e.g. your possibilities to work, equal rights, etc. Pay attention to the structure of your letter and finish your text with an appeal to improve the status of holders of a Green Card.

Task support

Für diese Aufgabe werden insgesamt 14 Punkte auf den Inhalt vergeben.

Form und Umfang meiner Antwort:
Write a critical letter …: Schreiben Sie einen Brief an Frau Jarrett in ihrer Funktion als Beraterin im Weißen Haus. Schildern Sie Ihr Anliegen und Ihre Situation als Immigrant mit einer Green Card und nennen Sie Ihre Forderung. Beziehen Sie sich auf Jarretts Blogbeitrag und Ihr im Unterricht erworbenes Wissen. Achten Sie auf die Textsortenmerkmale eines formalen Briefs (Anrede, Schlussformel, formelle Sprache etc.).

Mögliche Inhalte und Struktur meiner Antwort:
- *Introduction: (Introduce yourself and the reason for writing.)*
- *Main part:*
  - *It was a long and difficult process to get a Green Card.*
  - *It is difficult to find a job even with a Green Card.*
  - *Without a job, I feel like I cannot fully integrate.*
  - *I feel insecure about my future since I am not a US citizen and do not have equal rights.*
- *End: (State your appeal.)*

Proposed solution:

25th April 2016

Dear Ms Jarrett,

Recently I read your entry on the White House blog "New Citizens and the American Dream". Thank you very much for this post. I came to the US with a Green Card and I really appreciate your support for immigrants. However, I think that a lot of things still have to be improved even for immigrants with a Green Card.
As you have explained on your blog, the immigration system must be reformed. I wholeheartedly agree to that. Unfortunately, I have experienced difficulties with immigration to the US. I am a young woman from Germany and it is my dream to live and work in the US. I am highly motivated and want to start my own company as a travel agent. I think America is the best place to start your own business. However, it took a long time until I managed to move to the US. I applied for a Green Card three years ago and it was a very complicated and lengthy process before I was finally allowed to come to the US.
On the whole, I am happy that I have succeeded in immigrating to the US. I have been in the US for two months now and I want to gather some experience first before I will start my own business. Unfortunately, I still have not found a job or even an internship, even though I am allowed to work and am highly motivated.

Tip
The body of the letter begins with a capital letter.

I just hope to find a job soon because, in my opinion, you cannot fully integrate in society without a job.

Of course, I will not give up immediately but I wonder what my future will look like. What happens if I am unemployed for a long period? For the time being, I am allowed to stay in the US but I am afraid that this law might change. I am not a US citizen; therefore, I do not have equal rights and I am afraid that I might lose my residence permit. This would be a huge problem for me if I had already started my own business. I could lose everything. Considering this scenario, it might be more secure to be employed in a big company.

As you have written in your entry, immigrants are the face of America. I want to be a part of that face. But as long as my status of residence is insecure, I can only partly follow my dreams, which means America's promise will not become true for me. In my opinion, it is also necessary to improve the status of immigrants with a Green Card.

Sincerely,
Anna K-

(435 words)

4 Mediation

Your class is hosting the exchange students of your partner school in the US. In class, you want to discuss the topic of immigration to Germany and the US. As one of the hosts, you are invited to give an informative speech about the recent developments of immigration to Germany. You have found the following article about Carolina López and decide to use her experiences as an example to inform your American guests about the group of young European immigrants in Germany.

18 VP Prepare a speech in which you talk about Carolina López's reasons for migration and her experiences as an immigrant in Germany. Add information where necessary. Write your speech.

Write a speech in which you inform your American guests about Carolina López's experiences in Spain and in Germany. Pay attention to the textual features of a speech (introduction, end, addressing the audience, etc.). Use formal language to write the speech.

Task support

Für diese Aufgabe werden insgesamt 18 Punkte auf den Inhalt vergeben.

Form und Umfang meiner Antwort:
Write a speech …: Schreiben Sie eine Rede, in der Sie anhand der Informationen aus dem Text und am Beispiel von Carolina López über junge und gut ausgebildete Migranten in Deutschland sprechen.
Informieren Sie Ihr Publikum objektiv, d.h. ohne eine persönliche Stellungnahme. Beachten Sie die spezifischen Merkmale für die Textsorte Rede.

Mögliche inhaltliche Aspekte:
- Ms Lopez is a young, highly qualified woman from Spain.
- She moved to Berlin in 2012 since she could see no future for herself in Spain.
- Primarily young people are suffering from unemployment in Spain.
- She did an internship in Berlin in 2009.
- She appreciates the modern and innovative atmosphere of the city.
- She has adapted well to the lifestyle of young people in Berlin.
- She wants to stay in Berlin permanently.

Proposed solution:

Good afternoon, students!

In order to prepare our discussion about immigration in the US and Germany, I will talk about the current developments in immigration to Germany. I'm going to refer to Carolina López, who epitomizes the experiences of many young European immigrants in Germany.

Carolina López is a young woman from Spain who decided to make Berlin her new home. She has a university degree in marketing and belongs to a growing group of highly qualified young immigrants who are coming to Germany to find work. For some years now, Spain has been experiencing an economic crisis and a lot of people are suffering from unemployment. Many young people have been trying hard to find employment, yet more than one in four people are unemployed. Ms Lopez wants to work and follow a career but did not see any chance to do so in Spain. That's why she decided to leave Spain and move to Berlin in 2012.

Ms Lopez had already done an internship in 2009 and knew the city before she moved there in 2012. After coming to Berlin for the second time, she decided to stay and make it her permanent home. So far, she has experienced Berlin as an innovative, modern and international city and enjoys living there. She likes the lifestyle of average young people in Berlin and she has easily blended into the capital's population.

I hope I could provide you with an overview of this new group of immigrants and I'm looking forward to your comments and additional information. Thank you very much for your attention.

(260 words)

Tip
Introduce the topic of your speech.

Tip
Thank the audience members for their attention.

Abitur 2017: **Global challenges – communication**

Klausurteil: Leseverstehen und Schreiben integriert

Alexa, who's in charge of my life – me or you?

Got an Amazon Echo for Christmas, just like every other basic-issue human. I'm under no illusion it's anything other than the larval cell of a cybernetic panopticon that will eliminate our species. But I love it, because it's allowed me to turn my home into a centrally heated jukebox, with snacks in. "Alexa, play Whiter Shade
5 of Pale," I bellow the instant I get in the door, before I turn cartwheels across the floor. And it happens, like magic. Majestic, organ-led magic, the vibrations of which make the neighbours experience a creeping sadness they didn't know they had. There's clearly Stasi-like potential to a networked machine that is always listening to you, yet it's also clear we'll put up with any sinister technology – if
10 it's cool enough. It also has to work, though, and Alexa users have reported a few problems. Such as her randomly crying out in the night, like a ghostly child. Or autonomously flirting with the voice of Google's electronic domestic, […]. Or adding "cancer" to one woman's shopping reminders, instead of Pampers. Of the ways to receive bad news, that has to be near the top of the list.
15 My Alexa and I have had our share of run-ins, like any two people who share a cell. I know smart assistants are still learning. That's clear from her voice-recognition abilities, which are both incredibly impressive, yet also comically inept. "Play Woke Up New by the Mountain Goats," I yell, before she starts blasting out Woke Up in a New Bugatti by Ace Hood, featuring Rick Ross. I spend 20 minutes convincing her
20 "marmoreal" and "memorial" are different words (don't ask how she did with "formication"). […]
I can report a horrific twist. Over the past few weeks I've started communicating differently. At a recent gathering, where a few people were talking at once, I slightly raised my voice, and immediately a familiar cadence entered it. "KATE," I
25 said to my friend Kate. "BRING ME SOME MALTESERS. MALTESERS." I'd got used to barking blunt requests, as if perpetually on speakerphone with an automated cinema-booking system, or ordering a beer in France. It wasn't the best way to talk to her, Kate replied, in her own words, using a bit of volume herself.
Still, things will get better. An Amazon executive recently noted, in glowing terms,
30 that since far-field microphones had been introduced to Fire TV, users were starting to speak in entire sentences, and asking her different questions. "They are starting to express a lot more intent." He's not talking about the machine, he's talking about you. That's where the current wave of AI is leading us. We're not training Alexa. She is training us.

(456 words)
Rhik Samadder, *The Guardian*, 2018

— Tip
→ Aus urheberrechtlichen Gründen wurde der Ausgangstext durch den Verlag ersetzt.

[1] **Amazon echo** brand of smart speakers which can react to commands
[2] **larval** a form of an insect that is not completely developed
[2] **panopticon** a circular prison with cells that can be observed from the middle at all times
[4] **Alexa** virtual assistant which is controlled with your voice
[8] **Stasi** Abk. von Staatsicherheitsdienst; Geheimdienst der ehemaligen DDR
[25] **Maltesers** chocolate, sweets
[30] **Fire TV** voice-controlled media player

1 Comprehension

12 VP   Describe the advantages and disadvantages of using a virtual assistant as mentioned in the text.

2 Analysis

16 VP   Analyse the author's intention for writing the article. Focus on the addressee, language and structure of the text.

3 Evaluation

Choose one of the following tasks:

14 VP   a) Discuss whether artificial intelligence is a boon or bane to humanity

14 VP   b) Write a letter to the editor. In your letter, criticise the author for playing down the threat which voice assistants pose to our privacy

Klausurteil: Sprachmittlung isoliert

4 Mediation

18 VP   Your British partner school's magazine prepares a special edition on the impact of mobile technology on the language of young people. Based on Irena Güttel's text write a report in which you outline how new media change the language of young speakers of German as well as reactions to these changes.

Bäm! Nom Nom!

A: „was machste we?", B: „gehn essen, nom nom", B: „jip!", A: „späta party?", B: „yup, bin dabei. bäm!". So oder so ähnlich könnte es aussehen, wenn sich zwei junge Leute über Facebook oder WhatsApp fürs Wochenende verabreden. Sprachpuristen kommt da das Grausen. [...]

5   SMS, E-Mail, Chat und soziale Netzwerke – ständig tippen wir irgendwelche Nachrichten. Statt mit der besten Freundin zu telefonieren, schicken wir schnell ein paar Kurznachrichten hin und her. Mit der Folge, dass wir schreiben wie wir sprechen: in Wortsplittern, Satzfragmenten und ohne genau auf Rechtschreibung und Grammatik zu achten.

10   Wir schreiben We statt Wochenende, Jip statt Jippie. Präpositionen und Pronomen werden weggelassen oder verschmelzen mit anderen Wörtern. Dazu kommt eine Fülle von emotionalen Ausdrücken wie haha, gähn, seufz, mmmh und nom nom für lecker oder bäm für totale Begeisterung. Denn wo Gesichtsausdruck und Stimmlage fehlten, müssten Worte Gefühle vermitteln, sagt der Hannoveraner
15   Sprachwissenschaftler Volker Schlobinski.

Forscher beobachten diese Abwandlung von Sprache schon seit vielen Jahren. Während früher vor allem Computer-Nerds Begriffe wie lol (Abkürzung für laut lachen) oder omg (Abkürzung für Oh, mein Gott!) nutzten, sind diese heute für viele selbstverständlich. [...]

Sprachbewahrer sehen angesichts dieser Entwicklung schwarz. Ihre Befürchtung: Gerade junge Leute, bei denen Rechtschreibung und Grammatik noch nicht gefestigt sind, könnten gar kein korrektes Deutsch mehr lernen. Schlobinski sieht da jedoch keine Gefahr. „Es macht keinen Sinn so zu schreiben wie Thomas Mann, wenn ich einen Tweet (Text auf Twitter) mit Zeichen verfasse." Trotzdem seien Jugendliche noch in der Lage, ordentliche Schulaufsätze zu schreiben.

Diese Einschätzung unterstützt auch eine Studie von Christa Dürscheid in der Schweiz. Sie hatte vor vier Jahren untersucht, wie sich E-Mail, Chat und SMS auf das Schreiben von Jugendlichen in der Schule auswirkt. Ihr Ergebnis: Die meisten Schüler können unterscheiden, ob sie eine SMS oder einen Aufsatz schreiben.

„Die Schreibkompetenz hat nicht nachgelassen – im Gegenteil. Sie ist breiter geworden", meint Dürscheid. Denn eine einheitliche Websprache gibt es nicht. In einer E-Mail schreibt man anders als im Chat.

(328 Wörter)
Irena Güttel, *Mitteldeutsche Zeitung*, 2014

— Tip
→ **Thomas Mann** deutscher Schriftsteller (1875 – 1955)

Erwartungshorizonte

1 Comprehension

12 VP   *Describe the advantages and disadvantages of using a virtual assistant as mentioned in the text.*

Read the text carefully and note down the pros and cons of using a virtual assistant. Then inform the reader about the advantages and disadvantages according to the author. Use your own words and leave out any additional information that is not mentioned in the text

Task support

Für diese Aufgabe werden insgesamt 12 Punkte auf den Inhalt vergeben.

Form und Umfang meiner Antwort:
Describe…: Beschreiben Sie in Ihrer Antwort die Vor und Nachteile eines Sprachassistenten laut dem vorliegenden Text. Nennen Sie in der Einleitung die Quelle. Um Ihre Antwort weiterhin übersichtlich zu strukturieren, können Sie die Vor- und Nachteile getrennt aufführen. Formulieren Sie Ihre Antwort möglichst in eigenen Worten.

Mögliche inhaltliche Aspekte:
- It makes life more comfortable (play a song spontaneously, prepare a shopping list).
- Sometimes it makes noises at night or connects to other devices.
- Misunderstandings are frequent (plays a wrong song, adds diseases to a shopping list).
- It records your words and poses a threat to your privacy.
- It changes how people speak and interact with each other.

Proposed solution:
In the article "Alexa, who's in charge of my life – me or you?" the author Rhik Samadder describes his experiences of using a virtual assistant.
Samadder got his virtual assistant (Alexa) for Christmas. His experiences have been very positive so far. He sounds almost enthusiastic when he writes about its ability to play music on demand. In addition, the device has many other features which make life more comfortable, like preparing a shopping list.
However, the virtual assistant is not perfect. It often misunderstands titles of songs or items for the shopping list. Besides, the virtual assistant sometimes connects to other devices or makes loud noises at night.
Another problem is that a virtual assistant constantly listens to what you are saying. Therefore they could be used to spy on you in your home.
Furthermore, virtual assistants have a strong impact on how we talk and interact with each other. Instead of the virtual assistant adapting to the user's language, users are increasingly adapting their language to make themselves understandable to the virtual assistant.

(180 words)

Tip
→ Mention the source you refer to at the beginning of your answer.

Erwartungshorizonte **125**

2 Analysis

16 VP *Analyse the author's intention for writing the article. Focus on the addressee, language and structure of the text..*

Focus on the impact of the text on the reader and explain why the author wrote the article (= his intention). Examine how the author chose the language, the structure and the addressee to achieve this impact. Refer to the text to support your findings.

Task support

Für diese Aufgabe werden insgesamt 16 Punkte auf den Inhalt vergeben.

Form und Umfang meiner Antwort:
Analyse …: Die klare Darstellung der Autorenintention bildet den Schwerpunkt Ihrer Antwort (mögliche Intentionen von Texten wären z.B.: Information, Appell, Kritik, Unterhaltung etc.). Arbeiten Sie die entsprechende Intention im vorliegenden Text heraus. Als weitere Unteraspekte Ihrer Antwort gehen Sie auf den Adressaten, sprachliche Eigenheiten (Register, Stilmittel etc.) und die Struktur des Textes ein. Stellen Sie mehrmals und wo sinnvoll dar, wie diese Unteraspekte die Autorenintention stützen.
Was den Umfang betrifft, ist der Adressat schnell ermittelbar und erklärt. Zu Struktur und vor allem Sprache hingegen bietet der Text mehr Inhalt. Belegen Sie Ihre Erkenntnisse mit Beispielen und Zitaten aus dem Text.
Schließen Sie Ihre Analyse mit einer knappen Zusammenfassung der wichtigsten Ergebnisse ab.

Mögliche inhaltliche Aspekte:
- Introduction: (topic of the article or most important facts of the student's answer)
- The text is written for the average consumer.
- The author intends to entertain the reader.
- He uses informal language.
- He personifies the virtual assistant.
- He employs humour (irony, sarcasm, personal funny incidents).
- He uses comparisons and specific language to stress pros and cons of smart speakers.
- In the second part he points out the worrying impact which Alexa has had on him.
- He admits that he is not training Alexa but she is training him.
- Conclusion: The author wants to entertain and warn the reader of the dystopian potential of smart speakers.

Proposed solution:
Obviously Rhik Samadder's article is not solely aimed at ardent supporters of artificial intelligence but also at the average consumer of electronic gadgets. The author focuses on how virtual assistants affect our lives. Therefore he illustrates his everyday user experience with the virtual assistant Alexa.
My analysis will show that the author intends to inform as well as entertain. Samadder employs a lot of humour, e.g. when he describes the numerous pitfalls

— Tip
→ Shortly introduce the topic of your analysis

— Tip
→ State the main intention and addressee.

which he experiences while engaging with the virtual assistant. Samadder's personal experience and amusing incidents make it easy for the reader to relate to the author.

Furthermore, Samadder's use of a colloquial style and informal language contribute to the entertaining nature of the text (e.g. "I bellow the instant I get in the door", l. 5). The author even presents the virtual assistant as a human being. Sometimes it cries at night like a child or starts "flirting" with other virtual assistants in his home (l. 11–12). Samadder continues in this anthropomorphic vein, giving the impression that he is in an intimate relationship with his chatbot. According to him, they have had their share of "run-ins, like any two people who share a cell" (l. 15).

> **Tip**
> → Examine the language and state its impact on the reader.

Humor and sarcasm are both evident in the text. Everyday communication with the virtual assistant provides numerous pitfalls for the user like playing a wrong song with a similar title. The text also contains a lot of sarcasm. Samadder mentions the "Stasi-like potential" (l. 8) of smart speakers and compares them to a "cybernetic panopticon that will eliminate our species" (l. 2–3). Such statements prove that the author is not naïve and knows about the threat tech companies like Amazon or Google pose to our privacy. However the author admits that he is too weak to resist the comforts of technological progress. In a sarcastic remark he points out that "we'll put up with any sinister technology – if it's cool enough." (l. 10).

In the first half of the text, the author describes how he deals with the virtual assistant. But in the second half, he describes how Alexa deals with him. This could be quite disturbing for the readers, but the author confuses serious issues with an entertaining writing style. His use of irony and confessional humour make this technophobic passage quite amusing to read. The author admits that he has begun to bark out "blunt requests" (l. 26) to his friends as if they were malfunctioning virtual assistants. Of course this does not improve his relationships with his real friends. According to an Amazon employee, these kinds of social faux pas will be a thing of the past. The latest virtual assistants are able to understand longer and more complex sentences. As a consequence, people are starting to speak to them in entire sentences instead of barking short commands. For the author this proves that we are not training our virtual assistants anymore. Now the virtual assistants are training us.

> **Tip**
> → Explain – only important – aspects of the structure of the text.

In writing the article, Samadder clearly wanted to entertain his readers. At the same time he draws the reader's attention to the huge impact of technological progress on human behavior. After all, he gives a dystopian answer to the question in the title. Soon, the virtual assistant will be in charge of his life.

(530 words)

> **Tip**
> → End your analysis with a resume of your most important findings.

3 Evaluation

14 VP **a)** *Discuss whether artificial intelligence is a boon or bane to humanity.*

In this task you should discuss the benefits and risks of artificial intelligence. You may refer to your own knowledge and to the information in the text. Give several arguments in favour of and against artificial intelligence.
Write a well-structured text that makes your line of argument concise and persuasive.

Task support

Für diese Aufgabe werden insgesamt 14 Punkte auf den Inhalt vergeben.

Form und Umfang meiner Antwort:
*Discuss …: S*tellen Sie in der Einleitung das Thema vor und wecken Sie das Interesse der Leser. Erläutern Sie im Hauptteil die Vor- und Nachteile von künstlicher Intelligenz. Sie können wählen, ob Sie im Hauptteil stärker den Nutzen oder die Gefahren von künstlicher Intelligenz hervorheben wollen. Ebenso können Sie eine neutrale Position vertreten. Wie viele Argumente Sie anführen, hängt von der Komplexität Ihrer Argumente ab. Als Orientierungswert können Sie davon ausgehen, mindestens drei Argumente zu erläutern. Achten Sie auf eine klare und überzeugende Strukturierung Ihres Textes.
Schließen Sie Ihren Text mit einem Resümee ihrer Punkte, einem Ausblick und/ oder einem Appell ab.
Der vorliegende Erwartungshorizont tendiert zu einer Hervorhebung der Vorteile von künstlicher Intelligenz. Andere Argumente sind natürlich möglich.

Mögliche inhaltliche Aspekte und Struktur meiner Antwort:
- Introduction: *Is artificial intelligence a boon or bane to humanity?*
- *Artificial intelligence takes control away from us. (con)*
- *It is used to manipulate the public. (con)*
- *It makes life more comfortable. (pro)*
- *It makes life safer. (pro)*
- *There is no reason to be afraid of technological progress. (pro)*
- Conclusion: *We have to stay vigilant.*

Proposed solution:
Self-driving cars, automated trains and voice assistants are just some examples of products which rely on artificial intelligence. For some people such developments are a blessing. They make life safer and more comfortable. For other people artificial intelligence poses a threat. They are afraid of losing control and being manipulated. Now, who is right? Is artificial intelligence a boon or a bane to humanity?
People are likely to give up control when relying on artificial intelligence. Think about a self-driving car. How comfortable would it be to watch a film with the family while your car takes you to your holiday destination? This fantasy is very attractive but it is wrong and potentially dangerous. Even while using a self-driving car, the driver should pay attention to traffic. The family could still get into an accident if the driver completely relies on artificial intelligence.
Artificial intelligence can be used to manipulate or even deceive the public. Just think about spam emails or chatbots which try to contact us. Their software is programmed to address a certain user profile. That is how we receive targeted advertisements which attempt to manipulate us into buying things we have never heard of before. In the same way we can even receive false information which is made to manipulate the public.
However, we also benefit from artificial intelligence. It can support us and make our lives more comfortable. For example a search engine provides us with better results if it learns to understand what kind of information we are looking for. In addition to this, it can make our lives safer. For example there are a lot of devices

Tip
→ Begin your text by stating the topic you are going to discuss.

Tip
→ First con argument with an example.

Tip
→ Second con argument with an example.

Tip
→ First pro argument with examples.

in a car which measure the speed or temperature and help us to avoid accidents. Artificial intelligence is just one aspect of technological progress. As the past shows, new innovations have often aroused criticism and fear among people who were afraid of change. Some people wanted to ban cars, other people doubted that we would ever be able to fly. Nowadays we use cars and airplanes as standard forms of transport and modern life would be unimaginable without them.

In my opinion, you cannot say whether artificial intelligence is a boon or bane. It can be both. Therefore it is crucial to pay attention to the way artificial intelligence is used. It is important that we, the people, do not trust blindly in artificial intelligence and that we remain vigilant in preventing misinformation and manipulation.

(400 words)

Tip
→ Second pro argument weakening criticism.

Tip
→ Personal résumé.

14 VP **b)** *Write a letter to the editor. In your letter, criticise the author for playing down the threat which voice assistants pose to our privacy*

Write a letter to the editor in which you point out the risks of voice assistants concerning privacy issues. Use formal and polite language to explain your arguments. Refer to the report and to your own knowledge.

Task support

Für diese Aufgabe werden insgesamt 14 Punkte auf den Inhalt vergeben.

Form und Umfang meiner Antwort:
Write a letter …: Beachten Sie die Textsortenmerkmale eines Leserbriefs wie z.B. formale Sprache, Betreff, Anrede, Schlussformel etc. Nennen Sie zu Beginn des Leserbriefs, im Betreff, den Artikel auf den Sie sich beziehen. Beginnen Sie Ihren Text mit dem Grund für Ihr Schreiben und erläutern Sie anschließend kompakt und präzise Ihre Kritik. Formulieren Sie Ihre Argumente entschieden und zugleich höflich. Beziehen Sie sich in Ihrem Text auf Ihr selbst erworbenes Wissen und den Erfahrungsbericht.

Mögliche inhaltliche Aspekte:
- Introduction: (Give the reason for writing your text.)
- The article is a common example of how we give away our personal data.
- Our personal data can be misused.
- End/conclusion: (résumé/appeal)

Proposed solution:

"Alexa, who's in charge of my life – me or you?"
by Rhik Samadder, in the Guardian, 2018.

Dear Mr Samadder,

Thank you for your article about using a voice assistant. I do not possess such a device but I think it is very important to keep up with the latest technological innovations. Your article was very amusing to read. However, in my opinion it was too amusing if you think about the seriousness of the topic. I think devices like smart speakers and voice assistants threaten our privacy and you should have dealt with them more seriously.

Your article is a very good example of how we expose our personal data to big tech corporations. The latest gadgets are just too tempting. You can access and share information quickly, which makes everyday life so comfortable. However, we pay a price for these services and often we pay with our personal data. Your smart speakers are a frightening example of how personal data is collected. As you wrote in your article, smart speakers are listening to you. Moreover, they can record what you talk about while sitting in your living room. In the past, only infamous secret intelligence services spied on their citizens and tapped their telephones. Now it is much easier to know what we say and think. You just have to analyse the data recorded by our smart speakers.

So far we are told that our personal data is safe. Unfortunately this has not always been the fact. There are numerous examples of personal data which has been stolen. In addition to this, even if it is relatively safe now, we cannot know what will happen in the future. Who can guarantee that our data will not be used by a company who will try to turn us into perfect consumers? Or by a political party who will try to manipulate elections? Our data is valuable and we should not give it away too carelessly.

I would be very thankful if you dealt with privacy issues more seriously in your texts about recent innovations so that consumers also learn how to use the latest products responsibly.

Owen Harper, Bristol   (355 words)

Tip
→ Reference line referring to the article.

Tip
→ Give your reason for writing the letter.

Tip
→ Write your arguments short and to the point.

Tip
→ Conclude your letter with a short résumé or an appeal.
End a letter to the editor only with your name and where you live.

Klausurteil: Sprachmittlung isoliert

4 Mediation

18 VP *Your British partner school's magazine prepares a special edition on the impact of mobile technology on the language of young people. Based on Irena Güttel's text write a report in which you outline how new media change the language of young speakers of German as well as reactions to these changes.*

Write a report in which you outline how new media change the language of young speakers of German as well as the reactions to these changes. Write a well-structured text by referring to Irena Güttel's text.

Task support

Für diese Aufgabe werden insgesamt 18 Punkte auf den Inhalt vergeben.

Form und Umfang meiner Antwort:
Write a report… : Schreiben Sie einen Bericht. Beziehen Sie sich auf die Informationen aus dem Text und konzentrieren Sie sich auf die für Ihre Aufgabe relevanten Fakten. Beachten Sie dabei die spezifischen Merkmale für die Textsorte report (z.B. Überschrift, klare Strukturierung durch Paragraphen, Nennung der wichtigsten Fakten). Vermeiden Sie in der Sprachmittlungsaufgabe eine eigene Stellungnahme und beschränken Sie den Inhalt Ihres Textes auf die Mitteilung der gewünschten Information.

Mögliche inhaltliche Aspekte:
- Young speakers of German don't pay attention to grammar anymore when they send each other text messages or emails.
- According to a German linguist, this kind of communication results when facial expression and voice are missing.
- People who want to save the language from this development are pessimistic. They think people cannot learn correct German anymore after they got used to texting.
- Other linguists and a study contradict them with the fact that young people could still write a good school essay.
- The study shows that writing literacy has not decreased.

Proposed solution:
How does texting influence your literacy?
In reference to Irene Güttel's newspaper article about the question how media changes the language of young speakers of German and the reactions to these changes, it can be said that young people don't pay attention to grammar when they communicate with each other online. Instead, they write as they speak, use abbreviations and leave out prepositions or pronouns. According to Volker Schlobinski, a German linguist, this kind of communication results when facial expression and voice are missing. People who want to save the language and literacy skills are very pessimistic about this development. They argue that young people cannot learn correct German anymore once they have got used to texting at a young age.
Linguist Schlobinski, however, doesn't consider it to be a huge problem. Young people can still write a good school essay even though they are texting a lot. His view is supported by a study carried out by Swiss scientist Christa Dürscheid. According to her findings, writing literacy has not decreased but actually continued to develop. *(180 words)*

Abitur 2018: **The US and the American Dream**

Klausurteil: Leseverstehen und Schreiben integriert

The Crossing by Gary Paulsen

This is the beginning of the novel.
Manny Bustos awakened when the sun cooked the cardboard over his head and heated the box he was sleeping in until even a lizard could not have taken it, and he knew, suddenly, that it was time. This was the day. He would make the crossing today.

Juárez, Mexico, was never quiet. As a border town it was made of noise – noise that filled all the hours of the day – but the noises changed, and he listened to them now without thinking. Honking horns, the market starting to fill with people trying to get fresh goat cheese or the thick coffee, people yelling insults and curses at each other – a hum of noise. Mornings were the best time, not a good time – there were no good times for him – but the best. He lived on the street, moving, always moving because he was fourteen and had red hair and large brown eyes with long lashes, and there was danger if he did not move – danger from the men who would take him and sell him to those who wanted to buy fourteen-year-old street boys with red hair and long eyelashes.

So now he rolled out when the sun warmed the cardboard of his lean-to, wiped his mouth with a finger, and stood to begin moving for the day. Another day in Juárez. But this time it was different. […] This day he would cross to the north to the United States and find work, become a man, make money, and wear a leather belt with a large buckle and a straw hat with a feathered hatband.

Hunger was instant, had never gone. He went to bed hungry, slept hungry, awakened hungry […].

"Later in this day I will be leaving," he said, lowering his voice as he thought a man would speak. "It is time for me to be crossing to the north and finding work."

[Old Maria] studied him through the screen. A dozen flies worked to get in, making a high buzzing sound that somehow matched the talking sounds of the café in front. "You are too young to make the crossing."

Manny shrugged. "It is not age. I am ready to make the crossing and so it is time. Age does not matter." "But you are small." "I am not so small." He bridled. "I have strength and I am fast and I know how to work hard. That is all that is required to cross to the north. They only wish you to work hard."

She sighed.

(419 words)
From: Gary Paulsen, *The Crossing*, 1987

---

[16] **lean-to** – *here:* improvised shelter
[25] **Old Maria** – a woman making and selling tortillas in a simple place to eat
[25] **screen** – *here:* transparent curtain used to protect against heat or insects

1 Comprehension

12 VP *Describe the situation Manny finds himself in, his plan and his motivation.*

2 Analysis

16 VP *Analyse the way Manny's situation is presented. Focus on point of view and use of language.*

3 Evaluation

14 VP *Choose one of the following tasks:*

a) *Comment on Manny's view of the United States. Refer to the text and work done in class.*

b) *Write a letter to Gary Paulsen, the author of the novel, in which you reflect on the effect the extract from his novel has on your view on Trump's plan to build a wall between the US and Mexico. Refer to the extract and work done in class.*

Klausurteil: Sprachmittlung isoliert

4 Mediation

18 VP *Your American friend is doing a school project on Underage Refugees in Europe and has asked you for information.*

Write him/her an email in which you summarise what D. Betzholz says about the situation of underage refugees in Germany and the problems they face.

Die Tragödie der Kinder-Flüchtlinge

Noch 2010 nahmen deutsche Kommunen 2822 minderjährige Flüchtlinge in Obhut, die ohne Begleitung aufgegriffen wurden. 2013 waren es bereits 6584 – eine Steigerung von rund 133 Prozent.

Ulrike Schwarz, Referentin beim „Bundesfachverband Unbegleitete Minder-
5 jährige Flüchtlinge" in Berlin, kennt die Schicksale hinter den Zahlen. „Entweder werden die Kinder auf der Flucht von ihren Eltern getrennt", sagt Schwarz. „Oder die Familie kratzt ihre Ersparnisse zusammen und schickt sie ganz bewusst alleine los, damit wenigstens die Töchter und Söhne aus dem Krisengebiet rauskommen und die Chance auf eine bessere Zukunft haben." Schlepper, gefälschte Papiere,
10 die Fahrt übers Mittelmeer kosten viel Geld – von Afghanistan nach Italien bis zu 10.000 Euro pro Person.

Kinder, Jugendliche allein auf dem weiten Weg nach Europa. „UMF", unbegleitete minderjährige Flüchtlinge, werden sie genannt. Schätzungsweise rund 18.000 leben derzeit in Deutschland; zwei Drittel sind Jungen. Die meisten von
15 ihnen kommen aus Afghanistan, Syrien, Somalia und Eritrea. […]

Franz Joseph Freisleder weiß, was passieren kann, wenn die, die aus dem Krieg kommen, keinen Frieden finden. Er ist Ärztlicher Direktor des Heckscher-Klinikums für Kinder- und Jugendpsychiatrie in München und Oberbayern, der größten Einrichtung dieser Art in Deutschland. Zu ihm bringen Polizisten und Sozialarbeiter
20 Jugendliche aus den umliegenden Flüchtlingsunterkünften, die auffällig werden oder die sie nicht mehr unter Kontrolle haben. Seit Januar nahm Freisleder bereits

30 unbegleitete minderjährige Flüchtlinge auf seiner Station in München auf. So viele wie im gesamten Jahr 2012. Für dieses Jahr rechnet er mit mindestens 120 Fällen. Jugendliche, die aggressiv werden, um sich schlagen oder in Angstzustände verfallen. […]

„Sie haben ein Maß an Gewalt erlebt, das wir uns nicht vorstellen können." Auf der Flucht hätten sie gelernt, dass nur die Starken durchkommen, erklärt der Arzt. Da sei es nicht verwunderlich, dass sich Aggressionen aufstauten. „In denen brodelt es", sagt Freisleder. Es käme jedoch nur selten vor, dass Jugendliche wegen gewalttätigen Ausfällen zu ihm in die Klinik kämen. Die meisten seien depressiv und selbstmordgefährdet. Viele sorgten sich sehr um ihre Familien.

(320 Wörter)
Dennis Betzholz, *Die Welt*, 2015

Erwartungshorizonte

1 Comprehension

12 VP *Describe the situation Manny finds himself in, his plan and his motivation.*

Read the text carefully and consider that your task consists of three parts. Your answer must include Manny's current situation as well as his plan and motivation. In your answer, use your own words only and leave out any comments or any additional information that is not mentioned in the text.

Task support

Für diese Aufgabe werden insgesamt 12 Punkte auf den Inhalt vergeben.

Form und Umfang meiner Antwort:
Describe…: In Ihrer Antwort müssen Sie die wichtigsten Inhalte sowie aussagekräftige Beispiele und Details des Textauszugs wiedergeben. Beschreiben Sie die momentanen Lebensumstände Mannys, seine Zukunftspläne und seine Beweggründe. Formulieren Sie Ihre Antwort möglichst in eigenen Worten und konzentrieren Sie sich auf die wichtigsten Fakten im vorliegenden Text.

Mögliche inhaltliche Aspekte:
- Manny Bustos is a 14-year old Mexican street boy living in the border town of Juárez, Mexico.
- He sleeps in a cardboard shed on the street and is always moving as he is afraid of being caught and sold to men who abuse young street boys.
- He leads a miserable life and lives from hand to mouth.
- One day, after waking up, he decides that this is the day he will cross the border.
- He is full of optimism.
- He is sure that his life will take a turn for the better in the US.
- He will find work, become a man and earn money.
- In short, he will be able to make all his dreams come true.

Proposed solution:
In the excerpt from Gary Paulsen's novel "The Crossing" published in 1987, the narrator tells the reader about the main character Manny Bustos, a 14-year old Mexican street boy, his living conditions, his plan and his motivation to cross the border between Mexico and the US.
Manny lives on the streets of the border town Juaréz, Mexico, where he sleeps in a shelter made of cardboard. He is always moving because he is afraid of being caught and sold to people who abuse young boys. In addition to this, he constantly suffers from hunger as he lives from hand to mouth. Basically, his living conditions are miserable.
But today, after waking up, he is sure that his life will change as he has finally decided to cross the border to the US. He is full of optimism. He is sure that his life will take a turn for the better in the US. According to his view, he will have all the things that make life worth living. He will find work easily, become a man and make money. In short, he will be able to make all his dreams come true.
(200 words)

— Tip
Mention the source you refer to at the beginning of your answer.

… Erwartungshorizonte **135**

2 Analysis

16 VP *Analyse the way Manny's situation is presented. Focus on point of view and use of language.*

After having described Manny's situation in the comprehension task, focus on *how* his situation is presented. In general, is it presented as optimistic or pessimistic? What kind of language (e.g. adjectives, nouns, images) is used? What is the point of view and how does it affect the reader's perception of the main character? Refer to the text to support your findings.

Task support

Für diese Aufgabe werden insgesamt 16 Punkte auf den Inhalt vergeben.

Form und Umfang meiner Antwort:
Analyse …: Nennen Sie zu Beginn Ihrer Antwort zentrale Aspekte wie die Erzählperspektive und belegen diese anhand von Textstellen. Erklären Sie anschließend wie die Erzählperspektive die Beziehung des Lesers zu den Figuren beeinflusst. Welche Informationen erhält der Leser? Inwieweit erhält er Einblick in die Gefühle und Gedanken der Figuren? etc. Überdies gehen Sie auf sprachliche Mittel (Wiederholungen, Bilder, Wortfamilien, Satzbau etc.) und deren Wirkung auf die Leser ein. Belegen Sie Ihre Beobachtungen mit Beispielen und Zitaten aus dem Text.

Mögliche inhaltliche Aspekte:
- Point of view: third-person narrator with limited point of view.
- Reader knows (only) about Manny's feelings and thoughts.
- Manny is portrayed as young, naïve and unexperienced.
- The author uses comparisons to describe Manny's situation ("lizard").
- He uses word families, images and repetitions to portray Manny's situation vividly (noise, movement, hunger).

Proposed solution:
In his novel "The Crossing", Gary Paulsen uses a third-person narrator with a limited point of view and several rhetorical devices to present the main character Manny Bustos and his situation.
The plot is told from Manny's point of view by a third-person narrator. The narrator informs the reader about "his" thoughts and plans and what "he" is going to do. Already in the first paragraph of the excerpt the reader is told about Manny that "he knew … that it was time. … He would make the crossing today." (ll. 4–5). The reader also learns about Manny's thoughts. Manny wants to "become a man, make money, and wear a leather belt … and a straw hat with a feathered hatband." (ll. 19–20).The focus on Manny makes it easy for the reader to understand the main character.
Furthermore Manny's dream of wearing a leather belt and a straw hat with a feathered hatband characterise him indirectly as a very naïve, young and unexperienced person. His imagination of life in the US is far from reality. The dialogue with Maria also reveals his naivety (ll. 23 ff.). Maria warns him that he is too young and small but despite her warnings, Manny holds on to his plan to cross the border that very night.
The author also presents Manny by characterising him directly. In lines 14–15

Tip
Structure your text using paragraphs. Include a brief introduction and conclusion.

he describes him as a red-haired 14-year old with large brown eyes and long eyelashes.

The author uses different word families and rhetorical devices to portray Manny's situation vividly.

He describes his shelter, which is made of cardboard, as extremely hot. It is so hot that he has to crawl outside because "even a lizard could not have taken it" (l. 1–2). The reader creates a strong image of life in the border town. It is very lively and noisy. He repeats the word "noise" several times (ll. 6–10: "made of noise", "noise that filled", "noises changed", "a hum of noise"). In addition to this he uses further words referring to noise. The town was "never quiet" (l. 6) and there are "honking horns" (l. 8) and "people yelling" (l. 9).

The author also emphasises Manny's restlessness and necessity to move continually. He repeats the word "to move" frequently (l. 10–11: "He lived on the street, moving, always moving", l. 13: "if he did not move", l. 17: "begin moving for the day"). Other phrases express the idea of movement as well like "he rolled out" (l. 16), "I will be leaving" (l. 23) and of course the title "The Crossing".

Manny's hunger is obvious in lines 21–22. The enumeration of situations when Manny is hungry, show his poor living conditions.

In summary, the narrative point of view and the author's use of language produce a clear image of Manny's character and his situation.

(425 words)

> **Tip**
> To support your findings, explain them and give examples from the text.

3 Evaluation

14 VP **a)** *Comment on Manny's view of the United States. Refer to the text and work done in class.*

In this task you have to decide whether you agree or disagree with Manny's view on the United States and give reasons for your decision. Refer to Manny's thoughts and what you know about the American dream from work done in class. Take care not to contradict yourself and write a well-structured text using a concise and persuasive line of argument.

Task support

Für diese Aufgabe werden insgesamt 14 Punkte auf den Inhalt vergeben.

Form und Umfang meiner Antwort:

Comment on …: Greifen Sie in Ihrer Einleitung die Vorstellung Mannys von einem Leben in Amerika auf. Erläutern Sie im Anschluss ihre persönliche und kritische Einschätzung von Mannys Plan anhand mehrerer Argumente, indem Sie Ihr erworbenes Wissen aus dem Unterricht miteinfließen lassen. Achten Sie auf eine klare und überzeugende Strukturierung Ihres Textes.

Mögliche inhaltliche Aspekte und Struktur meiner Antwort:

- *Introduction: Manny has got false ideas about life in the US. The reality looks different for undocumented workers.*
- *Though lots of them find work, they are in constant fear that they will be detected and deported. → no security*
- *Employers exploit them. → no wealth*
- *Conclusion: Manny's ideas of a better life in the US are based on false assumptions and not on real facts. It is likely that he will fail in the US and that his dream will turn into a personal nightmare for him.*

Proposed solution:
In Manny's view, it is easy to be successful in the US after crossing the border. Like a lot of other immigrants he believes in the American Dream. He thinks that it is sufficient to have strength, to be fast and to know how to work hard in order to make his personal dreams come true. However, I think that he is rather naïve, which can be attributed to his age as well as to frequent success stories he might have heard on the streets of Juárez. The reality is quite different for most illegal immigrants like Manny.

A lot of Mexicans cross the US border illegally in pursuit of the American Dream. They believe the US is a wealthy and safe country where job opportunities are plentiful. Their success just depends on their own initiative and soon they will even be able to send money to their family members in Mexico. Unfortunately this view quickly turns into a nightmare for most illegal immigrants after their arrival. Though a lot of immigrants find work in agriculture or other menial jobs, they live in constant fear that they will be detected by the police and deported back to Mexico. They can never live a secure life or plan their future.

In addition to this, some employers exploit undocumented employees since the workers have no rights and there is nobody they can turn to for help. Therefore undocumented immigrants are often paid the lowest wages and it is not uncommon that they have to work extra hours without being paid for them. Though they spend all their time working, they still struggle to make ends meet. It is certainly not the wealthy life they had imagined before they illegally crossed the border.

In my opinion, Manny's ideas of a wealthy and secure life in the US are only based on false assumptions, not on real facts. He believes blindly in the American Dream because of his youth and inexperience. Unfortunately, he has no idea what life is really like in the US. I think that he will suffer many hardships in the US and that his dream will turn into a personal nightmare.

(375 words)

Tip
Begin your text by stating the topic you are going to comment on.

14 VP **b)** *Write a letter to Gary Paulsen, the author of the novel, in which you reflect on the effect the extract from his novel has on your view on Trump's plan to build a wall between the US and Mexico. Refer to the extract and work done in class.*

Write a polite and well-structured letter to Gary Paulsen in which you express your personal opinion about Trump's plan to build a wall. Refer to the extract of the novel and to work done in class.

Task support

Für diese Aufgabe werden insgesamt 14 Punkte auf den Inhalt vergeben.

Form und Umfang meiner Antwort:
Write a letter …: Schreiben Sie einen formellen Brief an den Romanautor von „The Crossing". Erläutern Sie ihre persönliche Meinung gegenüber dem geplanten Mauerbau unter dem Eindruck der Lektüre des Romanauszugs und mithilfe Ihres im Unterricht erworbenen Wissens.
Achten Sie auf die Textsortenmerkmale eines formellen Briefs (Anrede, Betreff, Schlussformel etc.)

Mögliche inhaltliche Aspekte:
- *Introduction: Refer to the extract from Gary Paulsen's novel and Trump's plan to build a border between the USA and Mexico.*
- *A lot of Mexicans like Manny Bustos live in poverty and have lost all hope for a change for the better in their country. Therefore they will not be discouraged by a wall as they will try everything possible to enter the US.*
- *No one can take away their dream of having a better life in America where they can find work and lift themselves out of poverty.*
- *End/conclusion*

Proposed solution:
Dear Mr Paulsen,
We have just read an extract from your novel "The Crossing" in class and I would like to tell you why I think that building a wall between the USA and Mexico won't reduce illegal immigration to the US.
A lot of Mexicans like Manny Bustos live in poverty and have lost all hope for a change for the better in their country. The Mexican government is unable to care for some of its most vulnerable citizens. Manny is such an example; he is a teenager living on the streets with no one to care for him. The government's failure to act finally drives many Mexicans to leave their home country and cross the border illegally. Therefore, they would not be discouraged by a wall as they will try everything possible to enter the United States, like digging tunnels or crossing the Rio Grande. No one, including President Trump, is able to crush the immigrants' dreams of a better life in America where they can find work, fulfil their dreams and lead a free and secure life. For them, America is a country which offers plenty of opportunities. Although most of them are poorly educated, they are willing to work hard and in jobs that other Americans don't want to do anymore.
In conclusion, I think it is the combination of the Mexican government's failure to improve the living conditions for their citizens as well the Mexicans' dreams of a better future in the US which makes them cross the border illegally. Consequently, in my view, a wall will not keep them from trying to realise their dreams in the US.
Sincerely,
(student's name)   (290 words)

— **Tip**
State the novel you refer to and the topic of the letter.

— **Tip**
End your letter with an appeal to the author, your personal opinion or your expectation for the future.

Klausurteil: Sprachmittlung isoliert

4 Mediation

18 VP   *Your American friend is doing a school project on Underage Refugees in Europe and has asked you for information.*

Write him/her an email in which you summarise what D. Betzholz says about the situation of underage refugees in Germany and the problems they face.

Write an informal email to your American friend in which you summarise Mr Betzholz' views on the situation of underage refugees in Germany and the problems they have to deal with.

Klausurteil

Task support

Für diese Aufgabe werden insgesamt 18 Punkte auf den Inhalt vergeben.

Form und Umfang meiner Antwort:
Write an email…: Achten Sie beim Schreiben einer E-Mail an Ihren amerikanischen Freund/Ihre amerikanische Freundin darauf, dass Sie die spezifischen Textsortenmerkmale einer persönlichen E-Mail einhalten (Anrede, Schlussformel, …) und formulieren Sie Ihre Antwort in informeller Sprache. Verfassen Sie eine E-Mail, die nur die gefragten inhaltlichen Aspekte umfasst.

Mögliche inhaltliche Aspekte:
- According to the article, the number of underage refugees increased by about 133 percent between 2010 and 2013.
- There are approximately 18,000 underage refugees living in Germany right now.
- Two-thirds of them are boys and most of them came from countries like Afghanistan, Syria, Somalia and Eritrea.
- According to a medical director at a hospital for child and youth psychology, the number of underage refugees who display social behavioural problems is increasing.
- Some underage refugees become aggressive, hit out in all directions or even sink into depression.
- Often underage refugees experienced violence in their home countries or when they were on the run.

Proposed solution:
Hi Dennis,
In your last email you asked me to give you some information on the situation of underage refugees in Germany and the problems they face in our country. Today I read an interesting article that was published in the German newspaper "Die Welt". I am sure you can make good use of my short report for your school project. In 2010, local German authorities had to care for 2822 underage refugees who came alone to Germany, but in 2013 this number of refugees increased by about 133 percent. All in all, there are approximately 18,000 underage refugees living without their families in Germany right now. Two-thirds of them are boys and most of them are from countries like Afghanistan, Syria, Somalia and Eritrea. According to Franz Joseph Freisleder, the medical director at a hospital for child and youth psychology in Bavaria, social workers and policemen regularly bring young refugees to him for treatment. His patients have previously displayed social behavioural problems or have not been in command of themselves. This year, it is estimated that at least 120 adolescents will be treated in his hospital.
According to Freisleder, some underage refugees will become aggressive, hit out in all directions or even sink into depression in the course of time. He thinks that the reason for such a development like becoming depressive or having suicidal tendencies is that they often experienced lots of violence in their home countries or when they were on the run.
I hope I could help you with these facts and I wish you good luck with your current school project.

(270 words)

Tip
Address your friend and refer to your source of information.

Wiederholen Sie zentrale Fakten des Grundwissens und elementare Methoden für die Textarbeit. Übungsaufgaben unterstützen Sie dabei.

Einfach trainieren

Grundwissen

The UK – tradition and change

How do judges, MPs and the government control each other?

The United Kingdom (which consists of England, Scotland, Wales and Northern Ireland) is a **constitutional monarchy** and its **Head of State** is the monarch (the Queen). At the same time it is a **parliamentary democracy** since it is the parliament which is the country's most powerful political institution. Its **Head of Government** is the prime minister who is elected by the majority in Parliament.

The British constitution
While most of the modern democracies have a **codified** constitution, the constitution of the United Kingdom is **uncodified**. 'Codified' means that the constitution of a state is written down in a single document, examples are the *U.S. Constitution* of the United States of America or the *German Basic Law* (*Grundgesetz*) of Germany. The British constitution is uncodified since a lot of **different documents form the constitution** and, in addition to this, parts of it are not even written down but rooted in **unwritten** understandings, precedents or customs. Often the British constitution is also referred to as an 'unwritten' constitution, but that is only true in so far as it does not consist of only one written document.

Throughout the centuries the constitution has been continually growing as new laws were passed. One of the most important documents contributing to the British constitution is the *Magna Carta* (1215). Other sources of the British constitution are e.g. the *European Convention on Human Rights* or parliamentary decisions. Basically, the sources of the British constitution are:

Statute law: Statute law is the principal source of the constitution. It comprises laws which were passed by the UK Parliament.

Common law: Common law is based on legal principles and judicial precedents, i.e. the judge has to consider decisions which were taken in other, similar cases in the past.

Constitutional conventions: Conventions describe **unwritten** practices and customs which have evolved over the centuries.

As a consequence of its various sources, the British constitution is **flexible**, i.e. it can be changed by parliamentary acts, judicial decisions or changing conventions much more easily than in countries with a codified constitution.

The British Parliament
The UK Parliament consists of two houses or chambers: an upper house (**the House of Lords**) and a lower house (**the House of Commons**), which are both situated in the Palace of Westminster.

The House of Commons
The UK public elects 650 **Members of Parliament** (**MPs**) to represent their interests and concerns in the House of Commons. They are voted to serve 5-year terms unless the House is dissolved earlier. In the **general elections** for the House of Commons, each constituency elects one representative to the House of Commons. The candidate with the simple majority of the votes wins the seat. Therefore, it is also called a **'first-past-the-post'** voting system.

Composition of the UK Parliament:

- 317 Conservative
- 262 Labour
- 35 SNP (Scottish National Party)
- 12 Liberal Democrat
- 10 Democratic Unionist- und Ulster Unionist Party
- 7 Sinn Fein and SDLP (Social Democratic Party and Labour Party)
- 8 Further parties e.g.
    - Plaid Cymru (4)
    - Green Party (1)
    - Other (2)
    - Speaker (1)

Total 650

Source: www.parliament.uk, 2017

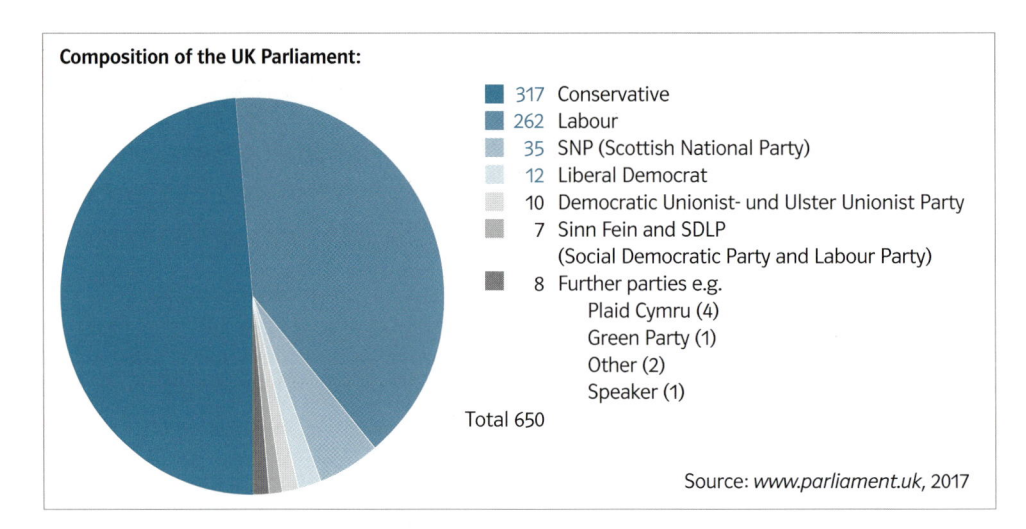

Since it is rather difficult for small parties to win the simple majority of votes in a constituency, the two main parties – the Conservatives and Labour – are by far the strongest powers in Parliament. Therefore the Parliament can be described as a **two-party-system**. The two-party-system is also reflected in the seating arrangement in the House of Commons:

The **Prime Minister** and his **government** sit on the front bench opposite the **Leader of the Opposition** and his '**Shadow Cabinet**'. The MPs who have no leading roles in the government or the opposition sit behind them (the backbenchers). So the MPs of the government and of the opposition (or likewise of the two major parties) sit opposite each other and confront each other in their debates.

The House of Commons has got the following main functions:
- holding the election of the prime minister
- controlling the government
- debating important issues of the day
- making and changing laws

The House of Lords
Currently the House of Lords consists of about 790 members who are eligible to take an active role in the chamber. The majority of the members (about 700) are life peers. They are appointed for their lifetime by the monarch on the advice of the prime minister. Other members are 26 archbishops and bishops of the Church of England and about 90 hereditary peers (hereditary peerage was abolished in 1999, only about 90 hereditary peers remained).
Part of the members of the House of Lords have a political background, while others have worked in various professional fields like medicine, law, business or public service. Additionally, many members are also involved with charitable, voluntary and civil society organisations as well.

The House of Lords has got three main functions:
- suggesting and amending laws
- setting up committees to investigate topics of public interest and to inform the public
- checking and challenging the work of the government during question time and debates

The Government
The Prime Minister is the **Head of the Government.** At the beginning of each legislature he appoints the ministers of the government who are also members of the Upper or Lower House in Parliament.
Tasks of the government include:
- The Government tries to implement its policy, i.e. it introduces bills into Parliament to turn its political programme into legislation.
- Government ministers make statements with regard to the government policy or to subjects of national importance to Parliament.
- The Prime Minister has got weekly meetings with the monarch whereby the topics they discuss remain strictly confidential.
- During the Prime Minister's question time, members of Parliament from all parties are allowed to question the Prime Minister on any important issues.

The British monarchy
The United Kingdom is a hereditary constitutional monarchy. As **Head of State** the monarch is neutral in political debates. The monarch's power is mainly limited to **constitutional duties** and **representational functions**.
Part of the monarch's constitutional duties are:
- to formally appoint the Prime Minister
- to appoint the ministers on recommendation of the Prime Minister
- to summon and to dissolve the Parliament (in practice, only on the advice of the Prime Minister)
- to give a speech at the opening of Parliament every year
- to sign bills which have already been passed by the government
- to appoint bishops, governors and judges
- to meet with the Prime Minister in order to talk about current events

Furthermore the monarch is the
- Head of State in the UK
- Head of the Church of England
- Commander-in-Chief of the British Armed Forces
- Ceremonial Head of the Commonwealth countries (an intergovernmental organisation that currently comprises 53 sovereign states. The monarch's role does not include any involvement in the day-to-day governance of any of the member states within the Commonwealth)

The monarch's representational functions include
- supporting voluntary services and charities
- visiting people in need and show sympathy e.g. after natural catastrophes
- taking a leading role in national celebrations
- making state visits overseas
- welcoming foreign Heads of State when they come to Britain

In fulfilling these representational duties the monarch and the royal family also serve as a symbol of national unity and identity, why the monarch also acts as **'Head of Nation'**.

How will Britain's social structure develop?

The age structure
The British population is ageing. There are currently more pensioners than young people under the age of 16. Though there will be a projected increase in the number of children aged 0 to 15 by 8.8% until 2039 again. The number of working people aged 16 to State Pension Age is expected to rise by 11.4% from 40.0 million in 2014 to about 44.6 million by 2039. According to national population projections of the Office for National Statistics (ONS) made in 2014, the number of people aged 75 years or older will almost double until 2039.
Moreover, it is assumed that net international migration to the UK will be +185,000 per year, compared with +165,000 per year in projections based on 2012.

Britain's class society
The traditional three **social classes** in Britain used to contain the working class, the middle class and the upper class. However, since society in Great Britain has become more **pluralistic** and lifestyles more **individual**, recent studies categorise British society in more different social groups. One important study, The Great British Class Survey published by the BBC and several British universities in 2013, categorised British society in seven groups. The social classes examined range from the 'elite' at the top to the 'precarious proletariat' at the bottom. The 'traditional working class' is just one of several social classes ranging between them and below groups like the 'technical middle class' or 'the affluent middle class'. The members of the seven social groups differ in **education**, **occupation**, **social environment**, **social behavior patterns**, **lifestyle**, **age**, **finances**, etc.

What ethnic minorities are there?

The 2011 Census found out that about 80% of the population in England and Wales are white and British. About 20% belong to **ethnic minorities**. The biggest ethnic minority among them are non-British white people with about 5% of the population. Other large ethnic minorities are as follows: Indians (2.5%), Pakistanis (2%), African (1.8%), Other Asian (1.5%), Caribbean (1.1%), Bangladeshi (0.8%), Chinese (0.7%), etc.

Ethnic minorities
Due to its relations through the Commonwealth to many different countries, the United Kingdom has been a destination for a lot of people leaving their home countries. The reasons for settling in the UK are varied. For example, after becoming independent and **the partition** of the British Indian Empire in India and Pakistan in 1947, a lot of people fled war and terror. Other immigrants have escaped poverty or political persecution or have come to study in the UK. At the same time a lot of immigrants have come to Britain to support its workforce. For example there are a lot of **second and third generation immigrants** whose parents were urgently needed by Britain's rapidly growing workforce from the 1950s to 70s. Considering Britain's aging population, immigration continues to be a crucial topic for its economy.

British black people
A lot of people from the Caribbean emigrated to the UK after the Second World War. Nowadays, they predominantly live in urban areas like London. People from Nigeria and Ghana followed them in the 1990s. Today, they make up about 3 % of the total population.

British Asians
This group mainly came from India, Pakistan or Bangladesh after their countries gained independence in 1947. Most Pakistani and Bangladeshi people live in or near former industrial cities like Manchester, Leeds and Bradford whereas most Indian people live in the south near Birmingham or in the London area.

British Chinese
As Hong Kong was a former British colony, a lot of Chinese came to the UK before it became part of the People's Republic of China on July 1, 1997. Until then it had been under British colonial rule. Today, lots of Chinese communities can be found in many major cities including London, Birmingham, Glasgow, Manchester, Liverpool, Newcastle, Edinburgh, Cardiff, Sheffield, Nottingham, Belfast and Aberdeen.

Non-British white people
The United Kingdom has always been a haven to European migrants too. For example, about one million Irish people emigrated to the UK due to a series of potato crop failures in the 1840s and during WW II, a lot of Jewish people fled continental Europe. In the last decade a lot of people have settled down from East European countries (e.g. Poland) which have joined the EU.

Racial inequality
A main problem seems to be racism in the workplace. A lot of black people and Asians are convinced that racism is the cause for their lack of job opportunities. Government statistics from 2015 show that the unemployment rate for all ethnic minorities is 11.3 % compared with 6.2 % of the overall population. The unemployment rate among black people is 15.4 % whereas it is only 5.5 % among whites.

The rates of unemployment illustrate the wealth gap between ethnic minorities and white people, which David Gillborn observed in his book *Racism and Education* in 2008. For example, 60 % of all Black and Asian households have no savings. Moreover, ethnic health inequalities can be seen too. The illness rates of women from some minority groups have been about 10 % higher than those of white women.

Acceptance and integration into British society
Today, a lot of things have changed for the better: there is less open prejudice, there are more mixed couples and friendships and people with an immigrant background have become role models for the youth while being successful.

Nevertheless, racism hasn't been overcome yet and amendments to the law do not automatically erase some people's hate and prejudices towards minority groups. Their attitudes have to change as well.

Useful phrases

Talking about the legislature, executive and judiciary power in the UK
constitutional monarchy • parliamentary democracy • to consist of written documents and unwritten conventions • to elect sb • Member of Parliament (MP) • to represent a constituency • to serve a 5-year term • the general election • the first-past-the-post voting system • to win the simple majority • to control the government • to debate the issues of the day • to introduce a bill • to make and change laws • to be appointed by the Prime Minister / monarch

Talking about Britain's society
a low birth rate • the population is aging • social classes / groups • pluralistic society • individual lifestyles • ethnic minorities • second and third generation immigrants • black people make up about 3 % of the total population • social classes range from … to …

Revision

1 *Match each political actor and two of their characteristics.*

1 The monarch

2 MP (Member of Parliament)

3 Prime Minister

a suggests MPs to become ministers in the government.

b passes bills.

c is the Head of State.

d is elected and supported by the majority in parliament.

e is elected by the people.

f does not belong to a political party.

2 *Point out possible consequences of immigration to Britain during the last decades.*

Solutions

1 1 c), f); 2 b), e); 3 a), d)

2 A lot of different cultures live together in British cities • Many British people have another mother tongue (other than English) • a lot of British people have close relations to foreign countries • British culture adopts aspects of foreign cultures, e.g. in music, cooking, etc. • there are many different religions in the UK • a lot of immigrants have come to work in the UK • British society is not aging as fast as it would without immigration since the immigrants are rather young • ethnic minorities can separate from British society • etc.

The US and the American Dream

What is the American Dream?

It is difficult to define the American Dream today, as it is a concept based on a dated idea which is open to individual interpretation and transformation.
Here are just a few possible meanings:
- the dream of **fame and fortune** and / or
- the dream of a **fulfilling life** and / or
- limited **government interference in private matters**.

Additionally, the dreams do not remain static but often change over the course of time due to a person's age and social standing. For a young girl the dream could be to get a well-paid job after graduating from university, whereas an elderly woman may dream of retiring comfortably and sitting contentedly in a rose garden.
The phrase "the American Dream" was coined in 1931 by James Truslow Adams in his book *The Epic of America*. According to Adams "[…] the American Dream is that dream of a land in which life should be better and richer and fuller for everyone, with opportunity for each according to ability or achievement. It is […] a dream of social order in which each man and each woman shall be able to attain to the fullest stature of which they are innately capable, and be recognized by others for what they are, regardless of […] birth or position."
The Statue of Liberty, which was given to the USA as a present by France in 1886, is a symbol of that dream of **freedom, liberty, enlightenment, independence** and **individuality**.

How did it all begin?

The Puritans
It began with the first **English Protestants**, also known as Puritans, who left England in 1620 on a ship called the *Mayflower*.
They left their homeland and settled in America primarily in order to:
- 'purify' their religion from any principles that did not originate in the Bible;
- worship God in the way they chose and not have to submit to the rituals and hierarchies of the Church of England;.
- regard *only* God and the Bible as their religious authority and *not* the English king;
- escape from persecution by the king on account of their religious convictions;
- settle down in their 'New Canaan', **'the promised land'** where, according to the Bible, "milk and honey flow";
- seek economic opportunities, reform their religion and, with it, society.

The Frontier Spirit
In the Puritans' wake more settlers arrived and gradually moved westward toward the frontier, an imaginary boundary between where civilization ended and wilderness began.
President Thomas Jefferson's **Louisiana Purchase** (1803) nearly doubled the size of the US and gave rise to the idea that Americans were destined to move west to the Pacific Ocean. The idea of **'manifest destiny'** took hold in the 1830s and 1840s, leading many to believe that the US was a **country chosen by God** with the **right to expand its territory** to the whole of the North American continent. By 1850, **California** had already become the 31st state. "The Last Frontier", **Alaska**, was admitted as the 49th state in 1959 and **Hawaii** added the 50th star to the flag that same year. Nowadays, when people talk about frontiers, they are usually referring to space exploration or significant scientific or technological breakthroughs.

The Declaration of Independence
- was written by Thomas Jefferson in 1776;
- declared the colonists' independence from their former mother country which led to a war with England;
- asserted that "all men are created equal" with the unalienable rights to "life, liberty and the pursuit of happiness";
- guaranteed that every American would have the opportunity to make their personal dreams come true;
- included only land-owning white men at first; did not include women, blacks or Native Americans.

In 1787, a formal **Constitution** was adopted, complemented by the **Bill of Rights** which consisted of 10 additional **amendments** guaranteeing the American people unalienable rights such as the **freedom of religion** and the **right to a trial by jury**.

Is the Dream still alive?
The reality of the American Dream takes on different qualities in the various social classes:
- Many **minority groups** feel they have been denied the opportunity to live free and equal lives.
- There is a gradually **widening gap between the rich and the poor**, making it increasingly difficult for the poor to realize the Dream.
- Whereas a **good education** is often a prerequisite for upward mobility, the relatively prohibitive costs of higher education leave many no choice but to stay where they are.

Additionally, **the middle class** suffered enormously from the economic crisis of 2008 and the ensuing **years of recession**, with the consequences that:
- many people became **unemployed** and then lost their property as they could not pay off their loans;
- the present generation doubted it would be better off financially than the previous ones, thus putting a **crack in the optimism** of the American Dream;
- Americans doubted whether a **university degree** was still worth the money it would cost;
- the **work ethic** and the **value system of** the Puritans became endangered as working hard and taking responsibility did not automatically result in financial well-being, which many still widely regard as a sign of God's grace.

Useful phrases

Talking about the American Dream
- to suffer from / to escape religious persecution
- to settle in a new land
- to find the promised land
- to enjoy religious freedom
- to seek economic opportunities
- to practice one's religion
- to regard sth as one's destiny
- to move the frontier (westwards)
- to expand one's territory
- to declare independence from
- to deny / grant rights
- to be equal in
- to guarantee sb unalienable rights

How did immigration affect the Dream?

Historical facts
Over the centuries many **diverse groups of immigrants** have settled in the United States at different times. These times can be roughly divided into **five large-scale waves**:

1. At the beginning of the 17th century, **European immigrants** went to the US to escape religious persecution and bad economic conditions in their home countries.
2. From the mid-19th century onwards the wave was made up mostly of people from **northern and western European countries**. Social and economic changes due to **the Industrial Revolution** made it hard for agricultural workers to earn a living. Moreover, **political instability** in some European countries as well as the **Potato Famine in Ireland** forced hundreds of thousands of people to leave their countries.
3. In the early 20th century the wave mainly consisted of **southern and eastern Europeans** who fled from poor economic conditions.
4. Before, during and after World War II many **refugees** hoped to escape political persecution.
5. Since 1960 it has mostly been **Asians** and **Hispanics** who have left their countries to escape political persecution, find work and better living conditions in the US.

In addition to the *reasons for leaving* their home countries, the immigrants were *attracted by*:
- the promise of work and cheap land;
- justice;
- political stability;
- the quality of life;
- educational opportunities.

Immigration laws
Several laws were enacted as a consequence of excessive, unregulated immigration into the USA in the 19th century.
The following timeline presents the most important milestones:
- 1921: A **quota system** was introduced to restrict immigration. The number of immigrants from any particular nation per year was limited to 3% of the number of people of the same national origin who were already living in the US.
- 1924: The quota system became stricter and the quota was reduced to 2%. It was designed to reduce immigration from southern and eastern Europe and Asia.
- 1965: The quota system was abolished due to heavy criticism that the quota could be a form of racial discrimination. It was replaced by a **limited number of visas** which were given to favored, skilled workers.
- 1996: The **Illegal Immigration Reform & Immigrant Responsibility Act** supported border enforcement. As one result of this law, the fence along the Mexican border was extended. Further, it increased the fines for illegal immigration and made it easier to send illegal immigrants back to their home countries.
- 2011: To amend the Illegal Immigration Reform from 1996 in favour of young immigrants, the Obama administration introduced the program **Deferred Action for Childhood Arrivals** (DACA). The major aim was to allow high school students who came to the US illegally to stay permanently in the US if they arrived before their 16th birthday and before 2007 in the US.
- Since 2017: The Trump administration has been cracking down on immigration. The president repealed the DACA program, imposed a travel ban on citizens from majority-Muslim countries and introduced a "zero tolerance" policy on illegal immigrants. Trump's plans have stirred controversy as opponents condemn the separation of families and the costs involved e.g. building a wall on the Mexican border.

The 'Melting Pot' and 'Salad Bowl'

The 'melting pot' is used as a metaphor to signify the assimilation of a diverse society. However, the melting pot concept may not be an accurate portrayal of American society. The idea is that immigrants assimilate with established Americans and **form one American Nation** in the end by giving up their old lifestyles and cultures.

More recently, another metaphor has been gaining attention, namely the 'salad bowl'. When you look into a salad bowl, you can see the separate ingredients even as it constitutes a whole. The idea here is that immigrants regard themselves as American but retain aspects of their heritage

Illegal immigration

The number of illegal immigrants in the USA has been constantly rising. According to information from the U.S. Department of Homeland Security based on the 2010 census, there are currently about 11 million people (ca. 3.5% of a total of 319 million people) living and working illegally in the USA.

The situation of illegal immigrants:
- They are permanently at risk of being deported.
- Without legal papers they face a lack of social security and often live in poor boroughs of big cities.
- They must work for low wages as many employers exploit their situation.
- Illegal immigrants are seen as a threat to other Americans who fear losing their jobs.

The political answers:
- More efficient border control should prevent illegal immigrants from entering the US.
- Offering illegal immigrants who have lived in the USA for a longer time legal ways to citizenship should help them escape their *illegal* status. (democratic party stance)
- Denying US citizenship and sending back all illegal immigrants should reduce their number in the US. (republican party stance).

Who is in the salad bowl today?

Until the 1960s, the huge majority (89%) of people in the USA were white. Since then there has been a dramatic increase in the numbers of Asian and Hispanic immigrants. Today, the white population makes up 62% of the people in the US. Hispanics are one of the biggest and still growing ethnic groups and make up about 17% of all Americans.

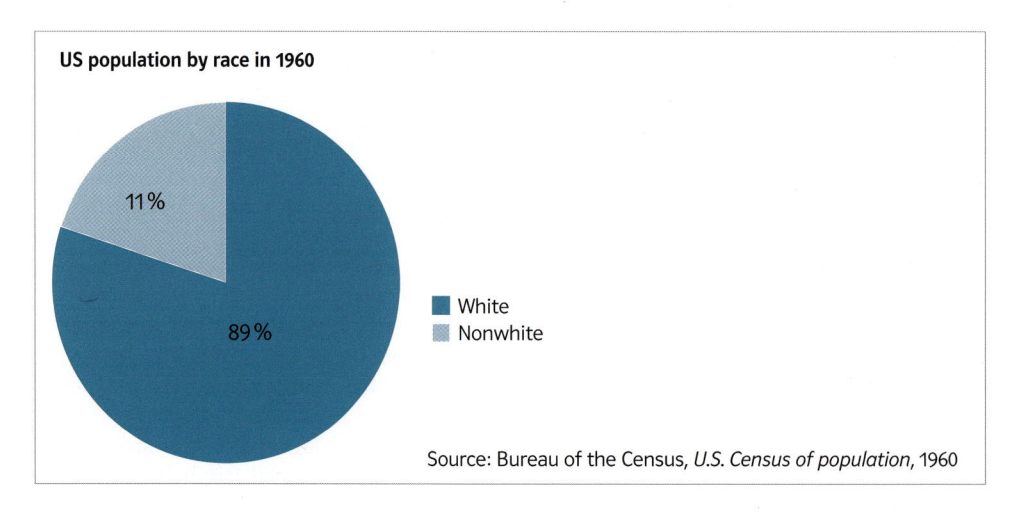

US population by race in 1960

- White: 89%
- Nonwhite: 11%

Source: Bureau of the Census, *U.S. Census of population*, 1960

US population by race in 2014 (Race and Hispanic origin)

- 62,1% White alone
- 13,2% Black or African American alone
- 17,4% Hispanic or Latino
- 5,4% Asian alone
- 1,2% American Indian and Alaska Native alone
- 0,2% Native Hawaiian and Other Pacific Islander alone

Source: *United States Census Bureau*, 2014

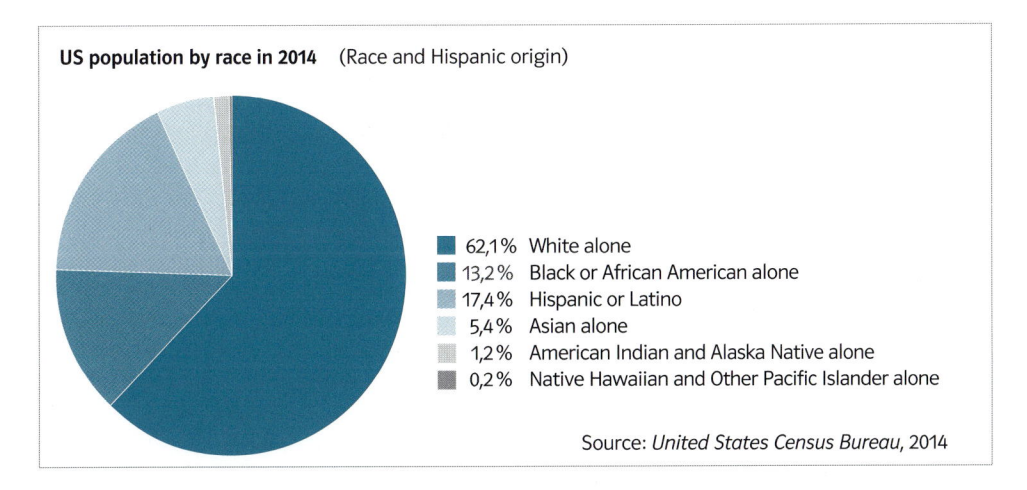

Native Americans

Millions of Native Americans were killed by diseases transmitted by European colonists or in wars with white settlers. In addition to this tragic past, the loss of identity and culture, alcoholism and a lack of prospects have led to depression, unemployment and a high rate of suicides among Native Americans. Today, Native Americans make up less than 1% of all Americans.

Problems:
- Living in remote settlements on the reservations, they lack prospects and opportunities.
- They suffer from bad living conditions in the reservations (poor health, lack of education, high rates of unemployment, low income, etc.).

Social Improvements:
- Steps have been taken to preserve their culture and heritage.
- Programmes for education and economic development have been implemented on the reservations.
- Some communities of Native Americans have established successful companies in their reservations, e.g., in the tourism industry.

African Americans

They make up about 13% of today's population.

Problems:
- About 26% of all black American families and about 41.2% of black families with a female head of household (and no male adult present) live in poverty (*See: Income and Poverty in the United States: 2014*, 2015).
- African American males make up the biggest ethnic group of prison inmates.
- Discrimination still exists in lots of areas of life e.g. on the job or housing market.

Social improvements:
- Programmes have been set up to support socially disadvantaged groups.
- There are many African Americans who are successful in politics, business, entertainment and sports and become role-models for other people in their communities.
- Civil rights organizations fight false prejudices against black men.

Hispanics

According to the *2014 U.S. Census* there are about 55 million Hispanics who live in the United States. The first Hispanic immigrants in the USA were Spanish colonists who started settling in Texas and California in the 16th century.

Today a lot of young people from South and above all Central America travel north to find work and better living conditions. If they manage to cross the border between Mexico and the US, most of them settle down in the southwestern states of the US.

Another big group of Hispanic immigrants come from Cuba, and the vast majority of them live in Florida. Besides fleeing from bad economic circumstances, a lot of them suffered from political persecution in their home country. According to the American Community Survey by the Pew Hispanic Center in 2011, most Cubans are well-off compared to other Hispanic minorities. Their level of income and education is higher than the average for Hispanics. However, there is still a gap to close to be on the same level as the white population.

Among Hispanic immigrants, Puerto Ricans have a special status. Puerto Ricans are US citizens due to the Spanish-American War in the late 19th century, when the US fought against the Spanish Empire. As a consequence of this conflict, Puerto Rico became a U.S. territory and its inhabitants were granted US citizenship. However, Puerto Ricans share much of the same problems as illegal Hispanic immigrants, like discrimination on the job market and poor housing. There are massive Puerto Rican communities in New York, Chicago and Boston.

Problems:
- About 24 % of all Hispanics live below the poverty line according to the report *Income and Poverty in the United States: 2014* published in 2015.
- Many Hispanics speak only Spanish. Since the Spanish-speaking community is quite big, it is not really necessary to learn English to participate in public life.
- Opponents of immigration fear a segregation of American society.
- Hispanics are regarded as cheap labourers and often have to work for low wages.
- In addition to the low wages, they often have to support their relatives at home with the money they earn.
- They live in poor city districts that do not receive adequate tax money with bad schooling and housing.
- The children suffer from a lack of a good education.

Social improvements:
- They gain more political influence as the number of voters of Hispanic origin is increasing.
- Programmes like the Deferred Action for Childhood Arrivals (see p. 149) Immigration laws) make it easier for young immigrants to stay legally in the US.
- A lot of Hispanic immigrants have become successful entrepreneurs. For example, a lot of the business in Miami has been set up by Cuban immigrants.

Asians

They make up a small proportion of immigrants (about 5 % according to the *2014 U.S. Census*) but are the fastest growing group in the United States. Many Asians have settled in California.

Problems:
- Like other minorities, Asians experience racial discrimination and prejudice.
- As well, some Asians conduct their entire lives within their ethnic enclaves, which results in segregation from the population at large.

Social improvements:
- A lot of Asians are well-educated and appreciate a good education for their children.
- They tend to be more successful in business than other ethnic groups.

Useful phrases

Talking about immigration
- to immigrate into
- to earn a living
- to find work and better living conditions
- to be attracted by educational opportunities
- to escape political persecution / bad economic conditions
- to be oppressed by / because of
- to flee from poor economic conditions

Talking about integration
- to give up / to keep one's cultural heritage alive
- to keep / transform / find one's identity
- to regard oneself as
- to have no documents
- to exploit sb
- to grant citizenship to sb
- to grant a work permit / residency permit

Talking about restrictions of immigration
- to enact a law
- to introduce a quota
- to limit / reduce immigration to
- to be a form of racial discrimination
- to obtain citizenship

Talking about ethnic diversity
- the number of … has increased
- the population consists of
- to suffer from separation
- to be discriminated against because of
- to be segregated along racial lines
- experience racial discrimination and prejudices
- to enforce / prevent racial prejudices against sb

How is the US dealing with terrorism in an insecure world?

Since the end of the **Cold War** the role of the US as a global superpower has changed from a global conflict with two protagonists (i.e., the Soviet Union and the US) to a global conflict with a lot of different smaller actors. Part of the shift in global powers has been the rise of new **regional powers** like China or India and the **increase of terrorist organisations,** e.g., in the Middle East. Terrorism has become a global threat and the USA has to redefine its role in the world, especially after the attacks on the World Trade Center on September 11th, 2001.

Security versus Liberty in US domestic politics
After the September 11th attacks on the World Trade Center, the government under President Bush adjusted the balance between liberty and security. However, opponents have been criticizing that the government's measures lean too far towards security over liberty.
Two examples will illustrate this:

- **The Guantanamo Bay detention camp**

  2002: The Guantanamo Bay detention camp was established in Cuba to detain terrorists or people suspected of being involved in terrorism. Human rights activists criticize the fact that detainees are being imprisoned without a fair trial and being tortured, which is against the Geneva Convention mandate protecting prisoners of war.

  2009: President Obama promised to close the detention camp but his plan was rejected by the Senate, one of the two chambers of Congress.

  2016: Although the number of prisoners has been decreasing from about 800 in 2002 to 91 in February 2016, it is rather unlikely that a majority in Congress will support closing the detention center in the near future. Some of the remaining detainees will be sent to other countries, while others will stay in Guantanamo to await their judgments from a military court.

- **The collection of private data**
  2001: The USA Patriot Act came into force, granting the intelligence services more rights in the fight against terrorism and allowing the government to collect the private data of any American citizen. In this way, the private data of millions of Americans were made accessible to the federal government.
  Opponents criticized that this act went against the **Fourth Amendment of the American Constitution** which guarantees the "right of the people to be secure in their persons, houses, papers, and effects, against unreasonable searches and seizures".

  2015: The USA Patriot Act expired but it was replaced by the USA Freedom Act. Due to public pressure to stop collecting and storing the private data of millions of Americans, the Freedom Act is a reduced version of the Patriot Act. For example, private data cannot be collected by the government but only by telecommunication companies. Furthermore, the government needs a reasonable suspicion to request and receive private data. The USA Freedom Act is effective until 2019.

The US and global security
As in the era of the Cold War, the United States still play a leading role in world politics with the mission to **expand freedom throughout the world**.
Regarding this mission and defending their security, it is their aim to:

- protect US citizens at home and abroad;
- fight terrorism abroad;
- weaken or abolish authoritarian dictators and oppressive regimes and replace them with a democratic government;
- protect US global interests (e.g., stopping the spread of nuclear weapons, geopolitical influence of the US in the Pacific, etc.).

But it faces and will continue to face many problems because
- pressuring other governments will lead to more criticism that the USA tends to control the world;
- many societies reject the American definition of democracy;
- its recent military involvements in Afghanistan and Iraq could not bring peace to the people but led to civil wars and even more terror by radical extremists;
- the failure to pacify regions of conflict and victims of military actions among the civilian population even created new enemies;
- terror attacks in its own country mainly driven by fanatical religious reasons have increased.

Nevertheless, the USA might prove to be successful in building a more cooperative world by taking the initiative to bring the nations of the world together in order to follow a common policy, especially in the fight against global terrorism.

Useful phrases

Talking about security
- to adjust the balance between liberty and security
- to lean (too far) towards security
- to detain sb without trial
- to collect and store data
- to limit the rights of secret intelligence services

Talking about global politics
- to expand freedom
- to protect interests
- to weaken authoritarian regimes
- to bring peace to
- to be criticized for

The US and the American Dream   155

Revision

1 Draw a mind map showing the major influences and sources of the American Dream.

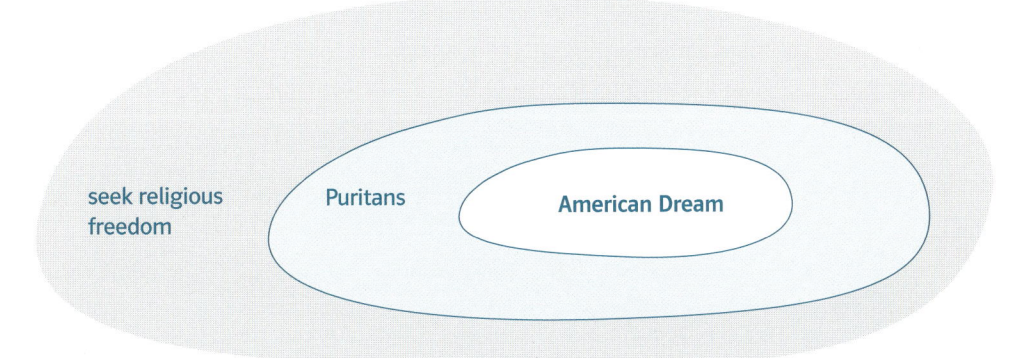

seek religious freedom — Puritans — American Dream

2 Complete the timeline with the major immigration waves into the USA and the reasons for migration.

Time	Regions of origin	Reasons for migration
after 1600		
after 1800		
after 1900		
after 1930		
after 1960		

3 Note down in keywords possible arguments of supporters and opponents of the measures to prevent terrorism.

The Guantanamo Bay detention camp

Advocates: _____
_____
_____

Opponents: _____
_____
_____

The collection of private data

Advocates: _____

_____

_____

Opponents: _____

_____

_____

Solutions

1 First circle: Puritans • 'promised land' • 'Manifest destiny' • frontier spirit • Declaration of Independence • Constitution • etc.
Second circle: seek religious freedom • purify religion • seek economic opportunities • believe in progress • expand its territory • Bill of rights (unalienable rights such as the freedom of religion and the right to a trial by jury) • etc.

2

Time	Regions of origin	Reasons for migration
after 1600	Europe / Africa	religious persecution, poor economic conditions / slave trade – slaves had no choice
after 1800	northern and western Europe (e.g. Ireland, Germany etc.)	political persecution, unemployment, famine
after 1900	southern and eastern Europe (e.g. Italy, Poland etc.)	poor economic conditions
after 1930	Europe	political persecution, terror, genocide, the Second World War
after 1960	Latin America, east Asia	bad living conditions, political persecution

3 The Guantanamo Bay detention camp
Advocates: protect the people, to prevent terrorist actions, to punish terrorists, to investigate terrorist actions
Opponents: men are detained even though they have not been found guilty of a crime yet, Human rights are severely offended (no trail, torture), the measures of the Guantanamo Bay Detention Camp might be applied by (authoritarian) future governments

The collection of private data
Advocates: it is a very effective measure to prevent terrorist attacks, you can act quickly, private data of innocent people is not misused since the police may only examine private data if they have a concrete suspicion
Opponents: private data can be misused by the government or by the companies, innocents are more likely to become suspects, the US Constitution protects the people against unjustified investigations by the police

India

What does it mean to be colonised?

Spices may have lured European explorers to the subcontinent, but India quickly became known as the "jewel in the British crown" for **yielding untold riches** for the British Empire. In addition to providing a cheap market for raw materials, India became a major market for English goods. Thus, colonisation came about because of economic motivations rather than **evangelical**.
Before the British claimed India as a colony in 1858 and Queen Victoria took on the title of Empress of India in 1876, other colonisers profited as well. Portuguese, Dutch, French, Danish and Norwegian business concerns and state governments ruled over segments of the country with military backing or with their own private armies. **Rebellions** against colonisers took place frequently.
By the 1850s the British had the biggest **claim** on India, and from 1858 to 1947 the colonial government was called the **British Raj**. Many Indian workers were **mistreated**, **exploited** and left without a voice in the government. After displaying their loyalty to Britain in World War I, many Indians hoped that they would be rewarded with **independence**.
This would not be the case. Following Mahatma Gandhi's lead, the Indian National Congress continued **to resist** British rule in the interwar years. Finally, on July 18th, 1947, King George VI signed the **Indian Independence Act**. The act gave India the right to **self-rule** and **partitioned** the country into two states, each with its own religious majority: India with Hinduism and Pakistan with Islam. East Pakistan split from West Pakistan in 1972 and became Bangladesh, while West Pakistan became what is known today as Pakistan.

Other effects of colonisation are complex and difficult to demonstrate. However there are some long-lasting **consequences** of British rule that are clear:
- English became the official language of India in 1844,
- **Development** of infrastructure was modeled after Britain, e.g., the British modernised the **transportation** system of the country in order to increase the efficiency of trade, in particular the railways,
- English-speaking Indians **were favoured** for certain jobs, many emigrating from India to other parts of the Commonwealth (it is estimated that India has the largest diaspora population in the world),
- **Western education** replaced traditional methods of learning, providing a limited opportunity to rise above the strict caste system,
- Indian people were exposed to western culture ("**westernised**") and **internalised** some British values including **beauty standards,** thus favoring people with lighter skin and other European features.

What is India like today?

Geography
India is the seventh largest country in the world. Shaped like a diamond, it is bordered by the Himalayan Mountain ranges to the north and the Indian Ocean to the south. Thus India is often referred to as a **subcontinent**, geographically distinct from the rest of Asia.

Climate
Conditions vary throughout the country, with tropical weather in the south and temperate weather in the north. The southwest summer monsoon season lasts for four months and accounts for 70–80% of India's annual rainfall, making it the most productive wet season on earth. The Indian economy is heavily impacted by monsoon rains. A good monsoon stimulates agricultural and economic growth, whereas a weak monsoon or drought can have the opposite effect. Climate

change could have a dramatic impact on the subcontinent as glaciers begin to melt in the north and sea levels begin to rise in the south. The government is **taking measures** to decrease the country's **carbon emissions**, keeping a close eye on **sustainability** as it will become a major issue in a country that is **surging with** growth.

Population
India's population is growing rapidly. Based on the Indian Census of 2011, there are 1.2 Billion Indian people (which make it the second-most populous country in the world) speaking more than 1,000 languages. English and Hindi are the two most often used in business and politics.

Economy
India has one of the largest economies in the world. The vast majority of Indian people (about half of the population) are involved in farming or other informal employment, but this is quickly changing as more and more people get involved in the **booming tech industry**.

Politics
India has the world's largest democracy. The Indian Parliament is modelled on the British parliamentary system with an upper and lower house. The Prime Minister is the head of government and the capital is in New Delhi.

Religion
Hinduism is the oldest living religion in the world. It is comprised of several philosophies based on the teachings of many founders and texts. One of the core teachings is **karma**, the concept that one's actions affect this life and the next. It is closely connected to the concept of **reincarnation**. Although Hinduism is the majority religion of the country with 80% of the population and 900 million followers worldwide, there are several religious minorities in India like Muslims, Buddhists and Sikhs and tensions can flare up at times. This is especially true between Hindus and Muslims.

What about Indian culture?

Originating in Hinduism, the **caste system** divides Indian society into a **hierarchy** based on status. These groups are expected to perform different functions in society. For example the **Brahmins** at the top are considered the intellectual and spiritual leaders whereas the **untouchables** at the bottom are supposed to be the **unskilled labourers** who perform the dirty work of society. Under the British Raj, the best jobs were granted to the higher castes and the system of **social stratification** was solidified. This policy of **segregation** began to change when social unrest in 1920 lead to the **allotment** of some jobs to the lower castes. After Indian Independence, the government outlawed **discrimination** and began instituting more **affirmative action** programs. Although the situation has improved since then, poverty and hunger remain major concerns. Estimates differ depending on the definition of the **poverty line**, but approximately half of the population is living in desperate circumstances or in **slums** without access to basic necessities such as permanent shelter, food, clean water, health care or education. This **deprivation** may be the source of vital creativity as many Indians must fight to survive every day. India has been called a nation of **entrepreneurs** with millions of **artisans**, street hawkers and **vendors** (such as *kabadiwallah* who sell junk or scrap, or *dhabawallah* who deliver lunch boxes called *tiffin*) working hard to live another day.

This is not to say that Indians are all work and no play. Indian culture contains such an immeasurable mixture of language, food, art, music, dance and customs that it would be impossible to include a full description here. But there are two aspects of Indian culture that are so beloved at home and abroad and they deserve mention: the films of **Bollywood** and the sport of **cricket**.

India – developing country or the next superpower?

A developing country is one that is primarily **agrarian** but seeks to **industrialise** and become socially and economically advanced. In that sense, India is indeed a developing country, one that is advancing at a breakneck pace. Nevertheless, the few exceptional cases of tremendous fame and wealth should not distract from the situation of the majority.

Much of Indian society is **patriarchal**. **Gender violence** is a major issue as girls who are victims of sex crimes do not always have access to justice. Many girls do not even have access to education. And arranged marriages give them even less choice in shaping their own futures.

Although it faces many obstacles on the way to becoming a fully industrialised country, history shows India to be a country of ideas, ingenuity and independence. The country of Buddha and Mahatma Gandhi will have to elevate its poverty-stricken masses before it can become the next super power.

Useful phrases

Talking about India

- to yield sth
- to oppress a rebellion
- to have a claim
- British Raj ['brɪtɪʃ rɑː(d)ʒ]
- to mistreat sb
- to follow sb's lead
- to resist sb / sth
- Indian Independence Act
- to self-rule
- to partition sth
- to be favoured for sth
- Western education
- to be "westernised"
- to internalise sth
- subcontinent
- to take measures
- carbon emissions
- to surge with
- to boom
- Hinduism, Islam
- karma
- reincarnation
- caste system hierarchy
- unskilled labourers
- segregation of
- allotment of jobs
- discrimination (against)
- affirmative action programs
- poverty line
- deprivation of
- artisans, vendors
- Bollywood
- agrarian, industrial, modern
- to industrialise
- patriarchal society
- gender violence

Revision

Draw a mind map of some of the challenges India may face in the future using the text as a source.

- population growth → **Challenges of India in the future**

Solutions

Challenges of India in the future: population growth, healthcare, finding a balance between the hierarchical caste system and the largest democracy in the world, religious tensions, climate change / natural disasters, overcoming poverty, gender issues, technological advancements, etc.

Shakespeare's life and time

William Shakespeare (1564–1616) was born in Stratford-upon-Avon and was an English entrepreneur, poet, playwright, and actor, widely regarded as the greatest writer in the English language. Shakespeare wrote poems and plays. His plays consisted of **comedies**, **histories** and **tragedies**. Shakespeare's best-known poems are the *Sonnets* which were first published in 1609.

Little is known about his childhood, but it can be assumed that he attended a grammar school in Stratford-upon-Avon where he became acquainted with classical ancient literature, the sources of inspiration for many of his plays.

At the age of 18, he married Anne Hathaway, with whom he had three children.

After moving from Stratford-upon-Avon to London around 1590, he began a successful career as an actor, writer, dramatist and shareholder of an acting company called the *Lord Chamberlain's Men* which was later known as the *King's Men*. Regular performances were given in the newly built **Globe Theatre**, which was built by a partnership of members of the company on the south bank of the river Thames in 1599. Wealthy and renowned, Shakespeare retired to Stratford-upon-Avon and died in 1616 at the age of 52.

How was Shakespeare influenced by his time?

During most of Shakespeare's life, Queen Elizabeth I (1533–1603) ruled England. The **Elizabethan Age** is also known as the "Golden Age" as it is characterised by its relative stability, economic growth and the flowering of literature, music and theatre.

The characteristics of the Elizabethan Age:
The age followed the English Reformation, an era when Elizabeth's father, Henry VIII, was responsible for the separation of the Church of England from the Roman Catholic Church. As a consequence, he himself as the king and Supreme Head of the Church of England also formally dissolved the monasteries and began the process of transforming England from a Catholic country to a Protestant one.

Elizabeth was crowned the new Queen at the age of 25 on 15 January 1559. The new age, which was also called the Renaissance, brought about a growing population in London, an exploration of foreign territories, new ideas and an increase of knowledge about science, technology and astrology. These developments also led to a renewed interest in the supernatural, including witches, witchcraft and ghosts.

In addition, the arts flourished under Elizabeth I. As she personally loved poetry, music, and drama, she helped to establish a climate in which it was fashionable for the wealthy members of the court to support the arts.

Shakespeare's tragedies, romantic comedies and history plays became a mirror of the Elizabethan Age as history and the supernatural were often used in his plays (e.g. the witches in *Macbeth* or the ghosts in *Hamlet*).

A lot of his plays like *The Tempest*, *Romeo and Juliet*, *Othello* and *The Merchant of Venice* were set in what is known today as Italy. In Shakespeare's time, Italy was still populated by various powerful city-states which represented a wealthy and exotic backdrop to the British audience.

Moral standards were changing at that time and the theatre's new rebelliousness resulted in some local and cultural authorities trying to forbid performances. There was especially a lot of criticism from Puritans toward the companies of travelling actors, acrobats and comedians, who wandered from place to place in their carts which they also used as stages for their performances. Puritanism in this sense was an activist movement within the Church of England during the reign of Queen Elizabeth I. Puritans believed that man existed for the glory of God and that his first concern in life should be to do God's will in order to receive future happiness. Therefore, Puritans were not pleased to see the performances which dealt with topics like love and authority liberally and disrespectfully. They claimed it would lead to bad behavior and that the plays would attract rowdy drinkers and other "impure" people. In their view, the plays were "the nest of the devil and the sink of all sins".

Even though the Elizabethan Age was also called the Golden Age, all that glittered was not gold as there were conspiracies and conflicts with other nations. Public executions were part of daily life and bear baiting became a gruesome act of "public entertainment" at that time. Shakespeare incorporates these themes in some of his plays, too.

The relevance of Shakespeare today

Shakespeare gives us an insight into the human condition which is unique and helps us to understand what causes people to behave in a certain way. Furthermore, the themes he dealt with in his plays are universally understood and his topics are timeless. They mostly deal with:

- Private aspects like love, marriage, injustice and distorted family relations (e.g. *Romeo and Juliet, Much Ado About Nothing*)
- Political aspects like tyrants and dictatorships (e.g. *Coriolanus, Macbeth*)
- Social aspects like the suppression of women and gender inequality (e.g. *Twelfth Night*)
- Racism (e.g. *Othello, Merchant of Venice*)
- (Post-)Colonialism (*The Tempest*)

Still today, artists are inspired by Shakespeare's plays. Some examples of famous adaptions are:

- *West Side Story* (1961) (a musical adaption of *Romeo and Juliet* set in the Latino quarter of New York)
- *Romeo and Juliet* (1996) (a film set in the present with two rivaling mafia gangs)
- *Shakespeare in Love* (1998) (a fictional film about Shakespeare himself)
- *Hrid Majharey* (2014) (an adaption of *Othello*, set in India in the present)

There are also lots of Shakespeare opera and ballet adaptions such as *Falstaff, Othello, A Midsummer Night's Dream*, etc.

Useful phrases

- playwright
- to write poems / plays / …
- to perform a play on stage / …
- to explore / discover foreign territories
- to support the arts (literature, music, theatre, painting etc.)
- to rebel against moral standards / authorities
- to influence / to have an impact on playwrights / … today

Revision

Describe the historical context of Shakespeare's life and work.

Solutions

Shakespeare worked and lived in the Elizabethan Age, also called the Golden Age • increasing interest in and support of the arts • discovery of new territories • discoveries in science • economic growth and wealth • changes of social standards and moral values (e.g. conflict between liberal tendencies in the arts and Puritanism) • violence was part of everyday life (executions, etc.) • etc.

Visions of the future

Imagine a coin. On one side you have all of the benefits that humankind has gained from **scientific progress** and **technological innovation**. On the other are the unanswered questions, the fears, and the outcomes of this rapid advance into the future.

With this coin in your hand, consider genetic engineering. Scientists could potentially develop gene therapies that could cure cancer, allow the blind to see, even stop the aging process. Food scientists could even create gene-modified foods that could end starvation in the world. But how do they make these discoveries and who pays for their research? Is it even safe? Do geneticists experiment on animals or human embryos? What if a gene therapy that was created to help desperately sick people was manipulated to allow wealthy people to design their own *Überbabies*? How will this effect society? Who loses and who wins?

This thought experiment can be carried out with any scientific discovery or technological breakthrough. It is especially important for **governing bodies** to be able to make predictions about the future, since ethical dilemmas proliferate when innovation outpaces our ability to contemplate the future implications of new science or technology. This chapter will prepare you for the *Abitur* and to look beyond the most recent discoveries to predict outcomes and weigh the legal, moral and societal implications of scientific and technological progress.

Science meets Technology

- It might be helpful to think of science as **theory** and technology as **practice**.
- **Science** is the study of the phenomena that make up our natural world.
- It is a systematic study that relies on facts and evidence – a process that involves observation, hypothesis and experimentation.
- **Applied science** is taking what is learned and using it to develop new **technologies** which solve our problems or improve our lives.

Science is basically an investigation of our physical world, and can therefore be considered neutral. However, the way science is then translated into technology can pose problems to humankind. There are myriad examples of this in history and popular culture. (For more historical background, research Arthur Galston or Dr. Gerhard Shrader.)

Critics point to the negative effects science has on the environment and to society at large. Taken to an extreme, people who fear or resist new technology are called **Luddites**. On the other extreme, some people, e.g., **technophiles** and **early adopters**, love new technology and associate it with progress and better living standards. No matter where one falls on the spectrum, it is undeniable that everyone should be concerned about security, privacy and ethics as we begin to use the instruments that will influence our future.

What challenges do we face?

As the world population continues to grow – depleting natural resources and causing catastrophic climate change – the concept of **sustainability** gains momentum. It calls for the balance between present and future generational needs.

Its cornerstones include:
- using renewable energy,
- reducing waste, recycling materials,
- urban and architectural planning, and
- forward-thinking farming practices.

Sustainability is not a **panacea** (one solution for all problems) but just one way of facing some of the challenges that affect our world. Other challenges include:

Internet and smartphone technology

The internet and smart phones have revolutionized the global economy and the way people communicate and socialize with each other. Incredible amounts of data are open and available to anyone with a connection. With this freedom of information come fears of **surveillance**, loss of **privacy**, espionage, and the commercial exploitation of personal data.

Genetic engineering

DNA is so small that one must use a powerful electron microscope to see it. However, the ability to edit a gene sequence has a massive effect on our world. From cloning to curing incurable diseases to genetically modified food – that tiny component has an inordinate impact on the future of humankind. Take GM foods, for example. Crops that are resistant to pests and bad weather could one day make it possible to end starvation and malnutrition. However, GM foods could have unforeseen effects on the food chain. And there have already been cases of multi-national biotech corporations suing small farmers for reusing GM grain.

Nanotechnology

Keeping with the microscopic theme, nanotechnology is science, engineering, and technology at an atomic or molecular scale. Scientists and engineers can manipulate matter to create medicine, biomaterials such as blood or bone, produce energy, etc. The possibilities are endless, and so are the doomsday scenarios that arise from this field.

Artificial intelligence

Robots have a bad reputation in popular culture. They are stereotyped as cold, raging machines, biding their time until rising up against their human overlords. This is because of something called the **singularity,** which denotes a time when AI (such as computer networks, robots, etc.) becomes self-conscious and autonomous, able to self-improve and surpass human intelligence. Until that time comes, robots are simple mechanical tools that are developed to make human life easier or more pleasurable. Think of driverless cars, drones, bionic body parts, robotic Santa Clauses who sing and dance and make your weird uncle laugh.

What stands behind utopias and dystopias?

Don't get too excited; scientists haven't developed a robot that can do your homework yet. Robots lack the human capacity for reasoning as yet. Our ability to imagine a future that is better or worse, while fun and diverting, can also give us clues about how to improve our current situation and what shameful actions we are doing now that may come back to bite us in the future. It is a thought experiment; like a scientist, you are making observations about society.
Sir Thomas More experimented with this thinking when he coined the term 'utopia' by combining two Greek words that mean 'no' and 'place.' His book '**Utopia'** was published in England in 1516 and many literary critics interpreted it as a critique of contemporary European society. The word is still used today to describe an imaginary perfect place or society in another time or space. Towards the end of the 19th century, industrialization threatened the livelihoods of skilled workers who were being replaced by machines. The **Luddites** were a group of English textile workers in the 19th century who protested the use of new machines because it meant people would lose their jobs. This is similar to what is happening in modern times. With the advent of computer software and robotic technology, many human workers are finding themselves obsolete. This phenomenon has been called 'disruptive innovation'.
People were starting to feel anxious about the future, which was only intensified by two world wars and the emergence of totalitarian states. This fear manifested itself in pessimistic visions of future societies, so-called 'anti-utopias' or '**dystopias**,' characterized by undemocratic governments oppressing the people they are supposed to serve by disenfranchising and dehumanizing them.

Famous examples include *Brave New World* (1934) by Aldous Huxley; *1984* (1949) by George Orwell; and *The Handmaid's Tale* (1985) by Margaret Atwood.
Dystopian works of fiction, film and art aim to criticize negative aspects of contemporary societies. The implicit threat is that if these problems are left unaddressed, the hellish landscape may come true. Modern dystopian fiction reveals the modern fears of environmental disaster, genetic engineering and surveillance technology. This can be seen in *Never Let Me Go* (2005) by Kazuo Ishiguro; *The Circle* (2013) by Dave Eggers; *The Hunger Games* trilogy (2008-2010) by Suzanne Collins; and the *Divergent* trilogy (2011–2013) by Veronica Roth.

Science fiction and fantasy

Utopias and dystopias are subgenres of **science fiction**, which is a form of fiction that extrapolates or concludes the logical course of scientific and technological developments and applies them to society and everyday life.
A science fiction story usually has the following elements:
- advanced technology (time travel, teleportation, space flight),
- non-human characters (aliens, androids, godlike figures), and
- action-packed plots (alien invasion, technology out of control).

The **fantasy** genre makes use of magical and supernatural elements to tell a story inside its own world. There is usually a clear distinction between good and evil. Many fantasy novels become bestsellers and get turned into movies or TV shows, like *Game of Thrones*.

Useful phrases

Talking about science and technology
- to develop gene therapies
- to experiment on
- ethical dilemmas
- to predict outcomes
- to weigh the legal, moral and societal implications
- to pose problems for
- to take something to an extreme
- technophiles
- to deplete natural resources
- catastrophic climate change
- panacea
- loss of privacy
- to cure incurable diseases
- genetically modified food
- to be resistant to something
- doomsday scenario
- to denote / connote something
- thought experiment
- to threaten the livelihood
- the advent of something
- to find oneself obsolete
- disruptive innovation
- to disenfranchise
- to extrapolate something

Revision

State the challenges presented by scientific and technological advancement listed in the text and point out the pros and cons of each scientific/technological innovation.

Solutions
Sustainability (pros: reduces waste, pollution, exploitation of natural resources, etc.) • internet and smartphone technology (pros: new possibilities to communicate and socialize with each other / cons: surveillance, loss of privacy, commercial exploitation of private data) • genetic engineering (pros: cure diseases like cancer, end starvation / cons: experiments on animals or human embryos, creation of *Überbabies*, unforeseen effects e.g. on the food chain, multi-national biotech corporations become too powerful) • nanotechnology (pros: create biomaterials such as blood or bone / cons: unforeseen consequences) • artificial intelligence (pros: make human life easier and more comfortable / cons: workers lose their jobs because they are replaced by machines, could surpass human intelligence and become autonomous).

Global challenges

dm is not just a store where you can buy makeup or deodorant. The initials *DM* used to signify a **currency** that people used in Germany before you were born. The transition of the *Deutsche Mark* to the *Euro* is an illustration of **globalisation**, or the process by which the world becomes increasingly integrated through **political**, **economic**, **technological** and **cultural channels**.

Where do bananas come from?

Political and economic
Nowadays, people can travel throughout the EU (and the world) without constantly exchanging their currency. The € and global lines of credit allow for increasing **mobility** for business travellers, tourists, immigrants and refugees. It also **facilitates** smoother **business transactions** between international markets. Think about bananas: This fruit is not native to Germany, so how did it end up in your smoothie? A complex interplay of **trade deals** between governments and **corporations**, international shipping routes, distribution warehouses and logistics technology came together to bring bananas to your local grocery store.
The most compelling evidence of economic globalisation is closer to you than you may realise. Would people from other countries recognise the brand name of the clothing or shoes you are wearing? You might be wearing the same outfit as someone in Kansas. **Multi-national** corporations manufacture their products wherever labour and **overhead costs** are the lowest and sell them all over the world. Oftentimes the pressure to cut costs has a greater priority than providing safe working conditions and **protecting worker welfare**. The result is often **social inequality**.

Technology
The World Wide Web is yet another form of globalisation. The internet began as a **medium** through which scientists could organise and share information with each other around the world. Now video games make it possible to steal cars or tend to a **virtual** farm with someone from Timbuktu. Technology such as computers and smartphones make it possible **to exchange ideas** not only with your neighbour but also with people you have never met before who live in an entirely different continent.

Culture
Advanced **communication technology** and global mobility make it possible **to spread ideas** around the world. Although academic and political discussions are important and impact the world, one of the most powerful and **problematic** aspects of globalisation is the spread of **cultural phenomena** such as sports (think of the Olympics or the World Cup), food (think of McDonald's or kebab shops), pop culture (How much of the music you listen to is in English? Where do your favourite movies and television shows come from?) and religion.

What are the dangers of globalisation?

After Germany won the 2014 World Cup, **international media outlets** reported on the exuberant displays of **national pride** that had long remained subdued, perhaps as an act of contrition for the events of World War II. Germans proudly wore their national colours and attached flags to their cars and homes and images of this appeared in news outlets around the world. The idea of nationhood is essential to the understanding of globalisation since many experts claim that globalisation **endangers** this idea. In their view, the logical outcome of globalisation is **homogenisation** of culture and language across the globe.
In addition to the loss of **local character**, workers all over the world are in danger of losing their jobs as multi-national corporations have no loyalty to people or place but rather profit, often transferring jobs to lower cost countries with no care about the environment or worker health

and safety. These companies have seats in many nations and can therefore **exploit** their legal situation **to create tax havens** to avoid paying taxes. A portion of that profit is then pumped into politics **to influence political decisions** in their favour. This reciprocal relationship between politicians and **corporate greed** widens the gap between the rich and the poor.

Technological globalisation presents its own problems. Criminal organisations have taken to the World Wide Web using blackmail, hacking, and cyber terrorism to threaten people and organisations. **Intellectual property** is threatened as companies that send their manufacturing to China put their products at risk of being stolen and copied. Furthermore the availability of smartphone technology is making it easy for governments to spy on citizens and each other, **eradicating** the concept of privacy.

Taken together, it could be argued that globalisation is a form of imperialism in that it exerts authority over the economic and political rights of nations. However supporters of globalisation say that it spreads democracy and wealth. Not to mention bananas.

Useful phrases

Talking about Globalisation

- to exchange currency
- globalisation
- political / economic / technological / cultural channel
- to increase (social) mobility
- to facilitate sth
- to make a business transaction
- trade deal
- (multi-national) corporation
- high / low overhead costs
- to protect worker welfare
- to cause social inequality
- medium for spreading culture
- to experience virtual simulations
- to exchange ideas

- communication technology
- to spread ideas
- to be problematic
- (cultural) phenomena
- international media outlets
- displays of (national) pride
- to endanger sth
- to homogenise sth
- to lose local character
- to exploit sth
- to create tax havens
- to influence political decisions
- corporate greed
- to own intellectual property
- to eradicate sth

Revision

Outline the examples of political, economic, technological and cultural aspects of globalisation that are presented in the text and organise the dangers of globalisation within those categories.

Solutions

Political / Economic aspects: currency / credit • increased mobility • easier business transactions around the world • multi-national corporations make greater profits • governments make trade deals with each other;
Danger: multi-national corporations have tax havens

Technological aspects: WWW • smartphones, computers, video game consoles • worldwide communication • medium to spread culture;
Danger: loss of privacy, problems with intellectual property, criminal activity

Cultural aspects: spread of ideas; phenomena such as sports, food, pop culture and religion;
Danger: loss of local culture, language

English as a lingua franca

The term "**lingua franca**" describes a language which is used as a common language between people whose **mother tongues** are different. English is used as a lingua franca in order to be able to communicate across different cultures and nationalities.

The importance of English

There are different reasons why English has become the dominant lingua franca on a global level. One source was the former numerous British colonies. Beginning in the 16th century, the first British settlers arrived in North America. In the 17th century more trade posts and settlements were founded in Asia and Africa and in 1770 James Cook landed on the east coast of Australia and claimed the land for the British Crown. At the height of the British Empire, the British Crown had colonies all around the world. English was used as a lingua franca in **trade**, **administration**, and **education** throughout the Empire. Separated from their mother country England and influenced by the local mother tongues, the people in the colonies developed different **varieties of English**. Best known are varieties like North American English, Australian English, Indian English or South African English.

Today English has an **official status** in about 80 countries in the world and with the US taking the leading role in the global economy its dominance is likely to increase further. Due to the process of globalisation in fields like business, culture, research, the media, entertainment, etc., the importance of English as a lingua franca is increasing. The importance of English as a lingua franca can be seen in job advertisements, for example. For higher positions and better paid jobs, English has become a key qualification.

In the vast majority of EU Member States, English as a foreign language is required within secondary education and in several EU Member States English is already taught at primary school.

Revision

State in which fields English has been used as lingua franca.

Solutions

trade, administration, education, business, culture, research, entertainment, the media, politics etc.

Skills

This section explains important skills for the different parts of your written exam in the *Abitur*. Do the training tasks after working on the *Übungs-Abis* if you want to repeat and practise specific skills.

Comprehension

Reading

To orient yourself, read the **title** and the **source** of the text. This is how to get the first clue about the content of the text, the text type (novel excerpt, newspaper article, etc.) and the origin of the text (date of publishing, author, quality / tabloid paper, etc.).
Then read the text carefully and try to understand the meaning of unknown words in their context. Read the text again and look up important words in a dictionary.
Mark any information in the text which is relevant to answering the comprehension task.

Writing

Structure the marked / relevant information for your answer to avoid repetitions and to form a coherent text. Use linking words to structure your text. Write a text in which you briefly inform the reader about the information asked for. Use your own language and present your answer in clear and concise language. The length of your text should be about a quarter to a third of the original text. As a general rule, write your text in the present tense.

> **Useful phrases to structure your answer**
>
> In the newspaper article / comment / speech / … the author presents / claims / speaks about … • In addition to this, … • Furthermore, … • Moreover, … • Finally, … • At the end of the article / speech, … • The author comes to the conclusion that …

Training

1 *To become familiar with the Operatoren of a comprehension, go to page 10 in* Einführung.

2 *To practise choosing and marking relevant information, go to page 30* (Übungs-Abi 2) *and do the comprehension task in* Erste Schritte.

3 *To practise structuring relevant information, go to page 81* (Übungs-Abi 6) *and do the comprehension task.*

Analysis

The analysis task usually requires you to examine an author's attitude towards a topic or how certain feelings and suspense are created when reading a text. You can find the most common *Operatoren* for the analysis task on page 11 in *Einführung*.
The most important aspects to analyse a text are presented below.

Referring to the text for proof

In the analysis task, you always have to support your arguments by referring to the original text. You can refer to the text by using a literal quotation, i.e. you restate the exact wording of the original text or by giving an indirect quotation, i.e. you reformulate the content of the original text in your own words.

When referring to the text, consider
- giving the line **(l.)** or lines **(ll.)**;
- marking literal quotations with quotation marks;
- using different verbs to introduce your quotation (not always "say / write").

Examples of indirect quotations:
- The author **emphasises** that the optimism for a better future was largely gone when President Barack Obama was planning his run for a second term as president **(l. 26)**.
- Moreover, he **uses** a rhetorical question to address the reader directly and to reveal the under-representation of Afro-Americans in TV **in ll. 29ff**.

Examples of literal quotations:
- In the first paragraph, the author **repeats** the pronoun **"we"** several times **(ll. 1ff.)**.
- The president **addresses** the audience directly **(l. 1, "My fellow Americans")**.
- The author **quotes** a policeman saying that he felt like **"a five-year-old holding onto Hulk Hogan" (ll. 6 – 7)**.

Line of argument

In newspaper **comments, editorials** or **speeches**, the authors try to convince the addressee of their point of view. They do so by choosing their line of argument deliberately. Usually, the **order of arguments** in a text begins with the less persuasive arguments (in the first half) and ends with the most persuasive arguments (in the second half). Sometimes the author gives **counter-arguments**. If so, focus on how he disproves them.

Moreover, authors support their arguments by referring to
- examples
- personal / second-hand experiences
- statistical data / surveys
- reports
- experts / scientists
- etc.

Training
To practise the analysis of a line of argument, go to page 30 (Übungs-Abi 2) *and do the analysis task in* Erste Schritte.

Language

In **comments** or **fictional texts** (short stories, novel excerpts, etc.) authors use language to create a certain mood or attitude towards a topic. For example, the **choice of words** influences the reader's perception of a text.
To examine the choice of words, focus on:
- register (formal, informal, neutral, vulgar, etc.)
- tone (sarcastic, angry, accusing, inspiring, etc.)
- style (sophisticated, complex / simple sentence structure, etc.)
- adjectives and nouns and their associations
- adverbs of degree (very, hardly, terribly, almost, etc) and comment (fortunately, hopefully)
- symbols (a rose, spring, a dove, etc.)
- stylistic / rhetorical devices
- etc.

Training

To practise how language affects the atmosphere of a text, go to page 18 (Übungs-Abi 1) *and do the analysis task **b)** in* Erste Schritte.

Stylistic devices

Stylistic (or rhetorical) devices intensify the reader's feelings while reading.
Frequent stylistc devices are:
- alliteration ("bold, bright and beautiful")
- anaphora ("I didn't like his hairstyle. I didn't want to tell him. I didn't think I ought to be unfriendly.")
- antithetical phrase / contrast ("a fire-and-ice relationship; a white star in the dark sky")
- enumeration ("old, grey, suave, majestic")
- hyperbole ("an absolutely fantastic book")
- irony ("Well, that was clever! Now it's broken.")
- parallelism "It's great for me, for you, for everyone."
- personification ("Huge cities never sleep.")
- metaphor ("She's a little monkey.")
- repetition ("March for your rights!" he cried, and we marched and marched.")
- rhetorical question ("Wouldn't we all like a holiday?")
- simile ("He behaved like a bull in a china shop.")
- synecdoche ("I need a new set of wheels." (=a car))

Training

To practise the use of stylistic devices and their effect on the reader, go to page 81 (Übungs-Abi 6) *and do the analysis task in* Erste Schritte.

Narrative perspective (fictional texts)

Dealing with **fictional texts** taken from novels or short stories, you often have to examine the narrative point of view. The narrative point of view influences how much a reader knows about the plot and his / her feelings about the events and other characters. Narrative perspectives can be mixed and they can change in the course of the story.
Talking about the narrator, do not confuse 'narrator' and 'author'. The author is the real person who wrote the novel, play etc. The narrator is a *fictional* character in or outside the story (e.g. a third-person omniscient narrator tells the story from the outside).

Third-person omniscient narrator
- This narrator is not visible in the story and tells the story from the outside but knows everything about the characters' thoughts and feelings as well as the background of the story.
- Sometimes the narrator will comment on the characters' behaviour, the events coming later in the story, or even on the writing itself.
- This style of narration is mainly neutral and more distanced than first-person or single perspective narration.

Third-person limited narrator
- This type of narrator tells the story from the outside, but only describes feelings and thoughts from the perspective of one particular character in a story.
- The narrator is not identical with this character.
- We sympathise more easily with the character we are told most about.

First-person narrator
- A character narrates the story from his / her own perspective. ("I …") We only know what this character thinks, knows, sees or hears.
- The first-person narrator is often, but not always, the main protagonist.
- We understand and sympathise most easily with this type of narrator.

> **Useful phrases to examine the narrative perspective**
>
> The author employs a first-person narrative perspective / … • The story is told from a third-person limited point of view / … • The story is told by a … narrator • The description of … is biased since the author uses a first-person narrative perspective.

Training
To practise the analysis of the narrative perspective, go to page 18 (Übungs-Abi 1) *and do the analysis task **a)** in* Erste Schritte.

Characterisation

Working with **fictional texts** like novel excerpts or plays, you are often expected to analyse the characters. Then consider the following categories:
- The **main character** (or **protagonist**) plays a central part in the plot.
  Less important characters are called **minor characters**.
- A **round character** is a complex character who is presented in detail.
- A **flat character** is rather simple and represents a stereotype.

A character can be described indirectly or directly. **Direct characterisation** takes place when the author explicitly states what the character looks like or feels like.

Example: Opening the door, the girl was terribly afraid.

Indirect characterisation is used when the reader has to interpret the character's actions, thoughts etc. to determine a person's appearance, feelings or attitude.

Example: Opening the door, the girl's hand was trembling.

Training
To practise the analysis of characters in fictional texts, go to page 57 (Übungs-Abi 4) *and do the analysis task in* Erste Schritte.

Analysing drama

A play is presented to the audience through direct speech, by the actors and actresses, on a theatre stage or in a film / radio play. Analysing a drama, pay attention to the following basic categories.

Types of plays
- Comedy has a happy ending.
- Tragedy has a sad or catastrophic ending.
- Tragicomedy is a mixture of both.
- One-act or short plays, like short stories, concentrate on one important moment / event.

Setting
Acts and scenes can be set in different places and in different times (ancient, middle ages, present, etc.)

Scenery
The scenery, for example, can be very detailed with lots of objects and images of landscapes or bare, i.e. there are no or hardly any objects on the stage.

Classic 5-act structure of the plot
1. The exposition introduces characters and theme.
2. The rising action increases tension / complications.
3. The climax / turning point starts a downfall (tragedy) or a turn for the better (comedy).
4. The falling action increases problems (tragedy) or works towards solving them (comedy).
5. The dénouement closes the play, with a catastrophe (tragedy) or a happy / open ending.

Poetry

Like songs, poems are short lyrical texts which aim to impress the audience emotionally. As with songs, poems consist of relatively short texts but they contain of a lot of information. The reader is confronted with symbols and images and even the form can convey a message. Therefore, you have to decode the content and the form of a poem. It is recommended to perform the following steps when analysing poetry.

1. *Read the poem and focus on its **content**. What feelings does the poem evoke? Who is the speaker, who the addressee? The information in the title and about its origin might help you too.*

2. *Focus on the **form** of the poem. Important formal elements of poems are the*
    - structure (number / length of verses, sonnet, free verse, etc.)
    - rhyme scheme, like alternate rhyme (ABAB), enclosed rhyme (ABBA), etc.
    - metre / rhythm (iambic, trochaic, dactylic, spondaic, etc.)
    - rhetorical devices
    - symbols
    - word choice

3. *Examine how content and form reinforce each other to support the message of the poem.*

Visuals

When analysing pictures (photos) or cartoons, stick to the following three steps:
First, describe the picture/cartoon.
Then, analyse the picture. Focus on symbols, messages, colours, the setting, the addressee etc.
Finally, evaluate the picture. State whether the picture/cartoon communicates its message effectively or not. Give reasons.

Useful phrases to describe pictures/cartoons:
The picture/photo/cartoon/painting portrays/shows/illustrates … • the photo was taken at/in … • in the background/foreground, you can see … • in the centre/bottom/top/upper left part/lower right part, there is … • the main focus of … • the cartoon deals with/illustrates the topic of … • the painter/artist/cartoonist uses light/dark colours • the picture looks realistic/old/ … • the person looks directly at the spectator • etc.

Useful phrases to analyse pictures/cartoons:
There is a contrast between … • the colours create a … atmosphere • … refers to (the world championship/…) • … is a symbol for (love/…) • … represents (their power/…) • conveys the impression of … • … catches the spectator's attention • its message is ironical/sarcastic/alarming etc.

Useful phrases to evaluate pictures/cartoons:
The picture conveys/communicates its message effectively because … • the artist's intention is to draw the audience's attention to … • the picture has a strong/weak impact on … because… • etc.

When analysing diagrams, start by describing them. Then go on to examine and interpret its data.

Useful phrases to work with diagrams

The **bar chart** shows … • the vertical axis shows … • the horizontal axis represents … • the longest/shortest bar is in year …

The **line graph** illustrates … • the vertical axis represents the number/percentage of … • the horizontal axis shows the time from … to … • the amount of … reaches its peak in year … and its lowest point in … • the graph/number of… steadily increases/rises/remains constant/decreases/falls •

The **pie chart** displays data about … • the largest segment is made up by … • the smallest segment represents … • … is a minority/the majority • … corresponds to only a half/a third of … • etc.

The **table** informs about … • in the first/second column/line, … • etc.

Evaluation

Comment

In a comment you are expected to express your own opinion on a topic. To do so, refer to your own knowledge and the information given in the text.
Basically a comment consists of the following parts:
- Introduction: Attract the reader's attention by referring to examples, news, quotes, surveys, personal experiences, future developments, etc. End the introduction by stating the question you will comment on.
- Second part: Briefly state your opinion.
- Third part: Present your arguments to support your opinion.
- Conclusion: End your comment by summarising the main facts, giving an outlook on future developments or mentioning possible solutions.

Training
To practise preparing for writing your comment, go to page 58 (Übungs-Abi 4) *and do the evaluation task **a)** in* Erste Schritte.

Argumentative essay or Composition

Like in a comment, you are expected to give your own opinion in an essay. In contrast to a comment, you are expected to include pro- *and* con-arguments in your essay. Depending on your decision, you may try to persuade the reader to agree with you or take a neutral position in your conclusion.

Often you are asked to **discuss**, **assess** or **evaluate** a statement in a comment or an essay. The most common ways to structure your arguments are shown in the table below. Always arrange your arguments beginning with the weakest and ending with the strongest, most persuasive argument.
The table illustrates a structure in which you argue in favour of the task (=pro).

Introduction	Introduction
Body: • con-argument 1 • con-argument 2 • (con-argument 3) • pro-argument 1 • pro-argument 2 • pro-argument 3	Body: • con-argument 1 • pro-argument 1 • con-argument 2 • pro-argument 2 • (con-argument 3) • pro-argument 3
Conclusion	Conclusion

Training
To practise preparing for writing your argumentative essay, go to page 82 (Übungs-Abi 6) *and do the evaluation task **a)** in* Erste Schritte.

Re-creation of text
Like in a comment, you have to brainstorm suitable ideas for the content of your text.

In a re-creation of text-task you are usually asked to
- refer to the setting described in a text;
- take on a role or express an opinion of a certain point of view;
- write to a specific addressee.

In addition you should write a certain kind of text which could be a
- letter (formal letter, letter to the editor, personal letter)
- speech script (talk, public / formal speech, [debate] statement)
- newspaper article (report, comment)
- (written) interview
- diary entry
- the continuation or completion of a fictional text (novel excerpt, play, etc.)

Training
To practise preparing for writing your re-creation of text, go to page 44 (Übungs-Abi 3) *and do the evaluation task **b)** in* Erste Schritte.

Mediation

In a mediation a sender passes on information to an addressee. This sounds fairly simple but depending on the context as described in the task there are some points to consider.
The following points will help you to analyse the task.

- **Context**
  A mediation always takes place in a certain **context**. To understand the context, read the task carefully and answer the wh-questions:
  – Who asks for information?
  – Why does he / she ask for information or for what purpose does he / she need the information?
  – What kind of information does he / she need?

- **Addressee**
  The form and the content of your mediation text depends on the characteristics of your addressee, e.g. the addressee's personal characteristics like education, nationality, etc. influence what kind of information you have to provide.

  Example: The form and content of your mediation text about national parks in Germany might change depending on whether you write to a professor of biology in London or to the little brother of your Indian pen pal in Mumbai.

- **Relevant information**
  Only inform your addressee about the information asked for.
  Do not add your personal opinion or further information which is not in the German text.

  Example: The German text might inform you about the advantages and disadvantages of a topic but your addressee only asks for the advantages of a topic. So leave out the disadvantages in your mediation text.

- **Text type**
  Each mediation task expects you to produce a specific text type (personal / formal email, newspaper article, etc.). Use suitable language for your text and add text parts if necessary (e.g. greeting and ending in a letter).

- **Intercultural understanding**
  Depending on the knowledge of your addressee explain or paraphrase facts and terms which are specific to German culture.

  Example: Talking about football, a British addressee might be familiar with clubs like Borussia Dortmund and FC Bayern München, but you will have to explain the importance of these clubs to German fans to an Indian addressee.

Training

1 *To become familiar with the* Operatoren *of a mediation, go to page 12 in* Einführung.

2 *To practise how to analyse points 1–4 above, go to page 19* (Übungs-Abi 1) *and 58* (Übungs-Abi 4) *and do the mediation tasks **a)–c)** in* Erste Schritte.

3 *To practise how to secure intercultural understanding, go to page 44* (Übungs-Abi 3) *and 82* (Übungs-Abi 6) *and do the mediation task in* Erste Schritte.